Researching on the World Wide Web

How to Order:

For information on quantity discounts contact the publisher: Prima Publishing, P.O. Box 1260BK, Rocklin, CA 95677-1260; (916) 632-4400. On your letterhead include information concerning the intended use of the books and the number of books you wish to purchase. For individual orders, turn to the back of this book for more information.

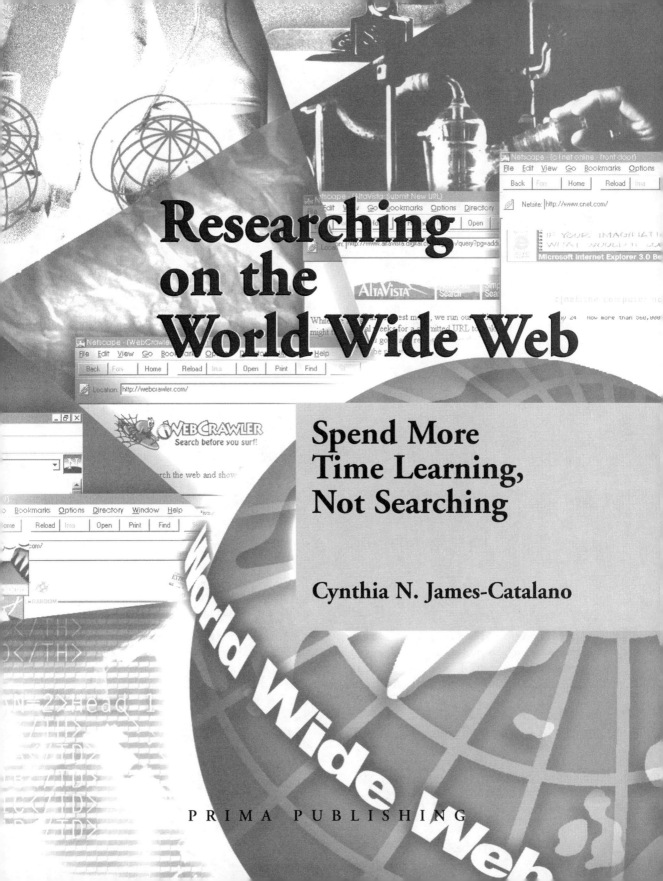

Researching on the World Wide Web

Spend More Time Learning, Not Searching

Cynthia N. James-Catalano

PRIMA PUBLISHING

Publisher: Don Roche, Jr.
Associate Publisher: Ray Robinson
Senior Acquisitions Editor: Alan Harris
Senior Editor: Tad Ringo
Acquisitions Editor: Julie Barton
Project Editor: Kelli Crump
Copy Editor: Theresa Mathias
Interior Layout: Marian Hartsough
Cover Design: Mike Tanamachi
Indexer: Emily Glossbrenner

ISBN: 0-7615-0686-1
Library of Congress Catalog Card Number: 96-70102
Printed in the United States of America
96 97 98 99 BB 10 9 8 7 6 5 4 3 2 1

To my family

Contents at a Glance

Contents

Acknowledgments

Every book is an effort of several people. In addition to the writer, there are the editors who keep it on track and get it to press. This books is no exception and I have several people to thank. I'd like to thank the Prima editors—Kelli Crump, Theresa Mathias, Tim Huddleston, and especially, Julie Barton—for all their work in bringing this book into being.

Several mentors and colleagues have encouraged my interest in computers and particularly, the Internet over the years. Without their constant nudging, I wouldn't be known as a cybrarian today. I'd like to single out the editorial research department of *The Orlando Sentinel.* That's where I first got a chance to practice my cybrarian skills professionally, although my official job title was news librarian. I often bemused my colleagues (Jill, Valerie, Susan, Cate, Patti, Becky, Kelly, Norman, Ric, and Judy) but I'm glad they gave me the environment to experiment.

Finally, none of this would have been possible without my family's support. I have been blessed with a loving family. My husband, Jack James-Catalano; my daughter, Victoria James-Catalano; and my parents, Betty and Charles James; have been my strength and inspiration. They're the ones who believe in me. Jack took the brunt of the house chores, grocery shopping, cooking, and yard work. He also listened to my frustrations and ideas as this book took form. Mom and dad were always willing to babysit. They kept telling me I could do it. And Victoria showed incredible patience for a 4-month-old baby who grew a few months older, a few inches taller, learned to eat solid food, pull-up, and cut two teeth all while her mommy wrote this book.

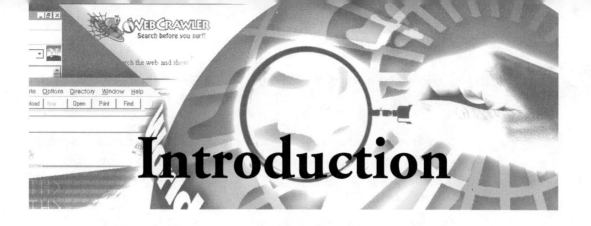

Introduction

Do you know where I can find. . . ? Insert the word or phrase of your choice there. I get lots of e-mail from parents, business owners, students, and fellow researchers. They're frustrated from endless hours of clicking from one screen to the next. They see my address at the end of my cyberlibrarian column in *Internet World* and in desperation send out a message hoping I can tell them that perfect spot on the Web that will answer all of their questions.

Unfortunately, I don't have as much time to answer e-mail as I used to. At first I would do the research and send back the answer. As my e-mail volume increased I started telling people where they could look on the Web. I would still check the site to see if it worked before recommending it. Then as even more e-mail came in, I started answering questions with general guidelines for Web research. I'd direct them to a search engine or index that I thought would be a good starting point.

Of course, they had probably tried to find it using Lycos or Yahoo! before writing to me. The problem was they didn't know how to use the research tools effectively. Many new Web explorers don't know the difference between an index or search engine. A few labor under the misconception that one research tool will chart the whole Web.

I remembered the old adage: "Give a man a fish, he eats for one day. Teach a man to fish he eats for life." The solution to my e-mail and the Web explorers' frustration is this book explaining how to do research on the World Wide Web.

I know that instructional books are supposed to be somewhat aloof. The authors avoid all mention of themselves. The tone is serious. The assumption is that you, the reader, don't know anything and must be talked to in that manner.

I never liked that style so I didn't write this book that way. I want this book to be educational, but not dry. I imagined that you and I were sitting down over a cup of hot chocolate on a rainy day. We got to talking about Web research. I explained to you what I know using examples from my experience.

This book is also written with the assumption that you're an intelligent person, quite capable of mastering Web research skills. You've already been on the Web. You know the basics of how to move around. You may already be an accomplished online researcher and the Web is just a new animal to you. Or you may be just getting into the field of research for professional or personal reasons.

Part I
Research Tools

1

What Is the World Wide Web?

The World Wide Web is undeniably popular. Often referred to as simply "the Web" or by the abbreviations WWW and W3, it has a catchy name. The Web has a following that rivals the devotion usually reserved for sports teams and rock groups. Many TV shows even end their broadcasts with Web addresses.

As the Web grows in popularity, businesses and schools are learning that it's a valuable resource of information. The Web is an ever-changing and growing collection of facts, opinions, pictures, and more. Unfortunately, it's easy to get caught up in the moving images and sound bites. It's also easy to get lost in the links that seem to promise the answer right around the corner but never seem to get there. If you don't know how to navigate, you'll spend more time seeking than learning.

To navigate effectively, you will need to know what the Web is and a basic idea of how it works. Also you'll need to know what can be found on the Web and what can't. This chapter will define the Web for you and tell you what you can expect from it.

Defining the World Wide Web

To make effective use of the Web, you first have to understand what the Web is. The Web is not a traditional resource. In fact, the Web is technically the software that uses *hypertext* to move from one point to another. This software uses the existing hardware that is networked together and known as the Internet.

The terms "hypertext," "hypertext link," and "hyperlink" are often interchanged with one another. Technically, a hypertext document contains hypertext links or hyperlinks.

A hypertext link is a word or phrase in a document that is linked to another document. Hypertext words are often a different color from the rest of the type onscreen. By clicking on a hypertext link, you can go to the other document—even if it is physically stored on a different computer. A VCR tape is not a movie; it's a medium to view a movie. Likewise, the Web uses a set of protocols that stipulate how computers can locate and obtain resources stored on a different computer. *Protocols*, simply put, are the ways computers "talk" to each other. The Web uses *HyperText Transfer Protocol*, which is commonly referred to as *http*.

But that's a fine distinction best saved for computer conferences. In practical terms, when someone refers to the World Wide Web, that someone means the information that can be found using Web software. In doing Web research, you'll only notice the technical aspects when there is a problem!

How the Web Works

The Web links sites together so you can jump from one page to the next. What does that mean? First, you have to realize that the Internet is not one big centralized computer network. Rather, it's a bunch of computers all over the world that are joined together by individuals and organizations that want to participate. You may have heard the Internet called the "network of networks" and that's an accurate description.

The Internet was never meant to be centralized. It was created in 1969 by the Advanced Research Projects Agency, an organization within the U.S. Department of Defense, and was originally known as ARPANET. It's purpose was to maintain open lines of communication in the event of a catastrophic war. If part of the network were destroyed or temporarily disabled, the computers would simply find ways to reroute and keep talking with each other. By designing the Internet this way, the lack of centralization set the stage for the biggest democracy this world has ever seen.

Home Pages

The Web became the forum for this democracy because anyone can publish on the Web. If you have access to an Internet Service

History of the World Wide Web

Where did the Web come from, you ask? Well, the idea of hypertext and the Web has been discussed in computer circles for a long time. The word, "hypertext," was actually coined in 1965 by Ted Nelson. Nelson, who is often called the "father of hypertext," had many theories on how hypertext should work and what can be accomplished with it.

The Web's birthplace, though, is CERN, the European Laboratory for Particle Physics, in Geneva, Switzerland. The abbreviation comes from the French spelling of the laboratory's name: Conseil Européan pour la Recherche Nucléaire. Tim Berners-Lee at CERN is credited with creating the Web. In 1980, while Berners-Lee was working at CERN, he wrote the computer program, Enquire. Enquire allowed hypertext links to be made. CERN's Web address is **http://www.cern.ch**.

Around 1983, Ethernet made its way to CERN. Ethernet set a 10MB standard for computer networks to run on and became a new way for computers to "talk" to each other. The CERN lab was the Switzerland gateway for e-mail, among other Internet protocols. In 1990, CERN was crowned the largest Internet site in Europe, the Web was named, and initial software developed. In 1993, the first version of Mosaic was released. Soon, Web conferences began and were sold out.

Since then, the Web has practically taken over the Internet. It has become the preferred method of information retrieval, and terms like "surfing the Web" have become commonplace in our language. For more details and technical aspects about the Web, go to the World Wide Web Consortium's Web history site at **http://www.w3.org/hypertext/WWW/History.html** and CERN's history of Internet protocols site at **http://wwwcn.cern.ch/pdp/ns/ben/TCPHIST.html**.

Provider, a computer, and the appropriate Web publishing software, you can put whatever you want online. It's kind of like a giant concrete wall and everyone has a spray paint can. When you squirt your message online, it's called a *page*. You can create as many pages as you like. Your main page is called a *home page*.

Home pages have become almost commonplace. Many business cards, which sported e-mail addresses a couple of years ago, now list a person's home page. Home pages serve as representatives of people who hope to reach others they don't normally talk with. Resumes are posted by those seeking employment. Names of friends and relatives are listed in the hopes of making contact with a long-lost friend or family member.

Home pages are used as a marketing tool by corporations, especially the media. Movie trailers are released with a home page listed on the bottom of the screen. Companies urge customers to get more information about a product by visiting their home pages. Radio stations advertise their home pages as a place to get contest entry forms. A lot of people have found a spray paint can and are spreading the paint liberally.

Sites

A *site* is a page or group of pages created by the same person. These pages often share a server but that isn't always the case. Pages at a site will have similar addresses, much as all the houses on a block share a street name. Sites are located on one or more servers. A *server* is a computer on the Internet and is physically located in one spot in the real world. Sites can have files on more than one server. Although the term *address* is used to describe a site's location on the Web, a site is not bound to a geographic location.

Sites can be *mirrored*. That means that another computer keeps an exact copy of the original site's files on its system and makes it available. This is frequently done across countries. A site in Japan might be mirrored in Germany. That way, when the site in Japan is busy, you can go to Germany. The German site is probably less busy

Figure 1.1
This page lists mirror sites for Views of the Solar System.

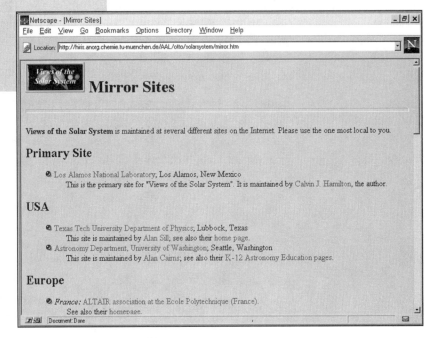

because of the time difference—not as many people are awake and online. That allows German networks to take more outside connections. There is a lag between the original site and the mirror when the original site is updated. Still, if you're not looking for today's news, the mirror site is accurate enough.

For example, Views of the Solar System is stored on a server in Los Alamos, New Mexico. However, it has become a popular site and the computer can handle only so many visitors so other servers around the world store the same files containing the Views of the Solar System information. Web users can go to any of the mirror sites and see the same thing that the one in Los Alamos would show them (see Figure 1.1). This mirror site's address is **http://hiris.anorg.chemie.tu-muenchen.de/AAL/otto/solarsystem/mirror.htm.**

Links

When a page is created, it rarely stands alone. The page creators use hypertext to *link* their pages with dozens, even hundreds, of other pages. This is a research boon. Now, when you see another source you think might be helpful, you just click to go there. If you want to go back to your original page, you can with another click. Your Web browser keeps track of where you've been so you can return to previous pages.

Say you're looking for the "how to's" of the Japanese paperfolding art origami. An expert in Japan has created a page detailing how to create origami and placed it on a computer at Keio University. You live in Minnesota. Fortunately, your Internet Service Provider's computer can talk to the computer in Japan using established protocols. You get on the Web and find an art site with "Origami Archive" listed in hypertext. Someone else made the link for you. You point to it with your mouse and the address **http://synap.neuro.sfc. keio.ac.jp/~aly/polygon/origami/origami.html** pops up. In less than a minute, you're there. For you, it's a seamless transition.

What's on the Web?

You now know a simplified version of how the Web works. And you know that the Web is a great repository of information. The question is, do you need all of that information? One person might use his spray paint can to explain the principles of temporal physics; another might simply paint "Jay loves Joni." Did you really need to know that? There are lots of gems out there in the virtual world. Unfortunately, there's also a lot of garbage.

There's almost no limit to what can be put online. Censorship isn't popular with Internet users, so the only limiting factors are usually technology and time. When Internet denizens felt their free speech rights were being threatened by government legislation, the usually chaotic group got organized. They established the Blue Ribbon Campaign to rally around the cause of freedom of speech

Figure 1.2
The Blue Ribbon
Campaign Home
Page explains the
purpose of the
blue ribbon
and offers
different styles
Webmasters can
add to their
own pages.

(see Figure 1.2). However, not everyone appreciates the unruly nature of the Internet. The Responsible Speech Campaign urges Web users to label material unsuitable for minors and to support browsers and software that allow users to avoid obscene material without seeing it. The white ribbon is its symbol (see Figure 1.3).

Web Organization

Until now, if you had a bit of research to do, you turned to a book. Sometimes it was as simple as looking in a dictionary for the spelling of a word. For more complex projects, you probably headed to the library. Libraries are marvelous places. Librarians work hard to make sure the books, magazines, videos, and other resources are organized in a logical manner. There's a catalog that tells you what's available and where to find it. If you have trouble, you ask a reference librarian who can often help you refine your research.

Figure 1.3
The Responsible
Speech Campaign
Home Page is an
alternative to the
Blue Ribbon
Campaign.

That method is still a good approach in the right situation, but the Web is quickly changing the way you look for facts. The library has the unfortunate limitations of space. Not every book can be stored in the building. One book may refer you to a another book that isn't in the library's collection. Libraries have the limit of timeliness. Even the most current resources, newspapers, and magazines will present information that is days old. Encyclopedia updates take even longer. If you need the latest statistic, a library probably won't be able to accommodate you.

The Web is current. Before a television show is over, fans are discussing its merits online. A bomb goes off in the Middle East and reports come in from eyewitnesses before the news cameras can set up. This lets you know first impressions of what happened and gives you contacts later if you want to learn more from the people who were there. However, one thing the Web is not is centralized. No one makes or enforces rules. There are a lot of conventions that generally everyone uses. But there's nothing to make everyone play nice together except common courtesy and a desire to help one another out. As the Internet community grows, it becomes more difficult to keep track of what everyone else is doing. It's a little like a small town that has grown into a sprawling metropolis.

Imagine a library where everyone donates a book. Instead of a librarian cataloging it and placing it on the bookshelf with like subjects, it's simply tossed in the nearest bin. Anyone who wants to donate a book can. The librarian doesn't review it or consider its merits; she simply tosses it into the next available bin. Would you want to do research in this institution?

When you look for facts on the Web, you're going into an institution organized much like that bin library. There have been attempts to organize the information online and some of these attempts are successful. Still, no one has been able to index every site in an easy, efficient system. (The Internet has been growing at about 100 percent per year since 1988 and doubles in size each year, according to Matrix Information and Directory Services, Inc.) There is so much information available that it takes skill to find what you want in a timely fashion.

If you do find it, you will discover it was most likely worth the effort. Much of what's online is there because someone really loves the subject. Like a gardener caring for her plants, most *Webmasters* (the people who create and maintain sites) make an effort to give you the most thorough page they can.

Multimedia World

Another big advantage of the Web is that it is a multimedia environment. Using hypermedia links, not only can you get the text of Martin Luther King Jr.'s "I Have a Dream" speech, you can listen to it. You can find the musical score of Canada's national anthem and listen to it while you read over it. You can turn an origami image to see how the paper is folded on the other side. You can watch a movie of the Olympic torch being carried into a stadium while listening to the crowds cheer.

To take full advantage of the multimedia environment, your computer must have the right hardware (such as a sound card) and software installed.

Web pages are colorful and often illustrated. Creativity is a hallmark of the Web. So are bad puns, with spiders illustrating many a Web site. It's easy to get sidetracked into fascinating diversions. Research hasn't been this much fun since the printing press gave us easy-to-read books. And you can do all this from the convenience of you own computer.

When Not to Look on the Web

Now that I've got you excited about getting online, let's discuss when to go online. Just because the answer might be on the Web, it doesn't mean that's the best place to look. The first part of research is to determine what you're looking for. If it's a simple, one fact answer, chances are a reference book would be quicker.

Ready Reference

For example, the dictionary is still the best place to look for spellings and quick definitions. What year did President Taft become president? An almanac or encyclopedia will quickly tell you 1909. Sure, these facts might be on the Web somewhere. If you're already online, it might be just as quick to look there. Chances are, however, that if you have a reference book handy, you'll save time looking there first.

For more information about reference materials on the Web, see Chapter 16.

As with any guideline, there are exceptions. If the word you want to define is new to a language (or has a new definition) you might have to look on the Web, where there are many specialized dictionaries. If you want the etymology of a word, you probably want to go to the Oxford English Dictionary (OED) on the Web at **http://www.oed.com**. (Unless you happen to have the OED in your personal library.) You can also find dictionaries you might not keep around your house, like rhyming dictionaries, slang dictionaries, reverse dictionaries, and foreign language dictionaries with idiomatic translations.

If you're interested in the current presidency, then an online source may be the only place you'll find information. Presidential speeches, proclamations, and executive orders get put online immediately. Opinions and reactions will instantly appear on the Internet. One place to start that kind of search is The White House itself—the Web version that is (see Figure 1.4). Just as the actual White House goes through the times of day, the Web image changes from morning to afternoon to evening. These kind of resources are moving beyond basic reference, however.

Forms

Forms are another item best left to the mundane world. Around tax season, Internet users get excited about being able to download IRS documents. Immigration and employment forms are other popular requests. The system should improve with time, but it often frustrates users now. Obscure documents are even more bothersome to find and it's doubtful that the government will have taken the time to put them online. In the time it takes to locate, download, and print a form, you could call the appropriate agency and request it be sent to you. If you want it immediately, libraries, post offices, and many government agencies have copies year-round to distribute. If you really have exhausted all other means or just want the novelty of online bureaucracy, try to get a form from the Internet. Otherwise, continue doing it the traditional way.

Figure 1.4
This is The White House Home Page in the morning. You can see how it looks in the afternoon in Chapter 12.

Phone Numbers

Phone numbers are another item that you can usually find more easily in a phone book. If it's a local phone number, your area phone book will usually serve you in good stead. Local listings may be more up-to-date. There are some phone number assistance sites on the Web. They generally rely on phone books (and you already have the local one), other directory listings, and voluntary registration. If you're looking for someone in another state or country and have an exact address, you might have some luck online. If you're looking for someone who has moved recently, the Web services probably won't have a listing. Unlisted phone numbers will not be online.

This is a difficult one for people to understand, especially because so many Web sites offer to find your long-lost college buddy. It seems that in the computer age a database of phone numbers would be relatively easy to produce and use. In my research experience, however, no online source (Web, commercial database, or CD-ROM) works as well the phone book. That doesn't mean you'll never find who you're looking for online—you might. For some reason, the people who create these databases have a hard time keeping them up-to-date and accurate. Part of the problem is the mobility of society and the fact that the person you're looking for may not be listed. (The phone was put in a spouse or roommate's name, for example.) Commercial databases that specialize in finding people (not simply directory listings) are your best chance of tracking someone down. That's a different field than Web research, though.

Timeliness

Another factor to consider is the age of your subject. Businesses and libraries started putting records online in the 1980s. Many libraries have put records prior to 1980 online, but there will be less consistency than more recent documents, that were probably created on a computer. Records originally stored on microfilm, such as census records, will probably not be on the Web. Librarians are working on ways to easily convert microfilm records to searchable databases. One day librarians will succeed and that kind of information will probably make its way onto the Internet. Until then, genealogists and other microfilm researchers are stuck squinting into microfilm readers.

On that note, if you want an original item, you're going to have to travel to whatever library or museum that handles it. If you're content to see scanned-in images of, say the original Gutenberg Bible, you can find it at **http://www.gigatech.com/sites1/gute1/ gute1.htm** (see Figure 1.5). If you want to see the real thing, you'll have to go there in the real world. If you're looking for anything that you must hold, inspect, or otherwise handle, then you have to stick to traditional research. Of course, you could still use the Web to find related information, such as the text of the Bible.

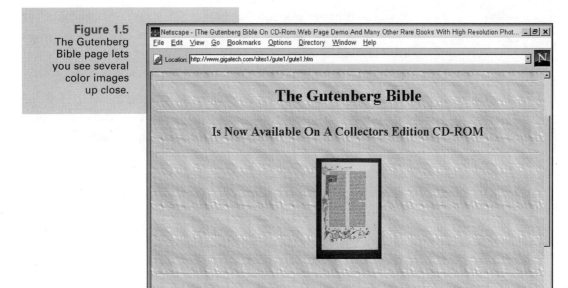

Figure 1.5
The Gutenberg Bible page lets you see several color images up close.

When and How to Look on the Web

Am I telling you to give up on Web research? Not at all. Just make sure you aren't overlooking the obvious. The Web is still a great place to go for current news, science, history, computers, entertainment, literature, and more. However, if you don't know how to approach online research, you'll spend a lot of time clicking from site to site and never answering your question.

Research starts with a question. It's easy to imagine a child looking up at the sky and asking, "Why is the sky blue?" That is essentially what adults do as well. We wonder about a political candidate's background or what the last line in *Gone With the Wind* is. It may be imposed on us, such as a research paper on Jupiter.

That research paper is a good example. Say you're a college student and your astronomy professor assigns a paper on Jupiter. You can go to an encyclopedia for basic facts, but your professor will expect more than that. So you decide to see what's available on the Web.

You first have to decide what it is you're trying to answer. "Tell me about Jupiter" is a little vague. Do you want to do a statistical report? Do you want to discuss theories of its creation? Will you cover myths that were once believed about it? You might want to touch on each topic. Once you decide what you're looking for and the order of importance, you must plan your search strategy. Keep in mind that just inputting the word "Jupiter" can also net you information about the Greek god or cities and businesses with that name. When you know what question you're trying to answer and have your search strategy outlined, you're ready to go online.

Summary

The Web is an expansive resource, full of information on just about any topic. However, you need to know your way around before you begin a search. A basic understanding of how the Web works will help you find resources and know where you are. You can learn more about the technical aspects (and probably will if you create your own home page), but the advantage of the Web is that you can locate the desired information without getting bogged down in jargon. Hypertext protocols allow you to click to the next source so you can concentrate on your subject and not have to remember complicated computer commands.

Just as important as understanding how the Web works is knowing when to use it. You can save yourself hours of research time if you first choose the right source, Web or not. Now that you're ready to get online, you need to learn the components of the Web. These are the tools you will use every time you research on the Web.

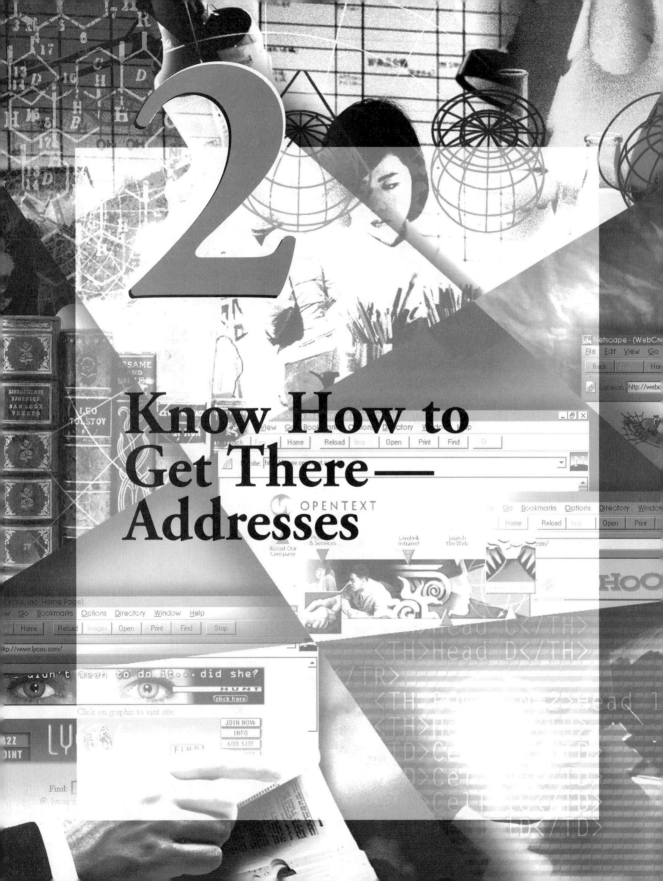

2

Know How to Get There—Addresses

To find your way around the Web, you need to know how to read the directions. Much of what computers do across the network is seamless and behind the scenes. You know that your computer has connected with another and is retrieving information, but you don't see the process happening.

However, addresses give you a window into this process because you know the path your computer is following. Addresses tell you where the information you're seeking resides. An address can tell you the name of the individual or group that has made the information available. You know at a glance if it is a government agency, company, or some other organization.

An address can help you decide when to follow a link. Web addresses can be research tools in and of themselves. Understanding them will aid your research and often speed it up. This chapter will explain the elements of an address and the significance of them. Once you know the elements, you will be able to read addresses and even figure out the addresses of the sites you're looking for.

Understanding Addresses

If you're going to a friend's house, you want to know what the address is. Likewise, if you're visiting a friend's Web page, you want to know the same thing. Web addresses can be simple (such as **http://www.yahoo.com**) or complicated (such as **http://www.cs. cmu.edu/Web/People/spok/in-progress.html**). You can maneuver through the Web without really understanding an address thanks to the links others have created.

However, it's better to understand the components of an address. There are two advantages. First, you can go directly to a source instead of hoping someone has made a link to it. Once you know the components of an address, you can often make an educated guess. It saves time looking it up if you can construct it yourself. Second, addresses have clues hidden in them that can help you evaluate the source of information.

If you have a list of hypertext links that does not include URLs, try pointing to it with your mouse. Your browser will probably show the address (usually at the bottom of the screen).

Defining URLs

Technically, an address is an *URL*. URL stands for Uniform Resource Locator. Http is the most commonly used URL on the Web. Http stands for HyperText Transfer Protocol. The part before the colon in an URL indicates the method being used to access the site. The URL http indicates that the file is stored on a Web server. Other methods and examples of sites are listed in the following table.

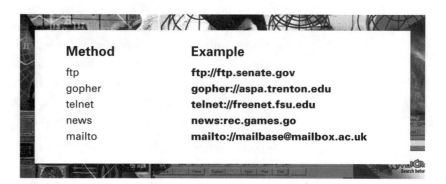

Method	Example
ftp	ftp://ftp.senate.gov
gopher	gopher://aspa.trenton.edu
telnet	telnet://freenet.fsu.edu
news	news:rec.games.go
mailto	mailto://mailbase@mailbox.ac.uk

Note that news does not have two forward slashes. Some mailto addresses also omit them. What does the method tell you? The following sections explain these addresses in further detail.

FTP

FTP stands for File Transfer Protocol. The file you're accessing is stored on an FTP server. At one time, it was the main way to get information on the Internet, but FTP sites still flourish now. FTPing requires you download a document before you can read it. Long-time Internet users will remember UNIX commands like *mget* and *more*. The Web allows you to view a document instantly, even if it is at an FTP site. The computer is still following the same route to retrieve it; you just don't have to oversee it.

What does an FTP URL mean? Chances are that the site you're visiting is an older one. That means it was not designed with the Web or hypertext in mind. FTP sites do not have graphics, although you may have the option of downloading them. Occasionally, an FTP site will not be updated because the creator has moved on to a Web site and treats the original FTP site as an archive. Sometimes an FTP site is the only place to get information. The word "file" may be used instead of FTP.

Gopher

Gopher sites were well on their way to dominating the Internet until the Web came along. Gopher, from a user's point of view, is similar to the Web in that it allows you to see the information instantly. Researchers follow a series of menus to get the desired document. The name "Gopher" comes from two places. The software, like the animal it's named for, burrows through the Internet to find the requested data. A gopher is also the mascot of the University of Minnesota, where the software was developed.

Gopherspace, when accessed through the Web, has much to offer. The files are stored on a Gopher server. You'll still get menus. The menus have icons that make them look similar to a Windows or Macintosh environment. You click on the icons to move around. Like FTP sites, Gopher sites will not have graphics and the text is plain. There tends to be a lag on retrieving documents, compared with sites that were created specifically for the Web. Some institutions have developed their Web pages and Gopher sites at the same time. Those hybrids work a little faster than "pure" Gopherspace.

Telnet

Telneting allows you to log on to another computer system. These systems have a connection to the Internet, but you're actually on their network when you log on. Typically, there is a visitor login with restricted privileges. You have to apply for an account on their network system to use all of it. Many of them offer free accounts or ones with minimal charges. Telneting on the Web isn't all that different from a straight telnet. Typically, your browser simply connects to your telnet application.

For research purposes, telneting is worthwhile if the information is available readily. If you have to get an account, it's only worth it if you think you will use this resource a lot. If it is a resource you will use frequently, it can be a boon. For example, a political reporter may access FedWorld on a regular basis (telnet to **fedworld.gov**).

News

News uses your news reader to go to a newsgroup. *Newsgroups* consist of a group of people who send and read e-mail about a particular subject. Everything here is opinion. Occasionally, someone will post a factual document that is properly cited, but newsgroups are mostly for conversation.

Mailto

Mailto URLs connect you to e-mail with the header already filled out. You can request that information be sent back to you through e-mail. There should be a page that gives you directions. You use mailto for specific research requests and when that is the only means you have to access the Web.

Domain Names

The second part of an URL directs your link to the proper site. Just as a friend might tell you to turn right at the first light, the address tells the software where to go. The next element, after the two forward slashes, contains the host and the domain. Domains are unique names that tell the computer's location. URLs are too varied to cover every possible combination, but there are some common things you can look for.

Let's start with a simple URL: **http://www.ufl.edu**. The *http* tells you the file is on a Web server. The *www* is the host machine. It stands for World Wide Web, of course. Host names are what the server computer is called. The domain is *ufl.edu:* the *ufl* means University of Florida, and the *edu* is a top-level domain name. When reading Web addresses for research purposes, the top-level domain name is the most important element in evaluating your source.

Top-Level Domain Names

Top-level domain names are limited to three- or two-letter codes. A period, called a *dot*, always precedes them. The two-letter domain names are country codes. There are seven top-level domain names that are determined by the type of site. Two of these top-level domain names are only assigned to computers in the United States. These domain names are listed in Table 2.1.

Table 2.1 Organizational Domains

Domain	Definition
.com	commercial
.edu	education
.gov	government
.int	international
.mil	military
.net	network
.org	organization

.com

The top-level domain .com is becoming more prevalent as more businesses launch sites on the Web. The domain .com is assigned to commercial enterprises. Companies have proliferated so much that there is a possibility that this domain name will be divided in the future. If you see .com in the address, keep in mind that any further information probably was put online as a marketing ploy. That does not mean it isn't trustworthy; I've found a lot of great resources in the .com domain.

Remember that most companies go online in the hopes of making money. They might get you hooked on a resource so they can charge for access later or they might allow only a partial search of their database and charge for full access. A growing number of companies sell advertising on their site. The advertising pays for the product, so their presentation is a little more straightforward. However, you have to wait for colorful ads to load before the chart, picture, or other item you're looking for appears. It's a little like the commercials in a television show you've recorded. You can zap by them, but you still catch a glimpse.

.edu

The top-level domain name .edu indicates education. It was originally intended for all schools, but with the availability of domain names rapidly disappearing it has been limited to four-year colleges and universities. Other schools and colleges have to use country domains now. When conducting a search, look for .edu in the domain name. Universities offer a wealth of information. You can usually be sure you're getting a reliable source. Still, universities do allow students to make their own personal pages, so make sure you tracked the correct source before quoting or otherwise depending on what you find. Universities also put a lot of information about themselves online. For example, you may be researching a health issue and see "nurse" with an .edu domain. You go there only to find it refers to the university's health clinic.

.int

This is the top-level domain name for international databases or organizations established by international treaties (although they may use .org instead). Sites that don't fit into a country domain name would be here.

.gov

The top-level domain name .gov means the U.S. government. Governmental agencies in other countries must use country domain names. As other domain names are becoming strained, so is .gov. It now refers to the federal government, with state and local agencies turning to country domain names. If you're looking for information from a particular U.S. government agency, you will most likely look for .gov in the name. If you're looking for an agency from a different country, look for the country code.

.mil

The U.S. military has .mil for its top-level domain name. This domain name is less common than the rest. (You will also find military sites under .gov.)

.net

The top-level domain name .net is meant to be used by computer networks. Internet Service Providers use it. Their users have .net in their e-mail addresses. However, if a company creates its own site, it should have .com as its top-level domain name.

.org

This is a miscellaneous category. Non-profit organizations tend to use .org as their top-level domain name. When you see .org in an address, it's a safe guess that it's a non-profit or social organization.

Country Code Domain Names

Country codes are two-letter, top-level domain names that offer a lot more variety. The United States code is "us." The second tier is what becomes important in determining the type of site you're visiting. An organization may choose to simply designate physical location. For example, **http://www.state.tx.us/DIR_homepage.html** is a site on a Web server in the state of Texas.

If Webmasters choose a descriptive domain for their site, there is more variety in the address. Descriptive domain names that make good use of the second tier can get a little more precise than the generic three letter ones. For example, .k12 is more specific than .edu. This address—**http://charleston.k12.sc.us**—tells you that you'll link to a site that deals with primary education in Charleston, South Carolina. Table 2.2 lists a few common second tier domains you might see.

Although using state codes for U.S. sites will become more common by necessity, you will see them more frequently when your research takes you to sites physically located in other countries. Other countries use similar codes in their domains, so be sure you always look

Table 2.2 Descriptive Domains

Domain	Definition
.k12	School (kindergarten through high school)
.cc	Community college
.cog	Councils of government
.lib	Library
.mus	Museum
.state	State government
.tec	Technical school

at the last two letters. For example, a site physically located in England might end in *gov.uk*. That's because in the United Kingdom, *gov* is the designation for government. Table 2.3 lists country codes.

Knowing where a site comes from won't tell you everything that's on it, but it does give you an important criteria for narrowing your search. The Internet is a global community and you can find information from just about anywhere. However, if you're looking for information on the Canadian parliament, a Canadian site stands a better chance of having what you're looking for than a Russian site.

If you're searching for a resource in a particular language, look for a country code in the URL. A site with **fr** as the domain name is more likely to be in French than an URL with **jp** as the domain name.

Paths and Files

Webmasters can be specific or broad in other levels of the address. Remember **http://www.ufl.edu**? That is a broad address that goes to the University of Florida's Home Page. For the libraries' page, the address reads **http://www.uflib.ufl.edu/uflib.html**. The *uflib* means University of Florida Libraries. This hierarchy is for the benefit of the people who design and maintain the system. It can be useful, if you can figure out the abbreviations. However, don't spend a lot of time trying to decipher them.

Sometimes you'll see a number after the top-level domain name. That is a port number and isn't important from a research perspective. (Of course, it's of great importance to the computer in knowing where to go.) Beyond the domain name, you can find clues as to where a link will lead you.

Table 2.3 Country Codes

Domain	Definition	Domain	Definition
ad	Andorra	ca	Canada
ae	United Arab Emirates	cc	Cocos (Keeling) Islands
af	Afghanistan	cf	Central African Republic
ag	Antigua and Barbuda	cg	Congo
ai	Anguilla	ch	Switzerland
al	Albania	ci	Cote D'Ivoire (Ivory Coast)
am	Armenia	ck	Cook Islands
an	Netherlands Antilles	cl	Chile
ao	Angola	cm	Cameroon
aq	Antarctica	cn	China
ar	Argentina	co	Colombia
as	American Samoa	cr	Costa Rica
at	Austria	cs	Czechoslovakia (former)
au	Australia	cu	Cuba
aw	Aruba	cv	Cape Verde
az	Azerbaijan	cx	Christmas Island
ba	Bosnia and Herzegovina	cy	Cyprus
bb	Barbados	cz	Czech Republic
bd	Bangladesh	de	Germany
be	Belgium	dj	Djibouti
bf	Burkina Faso	dk	Denmark
bg	Bulgaria	dm	Dominica
bh	Bahrain	do	Dominican Republic
bi	Burundi	dz	Algeria
bj	Benin	ec	Ecuador
bm	Bermuda	ee	Estonia
bn	Brunei Darussalam	eg	Egypt
bo	Bolivia	eh	Western Sahara
br	Brazil	er	Eritrea
bs	Bahamas	es	Spain
bt	Bhutan	et	Ethiopia
bv	Bouvet Island	fi	Finland
bw	Botswana	fj	Fiji
by	Belarus	fk	Falkland Islands (Malvinas)
bz	Belize	fm	Micronesia

Table 2.3 Country Codes

Domain	Definition	Domain	Definition
fo	Faroe Islands	iq	Iraq
fr	France	ir	Iran
fx	France, Metropolitan	is	Iceland
ga	Gabon	it	Italy
gb	Great Britain (UK)	jm	Jamaica
gd	Grenada	jo	Jordan
ge	Georgia	jp	Japan
gf	French Guiana	ke	Kenya
gh	Ghana	kg	Kyrgyzstan
gi	Gibraltar	kh	Cambodia
gl	Greenland	ki	Kiribati
gm	Gambia	km	Comoros
gn	Guinea	kn	Saint Kitts and Nevis
gp	Guadeloupe	kp	Korea (North)
gq	Equatorial Guinea	kr	Korea (South)
gr	Greece	kw	Kuwait
gs	South Georgia and South Sandwich Islands	ky	Cayman Islands
		kz	Kazakhstan
gt	Guatemala	la	Laos
gu	Guam	lb	Lebanon
gw	Guinea-Bissau	lc	Saint Lucia
gy	Guyana	li	Liechtenstein
hk	Hong Kong	lk	Sri Lanka
hm	Heard and McDonald Islands	lr	Liberia
		ls	Lesotho
hn	Honduras	lt	Lithuania
hr	Croatia (Hrvatska)	lu	Luxembourg
ht	Haiti	lv	Latvia
hu	Hungary	ly	Libya
id	Indonesia	ma	Morocco
ie	Ireland	mc	Monaco
il	Israel	md	Moldova
in	India	mg	Madagascar
io	British Indian Ocean Territory	mh	Marshall Islands
		mk	Macedonia

Table 2.3 Country Codes

Domain	Definition	Domain	Definition
ml	Mali	pl	Poland
mm	Myanmar	pm	Saint Pierre and Miquelon
mn	Mongolia	pn	Pitcairn
mo	Macau	pr	Puerto Rico
mp	Northern Mariana Islands	pt	Portugal
mq	Martinique	pw	Palau
mr	Mauritania	py	Paraguay
ms	Montserrat	qa	Qatar
mt	Malta	re	Reunion
mu	Mauritius	ro	Romania
mv	Maldives	ru	Russian Federation
mw	Malawi	rw	Rwanda
mx	Mexico	sa	Saudi Arabia
my	Malaysia	sb	Solomon Islands
mz	Mozambique	sc	Seychelles
na	Namibia	sd	Sudan
nc	New Caledonia	se	Sweden
ne	Niger	sg	Singapore
nf	Norfolk Island	sh	Saint Helena
ng	Nigeria	si	Slovenia
ni	Nicaragua	sj	Svalbard and Jan Mayen
nl	Netherlands		Islands
no	Norway	sk	Slovak Republic
np	Nepal	sl	Sierra Leone
nr	Nauru	sm	San Marino
nt	Neutral Zone	sn	Senegal
nu	Niue	so	Somalia
nz	New Zealand	sr	Suriname
om	Oman	st	Sao Tome and Principe
pa	Panama	su	USSR (former)
pe	Peru	sv	El Salvador
pf	French Polynesia	sy	Syria
pg	Papua New Guinea	sz	Swaziland
ph	Philippines	tc	Turks and Caicos Islands
pk	Pakistan	td	Chad

Table 2.3 Country Codes

Domain	Definition	Domain	Definition
tf	French Southern Territories	uz	Uzbekistan
tg	Togo	va	Vatican City State
th	Thailand		(Holy See)
tj	Tajikistan	vc	Saint Vincent and the
tk	Tokelau		Grenadines
tm	Turkmenistan	ve	Venezuela
tn	Tunisia	vg	Virgin Islands (British)
to	Tonga	vi	Virgin Islands (U.S.)
tp	East Timor	vn	Viet Nam
tr	Turkey	vu	Vanuatu
tt	Trinidad and Tobago	wf	Wallis and Futuna Islands
tv	Tuvalu	ws	Samoa
tw	Taiwan	ye	Yemen
tz	Tanzania	yt	Mayotte
ua	Ukraine	yu	Yugoslavia
ug	Uganda	za	South Africa
uk	United Kingdom	zm	Zambia
um	U.S. Minor Outlying Islands	zr	Zaire
us	United States	zw	Zimbabwe
uy	Uruguay		

Beyond the Domain Name

The forward slash following the domain name lets the computer know the address has ended. The rest of the address is the path and filename. It tells the computer where to look for a document and can get quite long. The address **http://www.ufl.edu/uf-active. html** is a short example. In this URL, *uf-active.html* is a filename. Here's a slightly longer one: **http://www.hsc.ufl.edu/shands/ sth.htm**. In this URL, *shands* is the path and *sth.htm* is the filename.

Tilde

Another character to look for is the tilde (~). A tilde identifies, by inference, the home directory of a web resource. It indicates to the server that the address is pointing to a particular physical directory.

A tilde in an address often indicates a user-created page. It resides on an Internet Service Provider's network, but is maintained by an individual. Although there are other reasons for a tilde to be in an URL, a tilde signals to researchers that the link may go to an individual home page.

A lot of home pages are simply people saying, "Hey! Look at this picture of my dog!" Fortunately, some have taken advantage of this medium to educate others on a subject they're experts in. The tilde appears before the user's name, like this: **http://www.iag. net/~oigarden**. Sometimes a user-created home page can be the best resource you can find. Companies, especially smaller ones, also create home pages this way.

Figuring Out URLs

Once you know the components of Web URLs, you can usually figure them out yourself. Let's say you're planning a trip to Six Flags. You're curious if it's online, but you don't have a address. There are ways to look it up, but you can probably figure it out. Chances are the Six Flags' Webmaster would use a Web server. So, start out with *http*. Next, *www* is a common host name. You know that Six Flags is a company and that *com* is the top-level domain name for commercial industries. Six Flags was probably made into one word, because spaces don't work in addresses. You come up with **http://www.sixflags.com** and try it. It works (see Figure 2.1).

Here's another example. Say you're interested in going to the University of California, Los Angeles. You know the abbreviation for the University is UCLA. Because it's a university, the top-level domain is .edu. You try **http://www.ucla.edu** and soon you're on the virtual campus (see Figure 2.2).

Figure 2.1
The Six Flags
Home Page
features popular
characters and
can be found
easily with its
simple address.

Figure 2.2
UCLA's Home
Page address is
easy to guess.

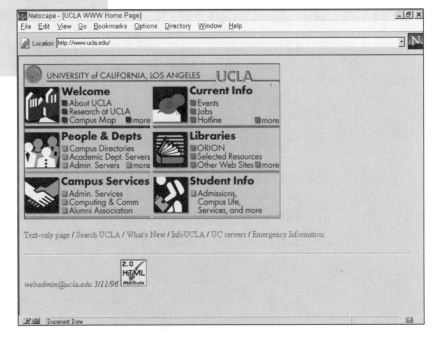

Figure 2.3
You can get to the
Arizona State
University Home
Page by using the
abbreviation,
"asu," in the
address.

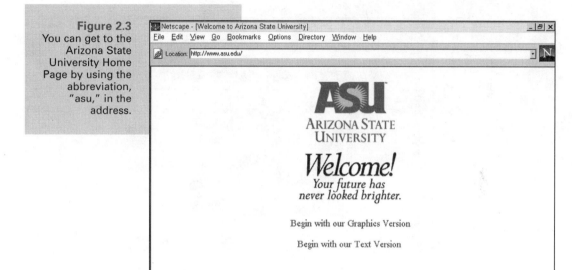

Figure 2.3
You can get to the Arizona State University Home Page by using the abbreviation, "asu," in the address.

You may have a few misses. The address for the University of Florida contains "ufl" and not just "uf." Organizations might also share initials. Looking for Arkansas State University, you could reasonably try **http://www.asu.edu**. That address, however, leads to Arizona State University (see Figure 2.3). The address for Arkansas State University is **http://www.astate.edu** (see Figure 2.4).

Benefits of Knowing URL Components

Knowing the structure of URLs helps you to remember addresses. One of the biggest complaints about the Web when it first premiered was how complicated the addresses were compared to Gopherspace, FTP, and Telnet. All Internet addresses use the same components and hierarchy. It was just that the Web addresses were so long because you typed everything in at once.

Figure 2.4
The Arkansas
State University
Home Page does
not use "asu" in
its address.

Addresses tell the computer you're on where to go to retrieve a file on another computer. They tell you the path that the computer is following and what kind of organization set up the site. Chapter 7 will tell you how addresses help you to evaluate the source of information for validity.

Summary

Web addresses are logical when you know how to read them. You can save time in your research if you make good use of addresses. The components of URLs let you know a little of what to expect, which helps you decide when to follow a link. You can also determine Web URLs on your own and avoid the search process altogether. When you do need to search, you can rely on indexes, libraries, and search engines. The next few chapters will cover those topics.

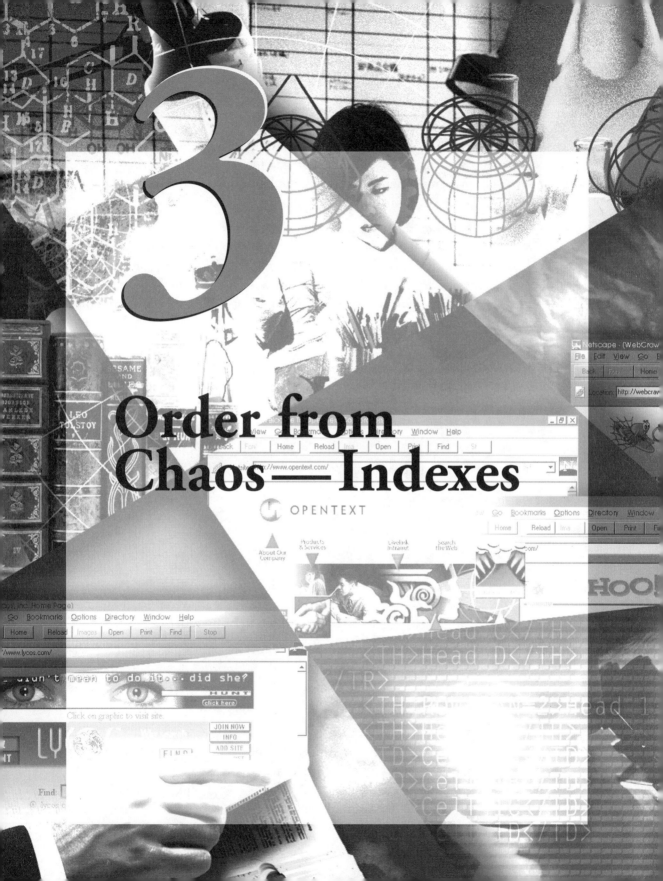

3

Order from Chaos—Indexes

The human mind likes to make patterns out of what it sees. That's why you can stare at a tile floor and start seeing designs that aren't there. It's the way the brain makes sense of something it perceives as chaotic.

Although many people embrace the free-wheeling spirit of the Internet, Web users quickly realized that without some organization there would be no easy way to find a Web site. More and more people were creating Web sites and there was no established agency to keep track of them all. So people began making lists of the Web sites they visited frequently. It wasn't long before these lists were being put online, and Web indexing was born.

There are thousands of indexes on the Web, created by professionals and novices. You will use indexes in your research. With bookmarks, you can create a personalized index that is in an order you understand with links to the places you visit most.

This chapter will explain meta-indexes and indexes and how to effectively use them. You'll also learn how you can create personal indexes by taking advantage of your browser's bookmark feature.

Grouping Web Resources

Although no one has been able to catalog the whole Internet, there have been some valiant efforts. Meta-indexes and indexes abound on the Web as librarians and others try to bring order to the chaos.

Remember the bin library I described in Chapter 1? Imagine a person coming along with a notepad and writing down every book in the first bin. Then the person moves on to the second bin, does the same thing, and continues until all the contents of all the bins are written down.

This diligent person returns to her desk. There she organizes the list so that subjects are together. When you come in and ask for a book about horses, she tells you that there's one in bin 4, another book in bin 7, and a related book in bin 9.

This is more helpful than having to dig through all the bins yourself, although regrouping similar books together would have been easier for you. When people create Web indexes, they are doing the same thing as this bin library organizer.

Web indexers don't have the option of moving similar sites to the same location. Fortunately, because of hypertext links, research this way isn't tedious. By grouping similar subjects together, indexers have given the illusion that all your resources are in the same place.

Cataloging the Web

Essentially, these indexers are cataloging the Web. However, "catalog" is not a popular word; maybe it gives people flashbacks to their elementary school days and the dreaded card catalog. Instead, these indexes are given interesting or descriptive names. Indexers work hard to keep their links current as addresses change and new sites are created. Web page creators both help and hinder by submitting their pages to be listed and creating reciprocal links on their own pages.

Many of these indexes are maintained by one person who does so in addition to other jobs and obligations. These dedicated people use their home page to present them to the Web public. Usually, indexes center on a subject that the person has an interest in.

Some indexes have grown quite large and must be maintained by large groups of people. A few have even become commercial enterprises. Traditionally, indexes have listed any related source under the appropriate subject division. Now, more of an effort is being made to consider the merit of the Web pages the index links to. Commercial indexes will rate their links and use that discernment as a reason why you should rely on them.

Indexes and Search Engines

Indexes are extremely popular with both researchers and the casual user. They allow you to benefit from someone else's experience. Why

go looking for a physics site when someone else has already found six and listed them together in one convenient spot?

Indexes should not be confused with search engines. *Search engines* look for sites in their Web database using the keywords you put in. Search engines usually try to include as many Internet resources as possible. Indexes give you a list to browse, usually divided into subject categories. An index is built around a central theme. Indexes will take you to links they've made in their subject category listing. When indexes offer a search option, you are only searching among the existing links. You will not find any site that is not part of the index.

If you want to read more about search engines and when to use them instead of indexes, go to Chapter 5.

There are two kinds of indexes on the Web. Both types of indexes can be good for research, but used incorrectly can slow down your research. Regular indexes may be dedicated to a single subject or cover many subjects. The links take you directly to the source. The other kind of index is a *meta-index*. It is a multi-level index. The larger meta-indexes try to incorporate as many resources as possible. Many meta-indexes offer links to search engines so that you can look for a site not listed in the index. Some self-named meta-indexes are nothing more than a grouping of search engines.

Meta-Indexes

You could call a meta-index a "mother of all indexes." It is an index of indexes. When you click on the hypertext link, you get another list of sources. Each click gives you a more narrow list to choose from. You may have to go through several layers before you get to the actual resource.

Many Web users make their favorite meta-index into their home page so that when they log on, the meta-index automatically pops up. If you do a lot of research and find yourself using one index in particular, you might want to consider this option. However, you may become tempted to always use the meta-index you see when you log on and forget the other options on the Web.

When to Use a Meta-Index

When should you turn to a meta-index? When you find a good meta-index that you trust, you'll find yourself using it again and again. When you need a quick reference, meta-indexes are the place to go. Some subjects lend themselves to indexes. For example, businesses want to be listed in as many places as possible. The marketers seek out indexes to be listed in. So, a business resource search is a natural candidate for a meta-index. If you don't know where to begin a search, meta-indexes will get you started.

Broad Searches

Broad searches are especially suited to meta-indexes. Perhaps you've been asked to find what's on the Web in the subject of health care. If you want dozens (or in this case, hundreds) of sites on health care, a meta-index is the perfect place to go. You'll get a lot of resources that you will probably want to pare down. If you're not sure how to narrow your search, the many levels of a meta-index may help you. As you go through the layers, you get an idea of which elements you want to concentrate on.

Current Events

Meta-indexes are also a good place to start looking for current events. Web publishing is so instantaneous that a page can be up within hours of an event. For example, after the bomb exploded in Oklahoma City, Web pages were up by that night to spread news and to coordinate relief efforts. One way to quickly publicize the new site is to send the URL to a popular meta-index, and then the meta-index makes the link. Frequently, a notice will be put on the meta-index's home page directing users to the new site. Ongoing events, such as the Olympics, will also have a special link where you can get the latest news. After the event is over, the link is removed from the meta-index's home page.

When Not to Use a Meta-Index

Don't use meta-indexes for places you already know about. It wastes time and eats up bandwidth to continually use a meta-index as a personal one. Besides, a meta-index could remove a link or shut down itself without warning. If you know the address of a site you will use frequently, go directly to that site.

Meta-indexes do not replace research on your part. You cannot assume that every related site will have links to the same meta-index. You might have to try several meta-indexes to find exactly what you're looking for.

Yahoo!

The most popular meta-index on the Web is Yahoo! at **http://www.yahoo.com** (see Figure 3.1). It has set the standard for meta-indexes. Yahoo has spawned off into a special site for children (Yahooligans!) and a magazine (Yahoo! Internet Life). It has even inspired parody sites such as Yippee!, Yankovic!, and !oohaY. The real Yahoo! has links to tens of thousands of sites. Most of these links come from Web page creators submitting their pages.

Yahoo! started as a hobby for David Filo and Jerry Lang while they were students at Stanford University. They used it to keep track of sites they were interested in. Their friends in the Internet community started using it too. As the saying goes "and they told two friends, and they told two friends. . . ." Yahoo! grew so large that Lang and Filo created a customized database to contain it all. In 1995, they moved it to its computer home at Netscape Communications.

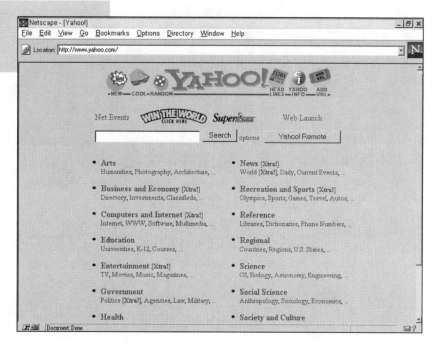

Figure 3.1
Yahoo! Home
Page.

Yahoo! produces no original content. Its sole purpose is to point people in the right direction. The success of Yahoo! shows the desire of Web users to have a little help sorting through everything out there. Yahoo! has a rudimentary rating system. Cool sites have a pair of sunglasses beside them. A cool site may be designated that way because of its thorough content and excellent presentation; or it may be designated a cool site because the Yahoo! staff found it entertaining.

Yahoo! is organized well. One nice feature is that it allows you to jump to its larger subcategories. For example, Health (a main category) has Medicine, Drugs, Diseases, and Fitness on the same line. By being able to go directly to Fitness, you skip one layer. The large number of sites, however, sometimes requires you to go through several lists before you get to your actual resource. The advantage is that

Yahoo! may have a site link that isn't available anywhere else. Consider if you want volume when deciding whether to use Yahoo! in research.

Yahoo! is not only a meta-index, it's a description. More than once, I've seen the phrase "a Yahoo!-like index" to describe a new site.

Other Meta-Indexes

How do you find meta-indexes? They do tend to link to one another. Once you know its address, you can go straight there. I've been asked why anyone would use a different meta-index than Yahoo!. The answer is simple: because for all the thousands of links Yahoo! has, it still doesn't have all of them. There are other considerations too. Yahoo! is so big that you can go through four or more screen lists before you actually reach the Web site you're looking for. Also, you might find a meta-index that has an organization you like better.

Some indexes have the word "library" in their name but aren't really online libraries. For a more complete discussion on what constitutes an online library, refer to Chapter 4.

The Categorical Catapult

http://www.clark.net/pub/cargui/links.html

The Categorical Catapult offers 160 categories with thousands of links. Graphical and push-button driven, it's initial categories are a little more sparse than other meta-indexes (see Figure 3.2). However, it's easy to use and does a good job within the subject listings it does offer.

Figure 3.2
The Categorical
Catapult Home
Page offers a
graphical
environment for
the researcher.

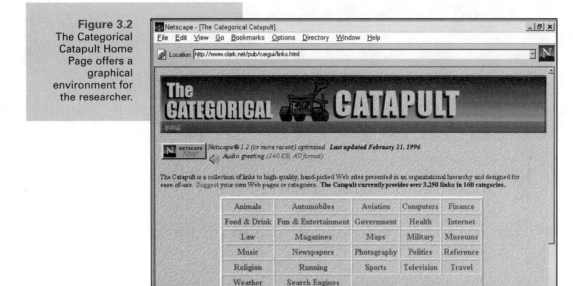

Essential Links

http://www.el.com

Essential Links has many categories and search tools available for Web research. It looks a little complicated at first but is actually easy to follow (see Figure 3.3). The Topical Links might be the most useful area for researchers, especially those looking for news on current events. Like Yahoo!, Essential Links has eschewed graphics for speed. It's a good tradeoff.

Galaxy

http://galaxy.einet.net/galaxy.html

Galaxy is another large site that covers the Web with some Gopher and Telnet links as well. You can search Galaxy's content in three dif-

Figure 3.3
The Essential Links Home Page looks confusing at first but is easy to use.

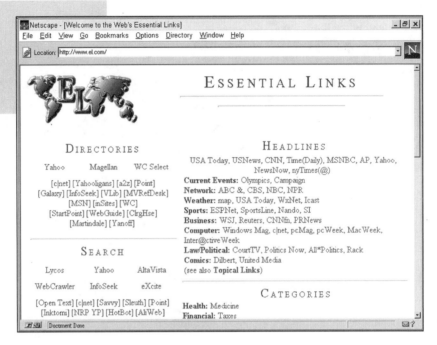

ferent fields or simply browse the index. This index seems more concerned with linking to practical sites than pure entertainment ones (see Figure 3.4).

The Mother-of-all BBS

http://wwwmbb.cs.colorado.edu/~mcbryan/bb/summary.html

The Mother-of-all BBS is a large listing of many topics (see Figure 3.5). The goal is to include sites from "Companies, Universities, Research Centers, Government Agencies, Research projects, Hardware or Software announcements etc. . . ." It reads a little like a phone book, with some listings being in bigger print or flashing to get your attention. It also covers a lot of Web territory.

Figure 3.4
The Galaxy Home Page is a good place to begin for academic research.

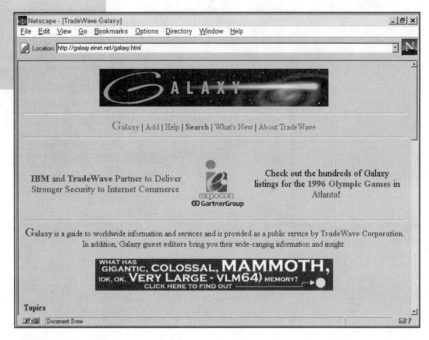

Figure 3.5
The Mother-of-all BBS Home Page offers a resource listing similar to a print directory.

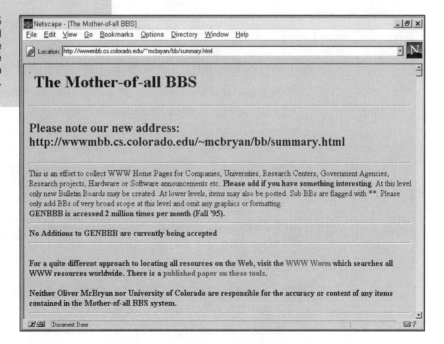

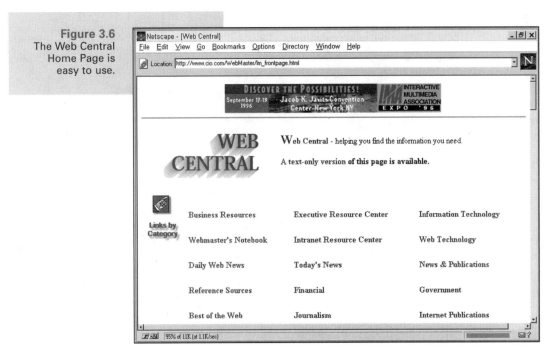

Figure 3.6
The Web Central
Home Page is
easy to use.

Web Central

http://www.cio.com/WebMaster/lm_frontpage.html

Web Central does not have as many links as other meta-indexes but it's easy to use. Well organized, it has long lists in the subject categories. This could be a good starting place if you want a meta-index that won't overwhelm you (see Figure 3.6).

The WWW Virtual Library

http://www.w3.org/hypertext/DataSources/bySubject/Overview.html

The WWW Virtual Library is more like a collection of indexes than a single meta-index because each subject heading is maintained by a different volunteer (see Figure 3.7). Quality varies because of this,

Figure 3.7
The WWW Virtual
Library Home
Page gives you
several browsing
options.

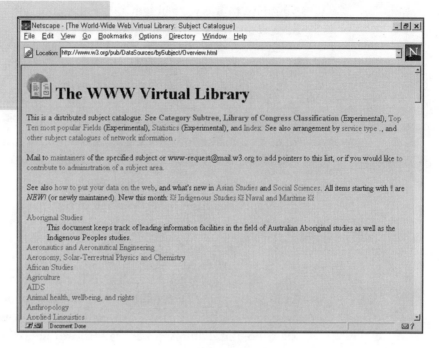

but you can find hundreds of topics with thousands of links. The WWW Virtual Library was created to keep track of the many Web sites blossoming almost overnight. It offers several organizational methods for you to browse by (alphabetical, Library of Congress listings, and popularity.)

Indexes

Meta-indexes will help you find indexes. Indexes are what will actually lead you to a resource site. Indexes do not have original content but may include commentary on the resources they link to. There are far too many indexes on the Web to compile a list here. Generally, the best indexes are compiled by individuals who center on a particular subject or theme.

You have to use your judgment when evaluating an index. The measure of an index is how useful you find the sites it links to. Also consider how often the links are updated. If several of the links have expired, chances are the index creator isn't looking for new ones to add. Left unattended, the old links aren't updated and new ones aren't added. Indexes can be like flower gardens that must be pruned and weeded for new flowers to grow. An uncared for garden can still produce a beautiful flower but is less likely to. An unmaintained index is less likely to have links to the best and more current resources.

A good example of a well-maintained index is The Costume Site at **http://ddi.digital.net/~milieux/costume.html**. The Costume Site has color and graphics. It's organized into easy to follow sections. The top of the site has hypertext links that let you jump to the section of your choice or you can browse through the list. It's updated on a regular basis. There is no content at the site; all the links lead to pages created by someone else. If you were interested in women's clothing in the 18th century, this would be the place to start looking. Figures 3.8 and 3.9 show the home page and index of The Costume Site.

As with meta-indexes, you should not rely on an index to always be there to take you to a favorite site. However, if you find an index that covers a subject you frequently research, you will use that index constantly. Be sure to send e-mail to the index's creator to say how much you appreciate it. Indexers will often respond to requests from users. By letting them know what you prefer, you will help them hone the index into a tool you can use effectively.

Personal Indexes

Relying on an index to always be up and have the link you're looking for is not a wise idea. However, you can keep track of sites you use by forming a personal index. You can arrange these sites any way you want: by subject, alphabetically, or an order only you understand. You can put your most frequently visited sites at the top so they are always a click away.

Figure 3.8
The Costume Site Home Page is illustrated with pictures and has an easy to follow organization.

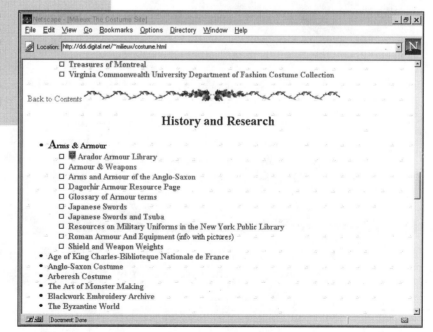

Figure 3.9
The Costume Site index is detailed and well-maintained.

You don't have to write down site addresses and names to form your index. You can use your browser's bookmark feature to create a personal index. You can save bookmarks under different file names to give you a subject category listing.

Bookmarks, Hotlists, and Other Pebbles

Did you read the story of Hansel and Gretel when you were a child? Their parents tried to lose them in the woods, but Hansel left a trail of pebbles to guide them back to their home. It's easy to follow links on the Web and then later forget how you got there when you try to return. You can waste valuable time retracing your steps. Even worse, you may have to conduct another search to find a site you visited just hours ago.

Note   You can read the story of Hansel and Gretel by going to:
http://www.mordent.com/folktales/grimms/hng/hng.html

Browsers offer a way to remember your favorite and informative sites. Bookmarks allow you to click on an URL and store it for future retrieval. Not all browsers call this memory aid a bookmark; you'll also see the term "hotlist." However, bookmark is more commonly used. Perhaps that is because Gopher servers offered them before millions of people were doing Web research.

Remember Where You've Been

Browsers will keep track of your Web travels during a session. However, once you leave your browser and go back in, that "travel log" is lost. Remember when Hansel left bread crumbs and the birds gobbled them up? You'll lose your trail just as easily.

If you think you will return to a site again, you will want to bookmark it. The bookmarks become your pebbles, guiding you through the Web. (Hansel and Gretel did not have the comfort of a home page to click to.)

Bookmarks as Research Tools

How can bookmarks aid your research? Primarily, by saving you time. You can bookmark the exact page you see. So in the future, you do not have to go through the levels of an index or query of a search engine to get there.

Bookmarks become your personal index of what's available on the Web. They're more than just time savers. They are a reflection of your tastes and research needs, just as a book library of the mundane world does.

Bookmarks are a record of where you've been and an indicator of where you will go. This can be essential for compiling bibliographies or conducting seminars later on. When someone asks you to name 10 good sites in your field, you already have an answer.

Making Good Use of Bookmarks

Bookmarks are a great memory aid but have to be organized in a manner so you can use them. You will quickly find page after page that you think you will use again. Most browsers will simply keep adding URLs to one, ever-increasing list in the order you click.

Do you have a lot of family photographs? Many well-meaning souls have piled up stacks of photos. When you look back on them later, you don't know the order they were taken in, the dates, the activities going on, or who is even in these pictures. You try to find a special baby picture and have to sort through a box of old school pictures, snapshots, and a stray negative or two.

Your bookmarks can easily look like that photo box without some order. Bookmarks are useless if you can't find the one you're looking for. You need to organize them in a way that makes sense to you and update the list periodically.

Logical Organization

Browsers allow you to create categories. They may be called folders, directories, or some other term. You can even create a hierarchy of categories and subcategories, depending on how detailed you want your personal bookmark index to be.

For occasional, personal research, use a few general categories. Professional online researchers will need a more detailed bookmark index. Remember to go from broad to narrow. For example, a medical researcher may have the general category of pregnancy and the more specific category of Cesarean deliveries.

You may find that several pages at one Web site can fit into different categories. Consider whether you need them all listed or if the home page alone will suffice. Whichever page you use the most often at a site should be the one you bookmark.

If a category starts getting large (about 10 bookmarks) you should break it into two categories or make subcategories. When you bookmark a page, make sure you put it into the correct category. Then, if you want to see what you have on science-astronomy you simply have to look at your bookmarks.

Bookmarks are for your advantage. Put the ones you use the most often at the top of each category. Don't overdue the indexing. You don't want to create a system so bulky you have trouble remembering which category a bookmark is in. However, well-chosen bookmark placement will aid your research.

Putting Bookmarks in the Menu

Most browsers will let you put a bookmark category in the menubar. You do not want to put all your categories on the menu! If you find that there are some sites you visit every day, however, you will appreciate the ease of clicking right on it.

Search engine URLs are a good example of what you might like to make part of your menu. Bookmark categories you put in the menu should be brief and limited to sites you use regularly. Give it a name so that you won't confuse with other menu commands.

Updating Bookmarks

Bookmarks are always in danger of becoming out of date. With the way Web sites come and go, an URL that is good today may be useless tomorrow. While that's a strong argument for bookmarking frequently-used sites, it is also a reminder to "clean house" on a regular basis.

If you discover that you don't use a bookmark as often as you expected, consider getting rid of it. Click on ones you really want to keep but don't use often to make sure they are still accurate. When a Web address changes, most Webmasters leave pointers to the new address. However, pointers won't remain in place indefinitely. You want to make sure you're aware of a new address before the pointer is gone.

There are few things more frustrating in Web research than believing you have the right address and getting an error. You then have to determine if the site you're looking for has moved or is gone permanently.

When a site does move, make sure you change its URL in your bookmark index. You should check on your bookmarks on a monthly basis. Of course, you won't have to check on the ones you use frequently.

Summary

Indexes, meta-indexes, and personal indexes you create with your bookmarks are all ways of bringing order to the chaos of the Web. When you have bookmarked a few good indexes related to your field of research, you will be ready for most questions that come your way. You will save time because the initial step has already been done. There's no need to decide on a search tool every time.

Indexes are compilations of Web sites organized in a logical manner. They are not the same as online libraries or search engines. Those tools will be discussed in the following chapters.

4

Libraries

Can you describe a library? Does a brick building full of rows of books come to mind? Maybe you go to the library only when absolutely necessary. Maybe it's your favorite place to spend a rainy day.

There are different types of libraries. Some have specialized collections, such as a law library. Others are quiet, scholarly places where you hesitate to cough out loud. Some libraries are noisy community centers, with story hours for children and power tool rentals for adults.

Now, the definition is changing to include the virtual world of computers. But what exactly is an online library? Some descriptions of the Web call it the world's largest library. Others think any collection of resources is a library. A library's home page is not the same thing as an online library.

This chapter will define what an online library is. It will tell you what resources are available on the Web and when you should turn to a Web library. You'll also see home pages of actual libraries on the Web and what you can use them for.

Online Libraries

For the purposes of research, there needs to be a more narrow definition. Online libraries, especially those on the Web, are the ultimate public library. They're designed to be used by the public. Anyone with an Internet connection can take advantage of an online library. An online library can be general or it can center on a single subject. An actual librarian should be involved in supporting it.

Online libraries must offer full-text resources or links to sites that do. They should link to sites that are free or label ones that might charge a fee. Online libraries should use a classification system, have a collection development policy, and be maintained by at least one information professional. That person might be called a *cyberlibrarian* or *cybrarian.* It's a nice touch if the librarian (or group of librarians) answers reference questions as well.

Classification Systems

Online libraries are a collection of full-text resources that are arranged by a classification system. The classification system is the key to a library's success. It directs you to exactly the right spot. It has references to related sources. For example, if you looked up Revolutionary War, it would tell you to see United States history also.

Many people still think of the Dewey Decimal System when they think about library classification. Some libraries continue to use Dewey, but even in the non-virtual world, most have dropped it in favor of the Library of Congress classification system. Called LC, it has been the delight and bane of librarians in the U.S. and countries that have adopted similar classifications.

However, the majority of online libraries do not use LC. CyberStacks and the WWW Virtual Library offer their holdings in the LC format for those who prefer it. Most online libraries present their collection in an index-like format. There are some general subject categories that are commonly used, such as reference or humanities. There is no standardization on what those terms mean.

Standardization on subject terms would be nice for online libraries but a more complex classification really isn't necessary. Hypertext links make it possible to have several subject categories lead to the same site if relevant to that category. This makes it a little less important where patrons begin their search because synonyms can link to the subject heading under which the sites are listed. Online libraries don't need a hierarchy as much as they need related resources linked together.

The important part of the classification system is consistency. Librarians must know what resources the library needs to have in the collection and classify them appropriately.

Cyberlibrarianship

What's a cyberlibrarian? How can you become one? What's the difference between a cyberlibrarian and a cybrarian?

I get these questions at least once a week. Let's start with the easy one. There is no difference between a cyberlibrarian and cybrarian. I write a column by the name of the former; I have a Halloween costume I wear in which I'm called the latter. You'll see both terms, although cyberlibrarian is slightly more common.

What is a cyberlibrarian? In my case, it means I do research on the Internet and write about my findings. When I worked in a news library, I had occasion to actually apply my research.

Cyberlibrarians are regular librarians who use online resources to answer research questions. Computer databases are our specialty. Even cyberlibrarians turn to book resources, however. We might have to look up a date or correct spelling before beginning a search.

Most cyberlibrarians use computer databases in addition to the Internet. An Internet librarian would be a subset of a cyberlibrarian. Some databases are not available on the Internet and may not be for a while. Credit reports, employment histories, driving records, and criminal histories are all available but not from the Internet. Due to the sensitive nature of the information, they're kept separate. This may change as more companies get online and Internet security improves.

Every computer database has its own terminology, organization, and search capabilities. It's a little like learning a language. I've learned how to use dozens of databases in my career and just when you think you understand one, the company will change the software!

A good cyberlibrarian determines what the patron is looking for, although that may not be the same thing the patron initially requests.

(See the section "Reference Interviews" in Chapter 7.) He or she then decides if this question really is best answered with an online source and which database will do it. Part of the job is finding it quickly with as few commands as possible. That's because most databases charge by the amount of time spent online.

Most cyberlibrarians do the online research themselves and then give the desired documents to the patron. Documents might be printed out or delivered electronically. Most requests are straightforward while a few will require going to several databases to find all the facts.

Rarely will you see an ad for a cyberlibrarian. It isn't a career choice in library school. Most library schools offer tracks for public, school, academic, and special librarians. However, library schools do offer database searching courses and new classes are being created as library schools see a need for computer skills. If you belong to a library association, they offer seminars to update your computer skills.

However, most cyberlibrarian experience is learned on the job. It helps to have an affinity for computers and an ability to think in Boolean logic. What kind of companies need cyberlibrarians? Any business that needs information found on a computer database.

Look for job descriptions that advertise computer research. Chances are your official title will be something more mundane, such as special services librarian or information specialist. Try to work for a company that produces something you're interested in. If you hate biology, you're not going to enjoy doing medical research for a pharmaceutical company whether its online or not.

Sometimes employers don't realize the amount of talent and hard work that goes into online research because the field is still growing. If your company doesn't realize the value of a skilled computer researcher, many times a demonstration of what you do will get their attention. Or you can do what I did, dress like a

Collection Development

A collection development policy is an academic way to say that librarians evaluate and choose sources for their content. Online librarians must also judge the merit of an item. Not every site that touches on a subject is included. If you use a library, you can be a little more certain of the source. Many online libraries allow you to ask reference questions and a librarian will help you find what you're looking for.

A collection development policy is simply a document in which the librarians state what the criteria is for selecting materials. A children's library may decide not to carry adult fiction. A public library may decide that videos should be part of their collection. Ideally, the collection development policy is written before materials are acquired. However, that is rarely the case in actual libraries that already have a building full of books left over from another era. Online libraries have the advantage in that aspect because they start with an empty slate.

• •

Read the collection development policy of libraries you frequently use. It will help you evaluate the resources you're browsing through if you know the librarian's criteria for selecting them.

• •

Librarians write a collection development policy for two reasons. First, both the staff and the public know what kind of materials can be found in the library. Staff members use the collection development policy to decide which resources to acquire. Second, having a policy helps avoid future conflicts. Patrons may be offended by a book and want it removed; or maybe a patron will request a book that the library is not going to purchase. In the real world, many librarians struggled with the controversy over Madonna's book *Sex.* Some patrons were demanding that the library buy it and make it available while other patrons were equally vehement that it not be brought into the library.

As the issue of obscenity on the Internet continues to be debated, online libraries will face similar challenges. If an online library provides a link to a site, is it responsible for the content at that site? I would say no, but these issues will continue to be hot topics at librarian conferences.

An online library that has a collection development policy will save itself from a lot of this anguish. Decide what will be in the collection and why. Make the policy known to the patrons and then stick to it. Patrons might still complain, but librarians can continue to build the library's holdings in good conscience.

Library Names and Images

Not every site that names itself a library is one; conversely some libraries don't have the word "library" in their title. (The WWW Virtual Library functions as a thorough, well-organized meta-index.) Just as few want to call their meta-indexes "catalogs," some libraries shy away from the word "library." Perhaps there is a fear they will appear stuffy or formal. Certainly the profession of librarian has evolved to the loftier titles of information broker and research specialist as librarians try to shake the shy-mousy-hair-in-bun-nose-stuck-in-a-book image.

Some online libraries have embraced the traditional image. In an effort to make online libraries more comfortable, they've divided them into familiar sections. You can visit places like the reference room or the children's reading room. They use words like "catalog" and even "stacks." Most of these sites were created by librarians and are maintained at a library or university.

Library or Index?

The main differences between indexes and libraries are twofold: the expertise of a librarian which lends itself to a more sophisticated

classification system. It's easy to maintain a bin library, which is how an index is organized. It's a lot harder to clean it up and make it a coherent collection, which a library must be. The difference between the two is reflected in the fact that online library links tend to be to information intensive sites.

•••

An index can be part of a library. A library cannot be part of an index, although an index may contain a link to a library.

•••

A couple of years ago, I would have made a sharp distinction between a library on the Web and an index. The line between the two is blurring. In fact, some researchers might make no distinction at all. Libraries and indexes are starting to do the same thing in practice. Several Web libraries present their collection in index form so they physically look a lot like an index. Certainly an index created by a devoted expert on a favorite subject will have taken care in choosing which sites to link to. The lines are especially blurred where meta-indexes are concerned.

Libraries and Meta-Indexes

Several meta-indexes have hired librarians to help with collection development. These librarians are starting to write policies regarding the meta-index's content. Some meta-indexes make it their policy to not include sites that don't meet a set standard. It is now common for meta-indexes to rate the sites they link to, although the criteria for these ratings vary greatly.

Meta-indexes and some indexes also offer references to related sites, just as a Web library would. And a few meta-indexes now offer help to Web-weary researchers, a similar service that Web libraries provide.

When to Use a Library

When you sit down to begin your research, you face a wide world of choices. Should you begin in an online library or with a meta-index? A simple guideline will help you decide in most cases. If you're looking for volume, a lot of sources at once, use the meta-index.

If you're more interested in the quality of the sources, start in an online library. Because the material is evaluated for content, you have a better chance of finding reliable facts. Libraries will also point you in the direction of related resources.

Meta-indexes are the better choice for entertainment. They link to everything: scholarly or silly. Libraries tend to lean toward the academic. Another thing to consider is the person doing the research. If your child is the one looking things up, you might want to stick with libraries. There will be less frivolous links to distract the young mind.

Internet Libraries

Even before the Web was created, people were opening up libraries on the Internet. The Virginia Military Institute's Libraries and Information Access at the Gopher site **vax.vmi.edu** comes to mind. Its collection is organized into "rooms" that contain related documents.

Pre-dating the development of Gopherspace, Internet libraries were available through Telnet or FTP. College libraries were early candidates for Internet sites and are still a strong and large contingent of libraries online. College students have been successfully using their university's Internet site for years. Many of the library Telnet sites are still popular.

Now the focus is on the Web and libraries are flourishing here as well. Some Gopher site libraries have converted to Web ones. Many libraries created a Web page that only listed links to the information it has on a Gopher site.

Librarian Home Pages

Librarians immediately saw the value of cataloging the Web. Someone needed to make sense of the information overload. That's what librarians do; they filter through the waves of new data and put it together in a way that others can make use of it. Librarians know how to evaluate sources for content. They wanted to make the "gems" stand out from all the rest.

To aid their own research, librarians began making lists of sites they frequently used. (Much as you build your own index using bookmarks.) Then librarians expanded these lists to include Web sites that others would find invaluable to their research needs. Librarians looked for sites that answered questions they frequently hear from patrons. Librarians began swapping lists and soon it became evident that simply putting their personal catalogs on the Web would be the easiest way to share resources. Several librarians have dedicated their home pages to carefully maintained links that mimic a library collection. It's a little like putting your personal library collection on the Web. One example is Margaret Vail Anderson's Home Page at **http://www.servtech.com/public/mvail/home.html** (see Figure 4.1).

Other librarians have created Web pages specifically for other librarians. Non-librarians will find them useful too because they have links to informative sites. Of course, these pages contain information that pertain to the field of library science. Librarians are constantly discussing their profession and the Web has just given them one more outlet. An example of a librarian's page for librarians is Anne Prestamo's Home Page at **http://www.uwm.edu/People/annepres** (see Figure 4.2).

The WWW Virtual Library

Tim Berners-Lee has tried to catalog the Web from the beginning. The WWW Virtual Library at **http://www.w3.org/hypertext/DataSources/bySubject/Overview.html** is an impressive listing of Web resources. Maintenance of the WWW Virtual Library passed to Arthur Secret, who oversees the project. As the WWW Virtual

Figure 4.1
Digital Librarian
lists one
librarian's favorite
Web sites.

Figure 4.2
Web Resources
for Librarians can
be used by non-
librarians too.

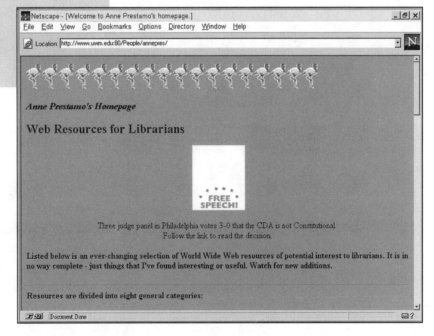

Library has grown, the maintenance of individual subjects is done by volunteers.

It's called a library, but I think of it as a meta-index. It doesn't have the cohesiveness of a library. However, the WWW Virtual Library has incorporated many elements of a library. There are a few "see also" references. And it even offers the Library of Congress classification system for those who don't want to use the alphabetical index.

Does it matter overall what it's called as long as it gets you where you want to go? Overall, no. For the casual researcher, someone who just wants to find a site every now and then, it doesn't matter.

For a more serious researcher, the quibble isn't over the name. It goes back to content (or, technically put, collection development). Because the goal is to catalog everything, you get linked to great reference material and not-so-great, essentially empty Web pages.

Individual maintainers might do a fantastic job on their section. The next section might have one link to that person's favorite Web site. When you have so many people developing a collection, you lose consistency. For that reason, I would call it a meta-index and not a library. The WWW Virtual Library is an ambitious and worthwhile project. I hope it keeps going because it is providing a valuable service.

Internet Public Library

The Internet Public Library was launched in March 1995. It started as a class project at the School of Information and Library Studies at the University of Michigan. It has grown to institution size.

Because of their background, the students naturally used the library metaphor. They stated a mission and created a collection development policy. In addition to the usual divisions (reference, youth, and teen) they created rooms, just as a physical library would have (see Figure 4.3). You can visit the Exhibit Hall, Reading Room, and Classroom. Librarians have their own area (although anyone can go there) and Web search engines are listed.

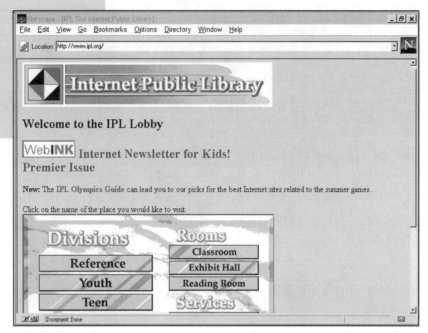

Figure 4.3
The Internet Public Library Home Page welcomes researchers and directs them to the appropriate area.

For those who miss the interaction of an actual library, the IPL offers a MOO. MOO is a Multi-User Object Oriented environment. You telnet into a MOO, where you join others who are currently on their computers. You can "move" around the library and talk with other patrons. A MOO is similar to a computer adventure game. Just imagine dozens or even hundreds of people playing at the same time. You're interacting with actual people, not characters in a computer file.

The Reference Center takes advantage of the Web's graphical environment (see Figure 4.4). A picture of a small library allows you to click on an object to move around the library. You can click on the librarian to ask a question or click on a bookshelf to see its contents.

Figure 4.4
The Internet
Public Library
Reference Center
gives you the feel
of being in an
actual library.

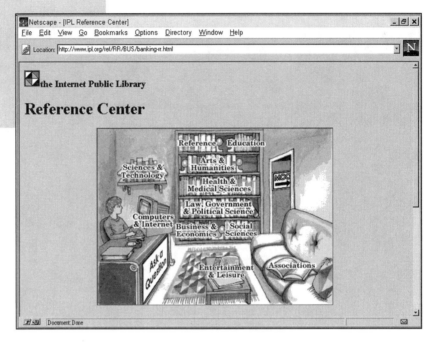

To save time while doing research in the IPL, use the text-only version of the lobby. You get the same materials and it's faster.

The Exhibit Hall, with its many color photos, gives the feel of actually being there. You can take a guided tour through an educational museum display, and links take you to related information.

The IPL is designed to make the patron feel comfortable. It's easy to use. Once you know where a particular source is, you'll probably want to go straight there rather than through the layers. As with indexes, you want to keep track of sites you frequently use, rather than counting on the library to always have a link. The IPL Ready Reference collection is searchable, so you can narrow down your research time if you know a name. IPL's address is **http://www.ipl.org**. IPL may be the closest site to what an online library should be. Not all sites have to use a library metaphor or graphics, however.

Other WWW Libraries

Carrie: A Full-Text Electronic Library

http://www.ukans.edu/carrie/carrie_main.html

Carrie is divided into traditional library departments (see Figure 4.5). It has a reference department, searchable stacks, a serials department, a documents room, and archives. Carrie also offers an exhibition hall with topics relevant to the field of library science.

Figure 4.5
The Carrie Home Page gives researchers traditional library departments to search in.

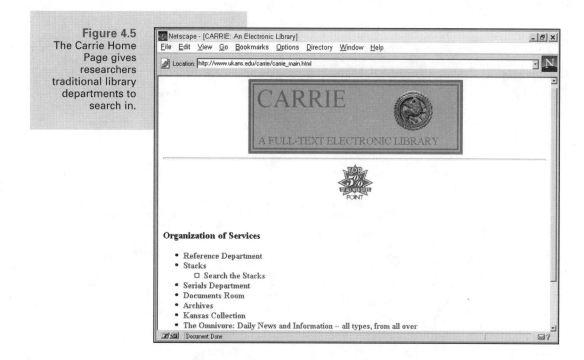

CyberStacks

http://www.public.iastate.edu/~CYBERSTACKS

CyberStacks has adopted the traditional library model and applies the example to its Web library faithfully. Using the LC classification system, CyberStacks catalogs Web and other Internet resources. All resources are full-text and of an academic nature. (see Figure 4.6).

Library Gazebo Kiosk

http://www.netins.net/showcase/gazebo/kiosk.html

The Library Gazebo Kiosk lists resources that have been recommended by librarians as reliable and easy to use (see Figure 4.7). It's organized like a giant index, but because it has a collection development policy and librarians evaluating the Web resources, it's a Web library.

Figure 4.6
The CyberStacks Home Page is a good library for researchers who cherish traditional library organization.

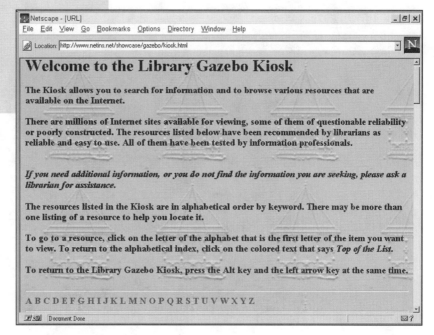

The Virtual Library

http://thorplus.lib.purdue.edu/vlibrary/index.html

The Virtual Library is maintained by the Libraries of Purdue University. It's elegant looking, with resources divided into traditional library departments accompanied by short descriptions of what to expect in each one. The sections are The Virtual Reference Desk, Subject Reading Rooms, Electronic Journals, Libraries World Wide, The Internet Gateway, and News, Sports, and Weather (see Figure 4.8).

Library Home Pages

Many libraries of all types have home pages on the Web. These pages are not online libraries; however, they may serve one or two functions that an online library does.

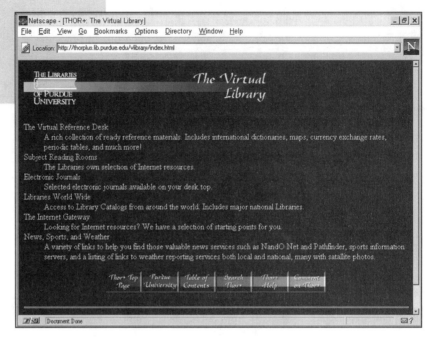

Figure 4.8
The Virtual
Library Home
Page provides a
clear organization
of resources.

Library home pages are not designed to be a library in and of itself. They're put online to tell you about the actual library and to complement it. Library home pages will give the physical location of the library, its hours and policies, and other facts that are useful only to patrons who can visit there. Library home pages might include reference sections, indexes to Internet resources, or links to search engines. These can be useful to an online researcher.

Library of Congress

http://lcweb.loc.gov

The Library of Congress is the one library that can fit into both categories. It is obviously a real, physical library. However, it has created its Internet presence to be an online library. You can learn about

Figure 4.9
The Library of
Congress Home
Page links to
many Web
resources that the
LC maintains.

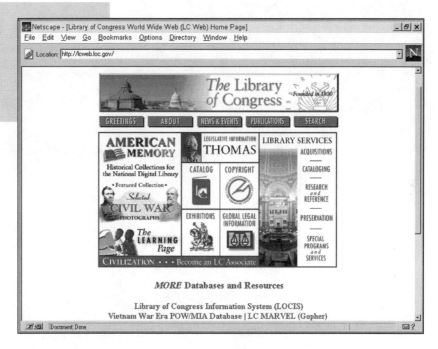

the actual Library of Congress and see exhibits online that you would see in person there (see Figure 4.9). If you're interested in U.S. government information, this is the online library to begin with. The Gopher site **marvel.loc.gov** is available on the Web as well. MARVEL is a reference collection that lives up to its name. The Library of Congress site is also a great source of copyright law in the United States.

The librarians at LC have been cataloging resources for almost two centuries. They have put that experience to use by creating Explore the Internet, a good search tool for researchers. Libraries have put examples of their collections and exhibits online (see Figure 4.10). This may whet your appetite to actually visit the real thing (if you do, the information about hours and lending policies is invaluable). But until you can go to the actual place, it's nice to see it online.

Figure 4.10
The Library of Congress American Memory page shows one of the exhibits the LC has created.

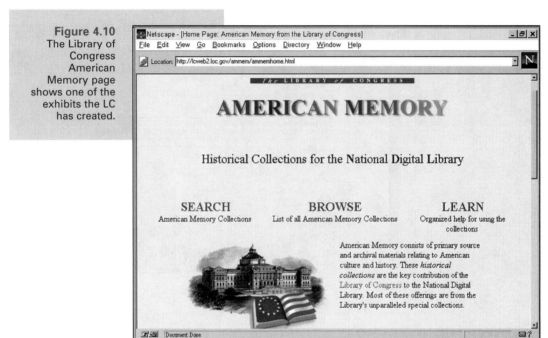

New York Public Library

http://www.nypl.org

The New York Public Library's Web page makes use of brilliant illustrations and its trademark lion (see Figure 4.11). It has samples from its research libraries and the librarians have created an index of useful Internet sites. You can even buy merchandise from the NYPL. For anyone planning a research trip to New York City, this page would be a great preview of what to expect. You can search the catalogs at home and go there with a list of books to look for already in hand.

Other Library Home Pages

When doing Web research, a library's home page might be useful for its Internet links. Some libraries offer reference services and allow

Figure 4.11
The New York
Public Library
Home Page lets
people around
the world
experience a
trip to this
famous library.

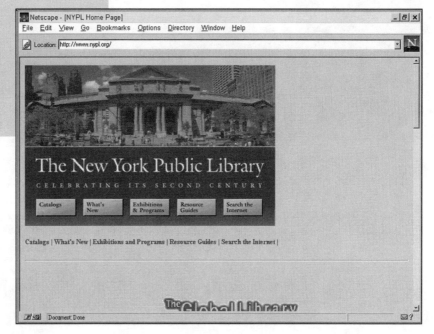

you to ask questions via the Internet. For example, the Alachua County Library at **http://acld.lib.fl.us** does this for both adult and youth services (see Figures 4.12 and 4.13). If you're willing to branch into the mundane world, library home pages are a good resource of where you can get materials through interlibrary loan. Of course, if you'll be traveling to that city, a library home page can tell you about both the library and city.

How do you find library home pages? Libraries tend to link to one another, so once you've found one, you can follow the links to others. However, that isn't always the most efficient way. You can try to construct the address or use an index. The Librarian's Meta-List has hundreds of listings, divided into categories. The address is **http://ainet.com/scfl/plethlib.htm**. Search engines, which are covered in the next chapter, are another way to find library home pages (or any other site.)

Figure 4.12
The Alachua
County Library
Home Page
makes the
library's services
available to the
Web community.

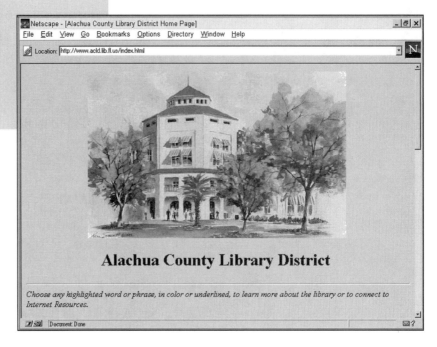

Figure 4.13
The Alachua
County Library
Ask a Librarian
page explains
how you can
solicit a
librarian's help.

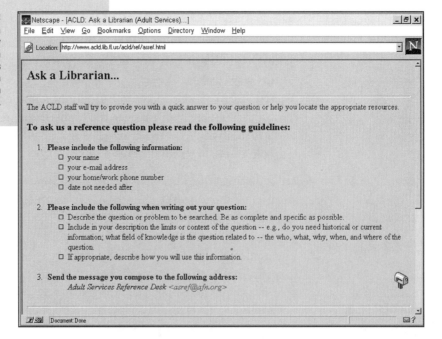

Summary

Web libraries are continuing the proud tradition of making information available to the public for education. Many libraries have a presence on the Internet. It's nice to touch base with physical libraries via their Web pages but it can be frustrating too. You can see great resources in the catalogs but unless you live nearby you cannot read them.

Web libraries erase that frustration. If you see it listed, you can get it in full-text. Online libraries give the public the benefit of a librarian's expertise. Web libraries are good research tools because you know the resource has already been evaluated and selected for its accurate content. (That doesn't eliminate your own judgement, but does make it easier.) Web libraries are the ultimate public libraries because they serve the world.

5
Search Engines

Excite, Magellan, and Open Text: what do these words have in common? They're all names of search engines. Search engines are well-known and misunderstood. Many Web users take advantage of search engines on a regular basis without realizing what tool they're using. Others call every tool they use to find information on the Web a search engine, without understanding the distinction between indexes, libraries, and search engines.

Even those who know the difference between tools don't necessarily know what a search engine does. They think search engines explore the entire Web or they don't know how to enter a search request in a way that provides concise results. Search engines have been the driving force behind Web research, but you have to understand one to make good use of this significant research tool.

Everything but Trains

When I first heard the term "search engine," I thought of the little train that could. I pictured this eager little train engine going out on the Web on the mission I'd sent it on. My imagination was erroneous, however. You'll soon learn that trains are the one metaphor not associated with search engines.

What is a search engine? It is software that looks for and finds Web (and other Internet) sites. You can search among its findings with keywords. It gives you a list of sites to choose from based on what criteria you entered. Search engines do not contain the information itself. They point you in the direction of Web sites that may have what you're looking for.

Search engines can cover newsgroups, Gopher, and FTP sites as well. Some also offer Telnet sites and e-mail addresses. Some programs allow you to specify which types of resources you want to look for. Web sites are the largest type of site you'll find with a search engine.

Engine's Double Duty

Essentially, search engines have two parts: the seeking part it does and the searching part you do. A search engine uses a software program called a *robot* to do its seeking. Robots are given some criteria to look for and then automatically visit Web sites. Qualified sites are added to its database. They are organized in several ways: by address, title, or words in the document.

Robots Create Databases

The goal is usually to include as many sites as possible, so these databases grow quite large. Meta-indexes and other sites with lots of pointers are popular places to scan. Robots are always looking for new sites to add. Robots go by a variety of names: spiders, crawlers, worms, and wanderers are the most frequently used terms.

When a robot adds a site to its database, it includes all the links that a page refers to. How those links are processed depends on the robot software. Web page creators can also ask that their page be included in a search engine's database. A human might consider the request, but generally the robot will handle submissions as well.

Database Organization

How a search engine organizes its findings varies greatly between programs. It's common for search engines to offer indexes of their contents to users. When you go to a search engine site, you can peruse the index rather than entering search terms. These indexes may not have a human overseeing them; the robot might just automatically assign a new site to a place in the index. You cannot rely on the index to contain cross-references.

Because of the automatic inclusion, search engines are good for bulk return but not qualitative content. You may have to search several engines to find a site, because one search engine cannot cover the entire Internet (although some have come close).

Keywords

A search engine will give you a form to fill out. You enter in words that you would like it to look for. These words might be called *keywords* or *search terms*. Keywords is a misnomer of sorts. In a more technical sense, keywords are added terms by indexers to aid consistent search results. Because robots are compiling the database you will be searching, there are no keywords added.

However, in a broader sense, keywords are any search term you put in. The search engine then looks through its database listing for any matches. It might look in the text of a Web page, the title of a Web page, or simply the address. It then gives you a list of sites that match your request.

Because it relies on the document itself to determine terms, you may have to do more than one search. For example, you could be looking for information on antique cars. However, one Web page may use the word "autos" and another one "automobiles." If you simply search on the word "cars," you will not find a site about antique automobiles.

The next consideration is how the search engine will interpret your keywords. If you put in more than one word, will it link them together? Most search engines will give you a site even if it contains only one word you entered. For example, say you ask for sites at the University of California, Los Angeles. Unfortunately, you will get a listing that includes sites that deal with universities, California, and Los Angeles. Because many universities have Web pages, you will get thousands of *hits*.

Boolean Logic

One way to avoid this is by using Boolean logic. Many search engines allow you to use "and," "or," and "not" to narrow or broaden a request. To find sites that contain all your keywords, your search term would look like this: "University and California and Los Angeles." You would still get a lot of irrelevant sites, but at least not as many as before.

To learn more about Boolean logic, visit the Online Internet Institute's Home Page at **http://arlo.wilsonhs.pps.k12.or.us/boolean.html**. It has diagrams and tutorials to explain the practical applications of Boolean logic in Web research.

You would use "and" to narrow a search, "or" to broaden it, and "not" to refine it. "Cowboys not football" would help you to find sites that deal with the Old West heroes and not the football team. Search request terms can become quite complex, but most search engines are not designed to accommodate the longer ones.

Plus and Minus Signs

Plus and minus signs are another way you can refine your research. Some search engines use these signs to indicate which words must be in a document and which ones must not. For example, "+cowboys –football" would tell the software that you want sites that include the word "cowboy" but not ones that have the word "football." Remember that if your search engine only considers titles or addresses you might still get a Dallas Cowboys site that didn't have the word football in the title or address. (In fact, a better search would be "+cowboys –football –Dallas.")

Search Engine Results

Search engines usually give you a list of best matches to least likely matches in descending order. The software has been designed to rank the sites in likely order of relevance. It does this by assigning a number to each word in a Web site title, address, and perhaps to all the words in a document. It's then a matter of matching numbers to your keywords. Some programs are more sophisticated than others.

Even if the search engine you are using does not allow limiting factors, such as Boolean logic, you will generally get the sites that are closest to your request first. This helps; however, you still may have to go through several dozen site listings, depending on how specific your original keywords were.

Result Lists

Generally, you will receive a list of 10 sites. At the bottom of the list will be an option to click for more hits. The software may have a limit to how many sites it retrieves. It might give you the first 100 sites it found that matched your keywords. There may still be other sites you'd be interested in, however, they did not get listed. Some search engines allow you to change the amount of sites listed.

As search engines allow for specific requests that let you fine tune your research, they will become more valuable. Many people use search engines but sift through countless lists of irrelevant (to them) sites. If you don't find one useful site in the first 50 listed, chances are the search request you put in is not going to give you the results you're looking for. You should start over.

Result Descriptions

Some search engines offer descriptions of sites to help you determine whether the link is worth following. Others will include the first few paragraphs of a document. You might be able to choose the level of description you get with a listing. Many search engines simply give you a listing with little explanation.

Special Considerations

It's difficult to give general instructions for search engines because they vary so greatly. Things to look for are the search term capabilities (can you use "and," "or," or "not") and database size. A search engine with an easy to use and reliable search structure won't make up for a limited database. Likewise, a large database won't compensate for imprecise results. Another consideration is how sites are indexed. Does your search request cover every word in a Web document or only the address?

Frequently-Used Search Engines

There are hundreds of search engines on the Internet, and more are being created every day. In the following section, I've included information on the most prevalent search engines. You will be able to determine which search engine best fits your needs after comparing all of them and checking out their sites on the Web.

AltaVista

http://altavista.digital.com

AltaVista went online in December of 1995. Created by Digital, it is an ambitious search engine. It's designed to be powerful and cover a lot of territory. The form is streamlined and simple to use (see Figure 5.1). AltaVista offers a different tip each time you visit, much like a technical fortune cookie.

Contents and Organization

AltaVista uses a robot named "Scooter" to scour the Web looking for new sites to add. AltaVista has decreed Scooter the world's fastest spider and a "well-behaved creature." Scooter manages to visit three million pages a day.

SOURCES

AltaVista not only covers the Web, it also keeps up with newsgroups. You can use it as a news reader, although you will probably be more interested in the search capabilities. You choose which database to search through: Web or Usenet.

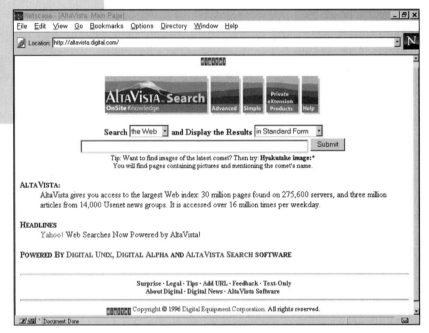

RATINGS

AltaVista does not rate its sites for researchers.

Search Abilities

All the words in a document are put into AltaVista's database. When you do a search, AltaVista considers the whole document. You can conduct an advanced search or a simple search. AltaVista offers both tips and help if you want to refine your search.

KEYWORDS

AltaVista will search for a word exactly how you enter it. That means capitalization matters. If you are interested in all forms of a word, you will have to truncate it. For example, you would search on child* to get results that include child and children. If you're searching for a topic that might have many words associated with it (such as dog, canine, puppy, or hound) you'll need to put in all of those words.

Punctuation, including accents, is ignored by the AltaVista search engine. It will interpret U.S.A. as U S A. You would not get sites that chose to leave out the periods (USA). The word "can't" would be considered two words: "can" and "t."

LIMITING FACTORS

There are several ways to narrow your search using AltaVista. If you enter two words but do not use a limiting factor, it will assume that you meant or. For example, "red roses" would be taken to mean "red" or "roses" by the search engine.

In simple searches, you can use the plus and minus signs. For example, "+red +roses −florist" would tell the engine that you want sites containing the phrase "red roses," but not "florist." This would help eliminate Web sites selling roses online.

In advanced searches, you can use Boolean logic. If you are adept at applying parentheses, "and," "or," or "not" to your search terms, you will prefer advanced searches. You can also give AltaVista the criteria by which to rank your search results.

RESULT DISPLAYS

You can look at a compact or detailed display of sites matching your query. AltaVista does rank the findings from the most words contained to the least. It will include sites that have only one word you were looking for if you used simple search and entered a phrase. You will see the first 10 sites. You can click on the next 10 to see more. AltaVista will link you to the Web site you click on.

When to Use AltaVista

You should use the AltaVista search engine when you want to scan many sources quickly. AltaVista gives results at a good speed and offers a large sampling of the Web. If you want to search a newsgroup for Web references, AltaVista is a good choice. For more experienced searchers, AltaVista's advanced search will meet your needs.

Excite

http://www.excite.com

Excite Inc. was founded in 1994, but Excite the search engine became available to the public a couple of years later. Excite's goal is not to index every Web site. Rather, it focuses on several different areas. Excite's innovation is to offer concept searching, which diverges from the traditional keyword search strategy. Figure 5.2 shows the Excite Home Page.

Contents and Organization

Excite does not try to include every Web site. It chooses popular, frequently-used ones. The goal is a high degree of cataloging on a

Figure 5.2
Excite's Home Page gives you several different categories to search or browse.

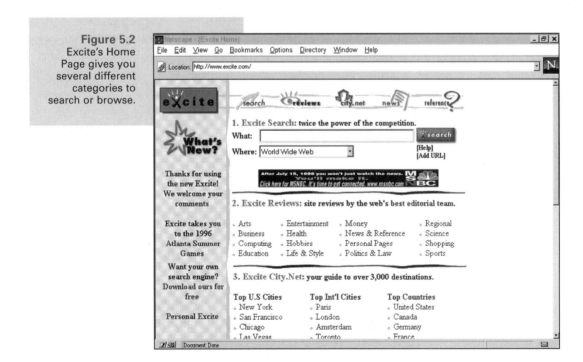

smaller database. Smaller is relative; Excite still offers millions of Web pages. It just stands out when other search engines try to concentrate on volume and include as many Web pages as possible.

SOURCES

Excite offers four categories to search in: Web, reviews, Usenet, and classifieds. Web, of course, is all the Web pages its robots have gathered. Reviews are written by professional journalists, and are summaries of two or three sentences. Usenet is the usual newsgroups. Classifieds come from the newsgroups and the focus is people selling stuff online.

RATINGS

Excite has a confidence rating that it gives with search results. The rating refers to how well the search engine has matched your search request. It does not reflect the merit of the site itself. You can search through Reviews if you want an opinion about a particular site.

Search Abilities

Excite's creators developed a search engine that can find sites based on a user-specified concept, not just keywords. Excite's software takes into account the proximity of keywords and phrases, then numerically determines context. It will retrieve documents that may not have the word you entered, but do contain words that are often associated with it. For example, gardening and pest control are often found together. Say you enter "gardening" in the search form. Excite's results include sites on insects commonly found in gardens, even if the word "gardening" isn't mentioned.

KEYWORDS

Excite also offers the more familiar keyword search. Excite's keywords come from terms frequently found in a document. The keywords are automatically generated by the software and updated once a week.

LIMITING FACTORS

Excite allows you to narrow your search in many ways. It supports both Boolean logic and the plus and minus signs. Exact wording is important however. If you enter "+automobile" you will not get a site that used the term "auto" because you told Excite's search engine that it must find sites that have the word "automobile" in it.

Excite does not offer truncation, so keep this in mind when you are interested in forms of a word. If you want information on both "child" and "children," you will have to enter "child or children" to be sure you get all possible resources.

RESULT DISPLAYS

Excite gives you the first 10 to 20 sites found. If there are more, you click on the next documents icon. Each one has a confidence rating and is listed in order by it. Web sites and reviews offer a summary; Usenet and classifieds have the subject and newsgroup.

When to Use Excite

Excite is good for searches when you're interested in the latest and largest the Web has to offer. It is also handy for newsgroups, especially sale items. You may want to look at the concept searching, but it does not make enough of a difference to justify using Excite over other search engines.

HotBot

http://www.hotbot.com

HotBot started out as Inktomi at the University of California, Berkeley. It went online as HotBot in 1996. HotBot is a quick search engine designed for the long-winded. It uses a scalable database that encourages you to enter as many search terms as possible (see Figure 5.3).

Figure 5.3
HotBot's Home Page is a study in contrasts with a simple search form in the center.

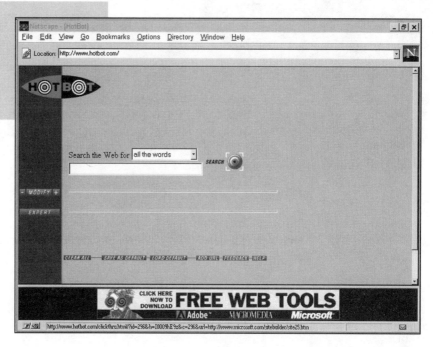

Contents and Organization

HotBot is built on a scalable model. What does that mean? Computer workstations are linked together with a high-speed local area network. Thanks to parallel computing technology, as more memory or computers are needed to keep up with the ever-growing Internet, they can be added into the system.

This is different than most systems, which rely on a huge computer server. HotBot does not have to go down while being upgraded because it is designed to be constantly upgraded. If HotBot's robots ever succeed in indexing the whole Web, they will have a place to store it.

SOURCES

HotBot focuses exclusively on the Web.

RATINGS

HotBot has a confidence rating that it gives with search results. The rating refers to how well the search engine has matched your search request. It does not reflect the merit of the site itself. If the keyword is in the title of a document, it will receive a higher rating.

Search Abilities

HotBot bills itself as the fastest full-text search engine available. I haven't clocked it, but results are returned quickly. The speed may be attributed to the scalable system.

You can do an expert search. That allows not only for limiting factors but also dates, media types, and location. You can even search for that Internet specific symbol, the sideways smile. :)

KEYWORDS

Unless otherwise indicated, HotBot will assume an "or" is between each word. The more words you put in, the more exact a match you will get, at least in theory. You can enter up to 20 words. You can indicate to HotBot if all or just some of the keywords must be in the document.

HotBot does not allow truncation. In fact, it does the opposite by leaving off the endings of words. For example, "swimming," "swimmers," "swims," and "swim" would all be searched for under the word "swim."

LIMITING FACTORS

In the expert search, you can use the form to specify if a keyword must, must not, or should be in the document. You can also specify where HotBot is to look (for example, the URL). Even if you don't choose an expert search, you can use the plus and minus symbols. There is a button to click for modifying searches and it will prompt you if you get stuck.

RESULT DISPLAYS

The confidence rating and page name with a little bit of description are listed in order of the rating. The address is listed, but you click on the name to link to it. You see about 10 sites initially but can keep going to see more.

When to Use HotBot

When you need something right away, HotBot is the place to go. It is fast. So far, it doesn't cover a wide range of the Web but that is changing as HotBot's robots busily scour the Web. HotBot might be helpful if you have a lot of keywords and aren't sure how to narrow it down.

Infoseek Guide

http://www.infoseek.com

Infoseek Corporation was founded in 1994 and soon began offering Web search products. Infoseek Guide is one of three services they offer (Infoseek Net Search and Infoseek Professional are the other two). Infoseek Guide has more than a search engine. Its database has been indexed for the public and you can follow those links if you would rather. It also can search a variety of sources (see Figure 5.4).

Contents and Organization

InfoSeek Guide tries to cover many different Internet resources and tries to present their findings in a variety of ways. Its robots index every word in a document.

Figure 5.4
In addition to its regular search form, Infoseek Guide's Home Page offers icons that lead to services and an index of its database.

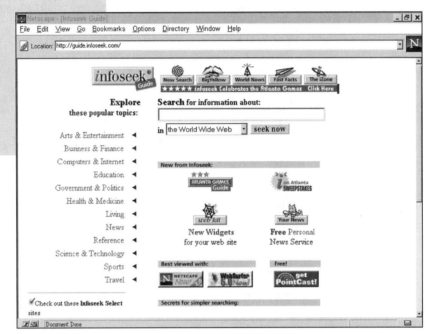

SOURCES

In addition to the Web, Infoseek Guide lets you search Usenet newsgroups, company directories, e-mail addresses, timely news (news stories from the last month), and Web FAQs (frequently-asked questions). You can also browse the Infoseek Guide index. The index is selected sites, not the full database.

RATINGS

Infoseek Guide does not rate its sites for the researcher although sites are ranked for relevancy. It does have checkmarks by Select Sites.

Search Abilities

Infoseek Guide is not one of the fastest search engines but it is one of the most thorough and accurate. Overall, it is good at returning sources you want based on your keywords.

KEYWORDS

Infoseek Guide is case-sensitive and does not allow truncation. Be sure to input exactly what you are looking for. Because every word in a document is indexed, you will probably get a return on nearly anything.

LIMITING FACTORS

Infoseek Guide is not set up for Boolean logic, but it does have many ways to narrow a search. You can use the plus and minus signs. You also have proximity delimiters, including quotes, hyphens, brackets, and commas. The following list describes these proximity delimiters:

- Quotes indicate that the words should be next to each other. For example, "stock option" would spare you many irrelevant sites.

- The hyphen indicates that two words should be within one word of each other. It could be used for stock-option as well.

- QBrackets keep words within 100 words of each other, such as [stock bond] to keep the focus financial.

- More than one name can be searched on at a time if a comma separates them. You could input Rosalyn Carter, Jimmy, Amy to get the whole family.

RESULT DISPLAYS

The Infoseek Guide results page is somewhat different from other search engines. It gives you 10 results it has ranked. The address is listed and you click on the site name to follow the link. You are also invited to hear from the experts and follow a link to a popular media site (such as *U.S. News*). A list of related topics—all links—runs down one side of the page. It's a lot of information but the search results are almost crowded out.

When to Use Infoseek Guide

Infoseek Guide offers one of the most thorough search engines on the Web. It's good to use when you're interested in the quality of your search results and have the time to take advantage of the search options.

Lycos

http://www.lycos.com

Lycos is one of the older and better known search engines (see Figure 5.5). You can somewhat tell by its name. Lycos comes from the Latin term for Wolf Spider. It was named in the days when anything to do with the Web had to have a cute spider/spiderweb reference. It started at Carnegie Mellon University but is now housed at the company, Lycos, Inc.

Figure 5.5
The Lycos Home Page has an index of its database and a search form. Watch the "o" in the word "Lycos" when you go there.

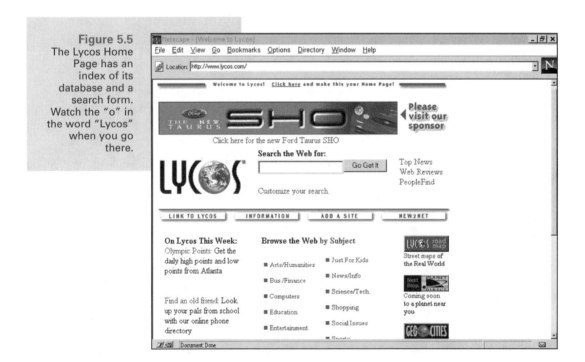

Contents and Organization

Lycos' creators want to cover the whole Web. They've been at it for a while so they may just make it. Lycos has over 90 percent of the Web indexed and stored in its database. It is updated continuously and rebuilt once a week. It has several servers that are load-shared. That means it doesn't matter which one you log in to.

Sources

Lycos focuses exclusively on the Web. You can browse an index of its database rather than keyword searching if you prefer.

RATINGS

Lycos has a confidence rating that it gives with search results. The rating refers to how well the search engine has matched your search request. It does not reflect the merit of the site itself. Lycos also lists how many of the keywords are relevant to the site.

Search Abilities

Lycos' strength is sheer volume. Every word in a document is indexed. You will get a lot of results for your keywords. Lycos depends on its ranking system to keep you from shifting through countless misses.

KEYWORDS

You can search on most terms but there are some exceptions. Lycos will not search for words of less than three letters. It also will disregard numbers. This means if you want to search for 4H Club Web sites, you can't use Lycos. You would only get results for the word club.

Lycos is not case-sensitive. It does allow you to truncate keywords using the $ symbol. For example, "child$" would get sites containing both the words child and children. (It would also pull up any word with child as the root: childish, childproof, childhood, etc.) You can also limit keywords with a period. For example, "park." would keep sites about parking out of your results.

LIMITING FACTORS

Lycos does not support Boolean logic. Curiously, you cannot use the plus sign but you can use the minus sign. So, you can eliminate words but you cannot insist that a word be present. There isn't anything else you can do to narrow your search other than choose your search terms carefully.

RESULT DISPLAYS

Lycos search results are ranked by relevance. You will see them 10 at a time and you can click for more. The address, name, and brief summary are included. You can click on the name of a site to go there. Lycos will give you a site even if it has only one keyword you put in. However, that site will be near the end of the result list.

When to Use Lycos

Lycos tries to cover as much of the Web as possible. When you need a high volume return on your results, Lycos is the search engine to choose. Lycos is also a good choice when you want a search on all of the text of a Web site, not just the title. Lycos does a good job of finding relevant sites in spite of not supporting many limiting factors.

Magellan

http://www.mckinley.com

I have classified Magellan as a search engine, but it could be called a meta-index as well. The McKinley Group was founded in 1993 with the express purpose of making an online Internet directory. Magellan is the result of their efforts (see Figure 5.6). It is named for Ferdinand Magellan because they see themselves as exploring and charting the Internet.

Figure 5.6
Magellan's Home
Page lets you
search its entire
database or limit
your search to
reviewed sites.
You can also opt
to browse
the index.

Magellan might be a good search engine to use in schools or at home with your children. That's because Magellan does not include sites that deal with pornography, pedophilia, or hate groups. Magellan's goal is quality as defined by its editorial guidelines, not quantity.

Contents and Organization

Magellan puts a lot of emphasis on rating sites. Because each site must be looked at by a person and not automatically indexed by a robot, it takes longer to build their database.

Magellan also offers an unrated database of Web resources. You select which one you want to search from. Obviously, the unrated one is larger and offers more results. Of course, if you're relying on Magellan for the rating, you must go with the smaller database. You can also browse the index of their database.

Magellan also comes in many languages; it has been translated into French and German. Magellan databases in other languages are being developed.

SOURCES

Magellan concentrates on the educational and practical side of the Web. That does not exclude entertainment, but it must fall within Magellan's editorial policies. Magellan also includes newsgroups, FTP, Gopher, and Telnet sites when warranted.

RATINGS

Magellan's strength is its rating system, which is family friendly. Sites are reviewed by writers and editors, and are rated on three areas. A site must be comprehensive, be easy to use, and have the vague criteria of "Net appeal." Each area is worth 10 points, for a total score of 30.

Points translate into stars, which is what you will see. One to 12 points gets one star, 13 to 21 points gets two stars, 22 to 27 points get three stars and 28 to 30 points get four stars. As you can see, there might be little difference between a three and four star site.

The writers and editors also write reviews which you can read before visiting a site if you want. In addition to reviews, green lights are assigned to sites considered to be OK for general audiences. Only the content of the particular page is judged, not the links it may go to. It is probably "safe" to let your children go to these sites if you're concerned about adult content. Just because a site does not have a green light does not mean it isn't OK for children too.

Sites are also ranked by relevancy so if you choose to search the unreviewed database, you will still have some guideline to go by. Magellan takes submissions from Webmasters, but they must go through the same review process as the other sites.

Search Abilities

Magellan's search engine is slow. If you're only interested in reviewed sites, you might want to stick with the index.

KEYWORDS

Magellan's creators suggest keeping it simple. It is not case-sensitive. You will get results on any sites that contain even one of your keywords unless you use a limiting factor. Keywords are referenced in the reviewed sites, so you could put in "dinosaurs" and get a site on "paleontology."

LIMITING FACTORS

Magellan allows you to use plus and minus signs to narrow your search but does not support Boolean logic.

RESULT DISPLAYS

It depends on which database you search as to how your results will look. For reviewed sites, you will get a summary of the review and can click on a review to read the whole thing. Magellan also offers a list of related topics. You will see stars and green lights indicating its rating. Both the address and the name of the site are in hypertext. You will see the first 10 and can click for more.

You will still have all those things in the entire database. However, you will also get sites that have not been reviewed and therefore do not have a rating on them. Results are ranked by relevancy.

When to Use Magellan

Magellan has a lot to offer in organization but unfortunately it's not as powerful a search tool as some of the others. It easily has one of the most comprehensive review policies. When you're concerned with quality and content, Magellan is a good choice. You might also enjoy the multi-language approach, especially if English is not your native tongue.

Open Text

http://www.opentext.com/omw/f-omw.html

Open Text Corporation produces Open Text Index as well as other Web services. It has a reputation for precision searching but not a lot of help or information about the search engine or the company (see Figure 5.7). It is linked with Yahoo! and is the default search engine for the meta-index when Yahoo! has no results.

Contents and Organization

Open Text does not offer an index, despite its subtitle. It does have a Japanese version. Open Text centers around the search engine form.

SOURCES

Open Text focuses on the Web but may include resources from newsgroups, FTP sites, and Gopher sites.

Figure 5.7
Open Text's Home Page is almost plain compared to other search engines, but the search form gets quick results.

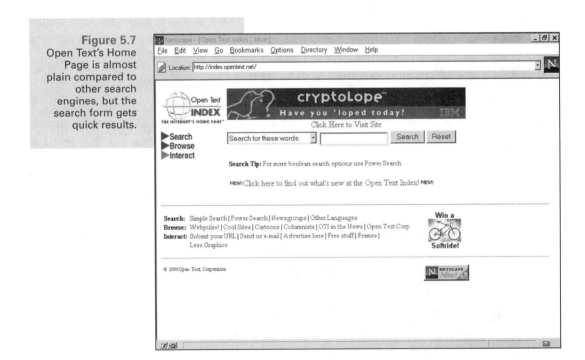

RATINGS

Open Text does not rate its sites for the researcher.

Search Abilities

The reason people use Open Text is its search form. It offers a power search, one of the most precise searches you can do on the Web, once you figure it out. You can also do a simple search, which is similar to ones offered by other search engines.

KEYWORDS

Open Text not only lets you put in keywords but it lets you designate where to search for them. You can truncate a keyword using the * symbol. For example, "walk*" will give you walk, walking, and walks. Other than that, you must enter precisely the term you are looking for.

LIMITING FACTORS

Open Text does offer Boolean logic, but you follow the predetermined forms rather than try to type in the search string yourself. You put in your first keyword then choose to search anywhere, summary, title, first heading, or URL. You then choose how it will relate to the next keyword. The options are and, or, but not, near, and followed by. You then enter the next word, choose where to search for it and continue until all your terms are entered.

It sounds more complicated than it is. For example, you want to find some good Web resources on how computer networks are used in hospitals. One search strategy would look like this:

```
computer within anywhere followed by network* within
anywhere and hospital within summary
```

Open Text comes back with 42 hits. A regular search engine simply using "and" to connect the keywords would have returned thousands. It could be narrowed further by putting the keywords within titles or URLs. This kind of precision search request is Open Text's strength.

When to Use Open Text

Open Text is an excellent choice when you have a specific subject and don't want to wade through thousands or hundreds of sites on a result list. A more experienced online researcher will appreciate it and be able to take advantage of its capabilities. The form makes it easy enough for anyone to use.

World Wide Web Worm

http://www.cs.colorado.edu/home/mcbryan/wwww.html

The World Wide Web Worm (WWWW) is almost like the elder statesman of search engines. It was online and winning awards when many of these other search engines were being designed. Say "the worm" to an experienced Web researcher and you'll usually get a grin (or a groan). Unfortunately, the WWWW has not kept up with the latest search engine trends. It's still useful for simple searches in which you know part of the address (see Figure 5.8).

Contents and Organization

The WWWW bills itself as "Serving 3,000,000 URLs to 2,000,000 folks/month." The WWWW uses addresses to build its database. URLs and hypertext links are the basis of this search engine.

SOURCES

The World Wide Web Worm, as the name suggests, focuses exclusively on the Web.

RATINGS

The WWWW does not rate its sites for the researcher.

Search Abilities

The WWWW offers four databases to search from. The difference between them is not always clear and depends on the researcher hav-

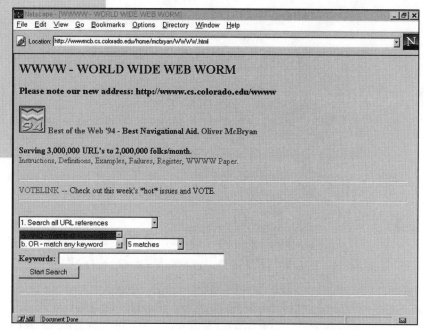

Figure 5.8
The World Wide Web Worm Home Page not only offers an easy to use search form, but it gives researchers a chance to voice their opinions via Votelink.

ing a good understanding of how the Web works. You can search all URL references, all URL addresses, only in document titles, or only in document addresses. The first two are larger than the latter two.

URL references means the hypertext links and this database will yield the most results. The latter two databases are concerned with HTML. HTML is "behind the scenes" when you're on the Web, so it would be difficult to know what to search for unless you are already familiar with a site.

KEYWORDS

The WWWW searches for character strings, not words. The advantage is that you can look for and find nearly anything— even graphic and sound files. Try to think of words that would appear in the site's address.

LIMITING FACTORS

The WWWW has a form that lets you select between and/or for how your keywords should be related. This is helpful, although not true Boolean searching. No other limiting factors can be used.

RESULT DISPLAYS

You will get back as many hits as you select, up to 5,000, before conducting the search. Of course, you may get less than what you asked for if the WWWW doesn't find more. The results are not ranked and have no description. You get the title and address for each site. You can click on either to go to that site.

When to Use the World Wide Web Worm

The WWWW is useful when you know the part of the address but can't remember enough to go straight there. It is also good for compiling lists. If you want all the sites having to do with the U.S. Census, you could search on the URL domain "census.gov" to get a results list. The WWWW can be a good tool for experienced Web researchers.

Meta-Search Engines

What if you don't want to enter your search over and over with each search engine? Robot programmers have thought of that. Meta-search engines have been created specifically to handle this problem. They allow you to enter your keywords once, but use several different search engines. Among the most popular meta-searchers are:

- All4One at **http://all4one.com**

- All-In-One at **http://www.albany.net/allinone**

- MetaCrawler at **http://metacrawler.cs.washington. edu:8080**

- ProFusion at **http://www.designlab.ukans.edu/ ProFusion.html**

- SavvySearch at **http://guaraldi.cs.colostate.edu:2000**

- Starting Point at **http://www.stpt.com**

Search Engines or Index?

What is the difference between an index and a search engine? The division is blurring. Many indexes, especially meta-indexes such as Yahoo!, offer links to search engines and even search robots of their own. Popular indexes have teamed up with search engines. Yahoo! and AltaVista are partners; CityNet and Excite have combined. Many search engines, such as Magellan, offer indexes of their database.

One of the key differences is the maintenance. Indexes are overseen by humans who thoughtfully review and place a new site into the organization. Indexers can reference a link to several categories based on the content, even if the word isn't in the title of the Web page. (Web libraries are even better for subject classification.) Search engines, which ideally try to include every possible site in the database, concentrate on volume. Robots add links automatically. Robots can be programmed to do some indexing, but it does not replace human judgement.

Indexes can also be subject-oriented and small. Search engines are designed to be general and large. Indexes allow you to see instantly which resources are included on a particular subject. Indexes and libraries are often created by individuals and non-profit organizations. (Although they may later become commercial, as in Yahoo!'s case.) Search engines are often created as a commercial enterprise. Companies hope to make money from selling advertisement space. Like network television, you have to put up with the commercials to use the search engine and view the results. Some even key the commercial banner to match the subject matter of your search.

When to Use a Search Engine

How do you decide which research tool to use? It depends on the kind of information you're looking for. If you have a specific topic, an index on the subject will be a better starting place. Of course, you may have to use a search engine to find the index. Also, if your topic is obscure, there may not be an index (or index entry) that covers it. A search engine will help you determine if there's a Web site on that topic.

If you're concerned with the quality of the content, you will want to use an index that rates sites or a library. If you want as many possible sites to look through as possible, use a search engine. It's also possible to find a good resource through a search engine that has not been placed in an index. Perhaps the site is new or the Webmaster didn't announce its creation to the index you're browsing through.

Personal Search Engines

Software companies are working on personalized search engines. These are programs that would continually search the Internet for sites that match your criteria. It would run for as long as you were logged onto the Internet. Over time, you could build up your own database which would be updated each time you go online. These personal robot programs are new, so their effectiveness in research hasn't been tested yet.

If you want to use an online personalized search engine, you can visit The Informant at **http://informant.dartmouth.edu**. You register your name and tell it the keywords you are looking for. The Informant will search using Lycos and e-mail you the results. It will continue to search and send you updated results so that you learn of new Web pages as The Informant finds them. You can also put in addresses of sites you want to keep track of. The Informant will send you e-mail when a change occurs at one of these sites.

If you're making your own index with bookmarks, you might want to put a personal search engine to work for you so you don't have to continually check the links. Remember, although a robot can do dreary work for you, it cannot replace your knowledge of what Web resources you need for effective research.

Summary

Search engines are indispensible to good Web research when you know how to use them effectively. Search engine databases, with the aid of robots, contain a majority of the Web sites. You may need to find a Web resource on a certain subject but you don't know if one exists, much less where it is. You will often rely on a search engine to answer that question. You will often hear or read about a site but not know what the address is. If you are not able to discern it, a search engine will track it down for you. Once you learn about the different ones, you'll be able to choose the precise research tool to meet your information need.

6

Background Material: Newsgroups and LISTSERVs

What do you do when the indexes fail you, the search engines give no results, and the libraries have no links to your ideal Web source? You might give up; maybe it just isn't out there. However, there is another place you can turn to.

Newsgroups and LISTSERVs existed long before the Web was created. In fact, they are the means for what the Web does best; they allow people to talk with one another. You can consider them an Internet version of the party-line phone. Anyone with a connection can listen and join in the conversation. Sites spread information and Internet Relay Chat gives immediate gratification, but newsgroups and LISTSERVs thrive because they're the primary means for communication between parties on the Internet. As with many other Internet features, the lines between the two have blurred with emerging technology.

Background Sources

Why would you use a newsgroup or LISTSERV? Because that's where people with the same interests meet. You've seen movies where the hero hangs out in a bar and hears the latest on criminal activity. This is a similar idea with a more positive atmosphere.

Discussions range from serious (**alt.save.the.earth**) to academic (**sci.geo.fluids**) to fun (**rec.games.mud.moo**). There are also simply inane discussions (such as **alt.tasteless**) but you would have no reason to use these kind of newsgroups for research. (Unless you were researching inane newsgroups, of course.)

Usually in these discussions, someone will post a message saying, "Look at my great Web site!" or "I found the best Web site for this." They share resources with one another and you will learn what the experts rely on.

The majority of the messages contain information and questions. By reading through them, you will quickly learn about the group that is participating. It's a good way to get "inside" information about a population—from professionals to fans brought together by a common passion. Newsgroup and LISTSERV participants write with surprising candor. They post what makes them happy and what concerns them. For example, if you begin reading a library LISTSERV it's only a matter of time before you read posts from librarians concerned about the public image of the profession. Participants sometimes discuss problems they normally wouldn't mention in public. There's even more of a willingness to discuss normally taboo topics, such as salaries.

Listening In or Lurking

You might find the answer to your question simply by reading other posts, especially if it's a current topic in the news. Certain subjects seem to be discussed eternally (the alleged JFK assassination conspiracy comes to mind) and if you just scan the whole newsgroup, you'll likely see mention of them. For example, a newsgroup on political science will by necessity discuss elections in an ongoing basis.

You can read newsgroups anonymously. This is often referred to as *lurking*. Most of the time, you will want to lurk. Your news reader might allow you to search newsgroup postings for a word or phrase. That can sometimes cut down on having to skim through hundreds of messages. A good phrase to search for is "Web page" because that phrase is frequently part of announcements.

You can listen in on LISTSERVs, but the moderator will know that you're there. Many LISTSERVs announce new members to the group. Usually, privacy won't be an issue. In general, LISTSERV subscribers are also expected to be participants. You may not want to join a LISTSERV unless you spend a lot of time researching that subject. (Or you may want to join a LISTSERV for researchers.) Many LISTSERVs can be read like a newsgroup. That is a better approach for a one time search.

Junk E-mail

Once you've spent some time on newsgroups and even LISTSERVs you'll notice that there are messages that don't apply to the topic being posted. These messages instead are trying to sell you something or just trying to get you to send money (via regular mail) to the address listed. These posts are known as *junk e-mail.*

Junk e-mail is especially irritating because the sender does not bear most of the cost; the Internet user does. It wastes bandwidth and it takes your time. A subset of junk e-mail is the chain letter. Yes, those portenders of doom and gloom if you don't pass the message on have made their way on the Internet.

Not only can you receive junk e-mail through a LISTSERV or newsgroup, you can end up on a mailing list where these insidious messages fill your mailbox and steal your quota. You can't avoid putting your real e-mail address on messages you send and post because you need people to respond to you. What do you do when the response is junk e-mail?

Some people have taken matters into their own hands. They send junk e-mail back to the sender after verifying the address. Others send bills to the junk e-mail offender for "proofreading" the

Asking for Help

If you have the time to wait for the answer, you can post a question. Most newsgroup and LISTSERV participants are helpful. They can answer your question directly or point you in the right direction on the Web. You'll probably get several responses, some directly to you, and others posted to the group.

When the answer to your question is a Web site, all you have to do is visit the Web site to see if it helps your research. When someone offending letter but I've never heard of anyone collecting. Chain letters get sent back to the people who originally passed it on. However, these techniques are time consuming and just add to the bandwidth abuse.

Probably the best thing to do is complain to the offender's Internet Service Provider (ISP). Most ISPs do not want their system used for junk e-mail and they will usually put a stop to it. If the offender gave you a local or toll-free number to call, you can call the company to say that their method of advertising isn't appreciated. In some cases, junk e-mail is illegal (pyramid money-making schemes, for example). For more information on dealing with junk e-mail, go to **http://www.mcs.com/~jcr/junkemail.html**.

What about those chain letters threatening dire consequences if you don't pass them on? They may request you send money or simply that you keep the chain going. You can counter with an anti-chain letter (one example can be found at **http://reality.sgi.com/employees/jed/things/chain.html**), but it may be best to simply delete and ignore them. If you're worried there's any validity to the bad luck curse, consider a chain letter I received via e-mail. It said I must pass it on within three days or I'd never have sex again. A few weeks after deleting the offending message, my husband and I found out that I was pregnant!

answers your question directly, you have to consider two things before accepting the answer. Can you rely on the person who replied to you and what do you need the answer for?

Did the answer come from someone you're already familiar with because you have been on the newsgroup or LISTSERV for a while? Did those who responded to your question list credentials or explain where they got the information from? Rarely will someone deliberately give you a wrong answer. However, other participants can

make a mistake. In some cases, they might be trying to sway you to their opinion. For example, a Republican newsgroup is the wrong place to ask what the best political web sites are. You would do that only if you pose the same question to similar newsgroups, such as the Democratic party site or the Libertarian one.

If you're asking a question for your own curiosity and you believe the person responding is answering correctly, then you don't need to keep researching. Let's say you participate in a country music LIST-SERV and you want to know who sang "I'm a Honky Tonk Girl." You can ask, someone replies that Loretta Lynn did, and the research is done.

But if the research is for your job or school project, you have to document the source. Unless the person who replied to you is an authority in the field and willing to be quoted, you will have to find another Internet resource to cite. For example, you can ask on an appropriate newsgroup how many American presidents had their mother's maiden name as their middle name. You get a reply from someone telling you the answer is nine, and that two of the presidents' first names were their mother's maiden name. That's nice to know, but unfortunately the person who responded is going on memory—she thinks she read it somewhere. That means you have more information to work with but you still need to document it with further research.

If you need to cite your Internet resources in a bibliography, see Appendix A, "How to Cite Internet Sites."

One hazard to watch for are fellow participants who *flame* people who ask general questions. (A flame is a snide, scornful response to a posted message.) Don't post a question to a newsgroup when you really could have found out the answer somewhere else. The tone of your request should be cordial and even a little earnest. Too many researchers have made the mistake of sounding imperial, as if they were demanding an answer. Your words might not sound that way spoken, but can convey a different impression when merely read. Newsgroup participants have grown wary of posts from reporters, students, and writers doing research about the Internet.

Always identify yourself and who you represent. There are almost no problems with using the responses simply for help in finding a Web site. If you plan to quote or refer back to someone, make sure they're aware of it. Technically, anything posted to a newsgroup is the same as someone standing on a sidewalk and speaking out loud. (E-mail is a private matter.) However, you don't want to get a bad reputation that causes others to shy away from you when conducting future searches.

Newsgroups

Newsgroups are topical discussions that anyone can read or respond to. Newsgroups reside on news servers. You use a news reader to access the groups. There are thousands, if not millions, of newsgroups in the world because they can come from a variety of places. Newsgroups do not have to originate on the Internet. They can be part of any computer network that has a gateway to the Internet.

Which newsgroups you can read depends on which news server you're connected to. You will rarely have a choice in this; your ISP has provided the news server that your news reader taps into. Of course, you can always make requests of your ISP.

Some Web sites have links to newsgroups that allow you to read them. For research purposes, however, it is better to simply go into your news reader. My experience has been that going through a Web site is slower and has more glitches. However, it may be the only way you can read news (or a particular newsgroup that your ISP doesn't carry.)

There are some Web guides to newsgroups. Newsgroups on the Net at **http://www.internetdatabase.com/usenet.htm** is one example (see Figure 6.1). Newsgroups may or may not be moderated. Moderated groups assure that irrelevant posts are kept out. Sometimes

Figure 6.1
Newsgroups on
the Net helps
you find the
newsgroup
you're looking for.

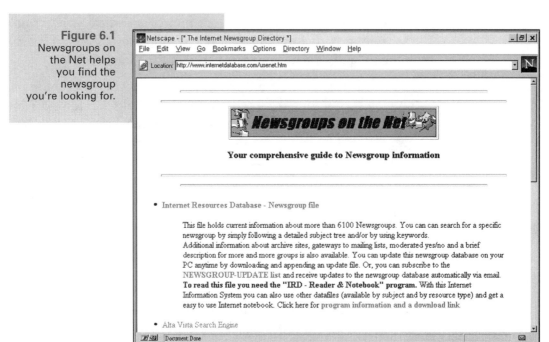

the more free-wheeling atmosphere of the unmoderated groups is more conducive to research because you get more input.

It's extremely easy to get sidetracked when doing research on a newsgroup. This is especially true if you find the subject interesting. Resist getting into the discussion unless you're able to devote your free time to reading and responding. If you do join in and you also plan to post questions in relation to your job, make it clear when you're speaking for the company and when you're speaking for yourself.

Public Forum

Remember that newsgroups are a public forum. Anyone can jump in the discussion. There are usually many more readers than posters. You might get an e-mail response from a lurker who would not post to the group when you ask a question.

You might also get several misleading or wrong answers. Always verify the responses you receive. Overall, you will use a newsgroup to get leads on where to go on the Web, not as the final resource.

How to Choose a Newsgroup

The first thing to do is determine how many newsgroups pertain to your subject. If there's only one, you obviously don't have much choice. If there are several, you should consider what kind of people a group attracts. Moderated groups might attract more serious-minded participants, but that isn't a guarantee.

You'll want to choose a group that's meant to inform, not entertain. A newsgroup that has "announce" in its name is a good place to look because that's what the newsgroup is dedicated to. A newsgroup with "creative" in its name is meant for fiction writing about a subject. Participants will not take kindly to a post asking for the best TV news Web site. Lurking won't do much good either; there's no reason for them to be discussing Web sites.

For the most part, you'll have to go by the newsgroup's title and description if one is given. You can usually get a feel for the tone in the first few posts you read. Even the subject lines will indicate if the participants are discussing facts and merits of a topic or merely whining to one another. Newsgroups that foster thoughtful discussions are more likely to contain Web pointers.

Larger groups offer more diversity. For the most part, if they're treating each other courteously, they'll probably help you out. If they're flaming each other, you would be treading into dangerous territory. It would be a waste of your research time.

You might want to consider the Usenet hierarchy in making your selection. It is called a hierarchy because related groups share ele-

If you will spend a lot of time reading newsgroups, you might want to read Usenet Help first. The address is **http://sunsite.unc.edu/usenet-i/usenet-help.html**.

ments. The more elements they share, the more related the two topics. For example, all newsgroups that begin with sci are about scientific topics. Newsgroups that begin with sci.geo are about geology topics. Some newsgroup names can be very specific (**sci.physics.computational.fluid-dynamics**) or extremely vague (**misc.misc**). A newsgroup that is part of the sci hierarchy (**sci.med.vision**) might have more experts and quality information. That's an assumption that can't be easily proven. Perhaps an alt group (**alt.med.vision.improve**) would be more helpful.

Unlike Web addresses, you do not want to try to discern the name of a newsgroup. It's easier to use one of the search utilities and put in the most important word. (Find Newsgroups at **http://www. cen.uiuc.edu/cgi-bin/find-news** is one place you can look on the Web.) Table 6.1 lists the more common group elements you will find in newsgroup names (not all of them are part of Usenet).

Table 6.1 Newsgroup Elements

Element	Purpose
alt	Alternative
bit	Bitnet LISTSERVs
biz	Business
clari	Clarinet news
comp	Computer
humanities	Humanities
k12	Kindergarten through 12th grade education
sci	Science
soc	Social issues
talk	Discussion of debatable or sensitive issues
news	News about Usenet and related software
misc	Miscellaneous
rec	Recreational
vmsnet	VAX/VMS

Figure 6.2
The Master List
of Newsgroup
Hierarchies
Home Page has a
thorough listing.

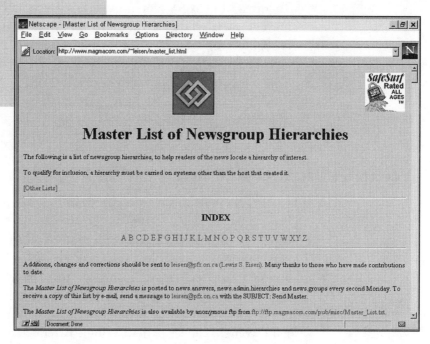

A more comprehensive listing is the Master List of Newsgroup Hierarchies, which you can find at **http://www.magmacom. com/~leisen/master_list.html** (see Figure 6.2).

LISTSERVs

LISTSERVs, also called mailing lists, are also topical discussions. However, they are carried on through e-mail. You receive messages and may respond through e-mail. LISTSERVs are often moderated and at the least, maintained.

The LISTSERV User Guide will tell you how to subsribe to, read, and send mail to LISTSERVs. The address is **http://www.earn.net/lug/notice.html**.

To join a LISTSERV, you must subscribe to it. This means you cannot completely lurk. If you don't send messages, most participants probably won't be aware of your presence. For quick research, LISTSERVs are not a practical choice. Perhaps you read a LISTSERV through Bitnet, which treats it like a newsgroup. LISTSERVs are useful if one covers a topic that you find of interest.

Your Selected Forum

LISTSERVs are an electronic form of the round-robin letter. Members can read what someone else wrote and then add their own thoughts. By the time you read your e-mail, you may find several versions of a thread in your mailbox. LISTSERVs can become almost intimate, as participants get to know each other's opinions and writing styles. Some LISTSERVs are designed as a support group for people going through a situation at the same time. Pregnant women, cancer patients, single parents, and other groups share ideas and encourage one another. Newsgroups can do this too, but LISTSERVs usually foster this environment better. Sometimes LISTSERVs end when the situation has passed (for example, the women give birth).

For the most part, you will find people well-versed in a subject on a LISTSERV. They will often have lists of Web sites they find useful and gladly pass them along. There are also fewer flames on a LISTSERV. Most troublemakers don't go to the trouble of subscribing to a LISTSERV just to hurl verbal attacks. There are too many newsgroups to choose from.

However, it's easy to forget that in most cases anyone can read and subscribe to a LISTSERV. If you want to keep your research discrete, a LISTSERV is not any more private than a newsgroup when it comes to posting questions. Like newsgroups, LISTSERVs should be used as a starting place for research, not the place to find the answer itself.

How to Choose a LISTSERV

As with newsgroups, you first must determine whether there is a LISTSERV that applies to the subject you're interested in. There are Web guides to LISTSERVs to help you choose one. Liszt, at **http://www.liszt.com**, is one place you can look (see Figure 6.3). If you find an appropriate LISTSERV, the next thing to consider is the volume of e-mail it generates. If you realistically can't keep up with it, don't subscribe. Many researchers have eagerly subscribed to several newsgroups, then logged on a few days later and discovered an overflowing mailbox.

Once you've chosen a LISTSERV, follow the directions to subscribe. Spend the next few days reading the e-mail generated. Have the messages been helpful? If the primary thing you're interested in is Web sites, do the participants discuss Internet resources on a regu-

Figure 6.3
The Liszt Home Page bills itself as the world's largest directory of mailing lists. You can search for the one you want.

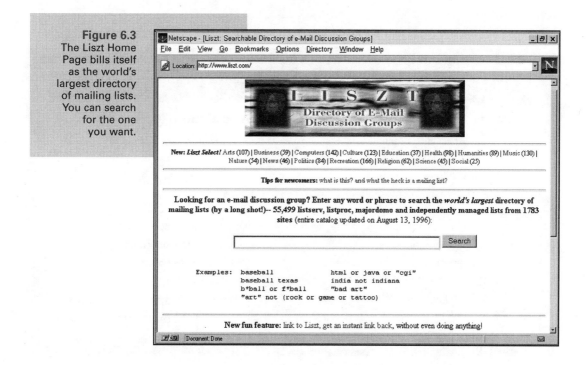

lar basis? Are they willing to answer questions when you get lost? You may like it so much that you join in the discussion.

You might also want to consider joining a LISTSERV that relates to your profession. There are several for librarians. (For example, a librarian for a hospital might want to get on a LISTSERV that discusses new medical practices.) Table 6.2 gives the addresses of some library-related LISTSERVs.

When to Use a Newsgroup or LISTSERV

Newsgroups and LISTSERVs are not a primary source for Web research. If you participate in a LISTSERV or read a newsgroup regularly, you might find out about a good Web resource. However, you should not rely on them to find all of your material.

Table 6.2 Librarian LISTSERVs

Name	Subscription Address
ALAOIF (ALA Office of Intellectual Freedom)	listserv@uicvm.uic.edu
CHILD_LIT (Children's and YA literature)	majordomo@email.rutgers.edu
KIDLIT-L (Children's literature)	listserv@bingvmb.cc.binghamton.edu
LIBCAL (Announcements of librarian activities)	libcal@ash.palni.edu
LIBREF-L (Reference librarians)	listserv@vm.usc.edu
LM_NET (School librarians)	listserv@listserv.syr.edu
NEWSLIB (News librarians)	listproc@ripken.oit.unc.edu
NNEWS (Internet library resources)	listserv@vm1.nodak.edu
PUBLIB (Public librarians)	listserv@nysernet.org
STUMPERS-L (Difficult reference questions)	mailserv@crf.cuis.edu
WEB4LIB (Web librarians)	listserv@library.berkeley.edu

Current Events

There is one situation in which you will want to turn to a newsgroup first. Current events often generate Web sites. It is so easy to publish a Web site that they're often put online within 24 hours of an event. The quickest way to find out about these Web sites is a newsgroup or LISTSERV.

If you already follow one, you will probably see references to Web sites immediately. For example, a news librarian LISTSERV might post messages directing you to an airplane crash Web site. This is the one time that crossposting is appreciated. You may discover after a national tragedy that people post Web pointers in unrelated newsgroups. For example, a message telling about a hurricane relief Web site might be posted in a philosophy newsgroup.

Time Factor

If you're trying to find something in a hurry and you're actively involved in a LISTSERV, you can post a question. Perhaps you regularly read a LISTSERV that discusses cancer research. Your manager asks you if there's a Web site that explains a new treatment. She needs to know in the next hour. One of your colleagues may have heard of, or even created, such a Web site. It is easier to simply ask. Just be sure you start looking while waiting for an answer!

Finding People in the Field

Sometimes it isn't a Web site you need. You're looking for an expert in the field. Web sites might list contact people. However, there's no guarantee that they're available or willing to help. If you post a query to a newsgroup or LISTSERV asking for volunteers, you will definitely get someone who wants to work with you. This is a rather broad approach. It's a lot like scooping beach sand and water into a sift, and then shaking it out until the shells are left. It may be the only way to track someone down though.

Attention Desired

Because both newsgroups and LISTSERVs are open to the public, they are good places to get the attention of a lot of people. If you're conducting a large survey, a newsgroup will help you reach interested volunteers. If you want Webmasters to give your their favorite Web sites, a newsgroup or LISTSERV dedicated to Web page creation would be the ideal place to go. When you want a lot of input or suggestions, newsgroups are a good research tool.

Make sure you pick the right newsgroups to post to or you will be guilty of spamming and your message will be treated as junk e-mail. (Spamming occurs when someone posts the same message to many newsgroups, regardless of the content of the newsgroup.) Some newsgroups and LISTSERVs specifically prohibit these kind of posts. It's good netiquette to heed those restrictions. If you post to newsgroups where general request messages are acceptable, you'll get a much better response.

No Other Sources

If you've tried the indexes and the search engines but haven't found a Web site, you might want to read through or even ask for help on a newsgroup. Perhaps someone knows of a Web site that you couldn't find because it's new. Possibly, the information you want is at a FTP, Gopher, or Telnet site, and a Web search wasn't able to pull it up. If the subject is important, don't give up until you have checked the groups.

When Not to Use a Newsgroup or LISTSERV

Newsgroups and LISTSERVs were not designed to be research tools; they're primarily to let people talk with one another. There are newsgroups dedicated to helping people find answers to their questions, but they are the minority. There are times to avoid newsgroups and LISTSERVs, even if you have exhausted your other resources.

Private Research

You might be conducting a search that needs to be kept private. Perhaps your company is developing a product and doesn't want the competition to see it. Perhaps you work for a newspaper and don't want to give the rest of the media your scoop. It could even be that you simply don't want someone knowing what you're reading online.

When privacy is an issue, do not rely on newsgroups for background research. You can still scan through them. However, it would be unwise to post questions that would make it obvious what you're looking for. A sharp competitor could figure out why. Naturally, their researchers would be utilizing the same groups as you.

General Requests

Broad questions should not be posted. You would not post to a teachers LISTSERV "Are there any good education resources on the Web?" Of course there are. Do you have a particular topic? Are there LISTSERVs or newsgroups that cover your topic specifically? It would be better to go to a literature newsgroup and ask "Are there any Web sites on Elizabeth Barrett Browning's poetry? I haven't found one and my 10th-grade English class is studying her work next week."

Now the participants know exactly what you're interested in, who your target audience is, and that you have a time limit. You'll get much more productive answers to questions this way. Remember to also return the favor to fellow researchers and answer their questions in the future.

Summary

Newsgroups and LISTSERVs can be the last resort or first step in Web research, depending on what you're searching for. Normally, they will be background material only because they're designed for communication, not research. Be aware of the culture and what is acceptable to the group before posting a question. When used properly, newsgroups and LISTSERVs enhance your search strategies.

PART II
Search Strategies

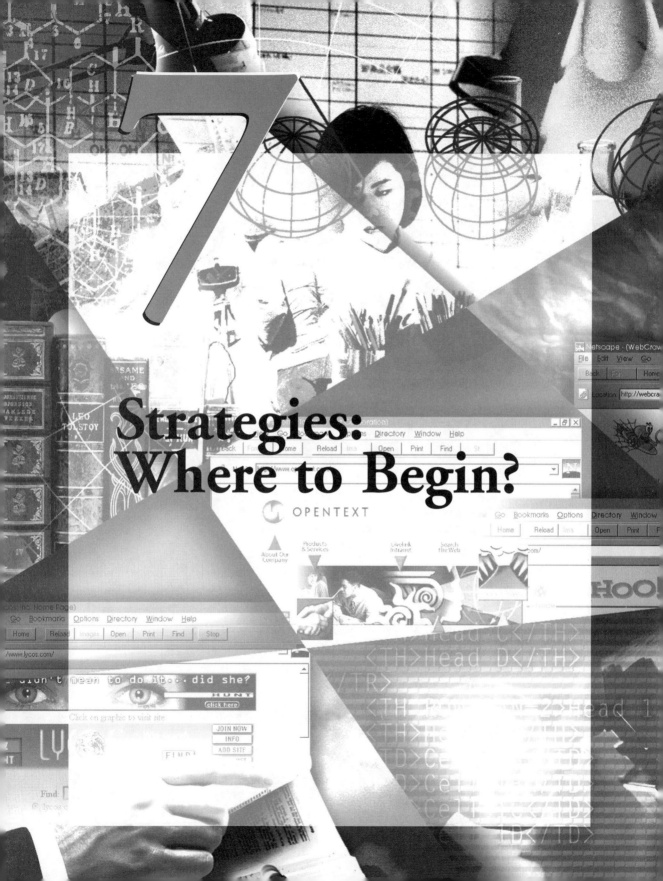

7

Strategies: Where to Begin?

Have you ever gone to an amusement park when you don't have a lot of time? You only have a day so you get the map and decide all the places you're going first, which ones are next, and which attractions you're willing to skip. You then try to guess where everyone else will go so you can go to an uncrowded area. You might even decide when you're eating and where. In other words, to make the most of your time, you plan a schedule of events.

A good deal of research is done before you even log on the Internet. Like that amusement park trip, you need a plan before you begin. You must decide what you're looking for and where you'll go to find it. This is called a *search strategy*. A good search strategy will save you time and frustration.

Determine the Search Request

All research begins with a question. You, or someone you're trying to help, wonders about something. However, a question is often broad. You probably don't think in outline form. To effectively search for an answer, you have to distill the original question to the germane fact being sought.

When helping someone else, it isn't always enough to ask them what information they want. Sometimes people think they know the resource they want but really don't. That's because they don't know which resources are available and what information they contain. When you're helping someone else, you have to consider the resources necessary to answer the question and the best way to obtain those resources. This strategy works for your own requests too.

What Is Being Asked?

When you start with an idea, you need to develop it beyond the initial query. Some questions are straightforward. How did my stock finish today? How do I spell eschew? However, most questions are more complicated than that.

Sometimes what a person asks for isn't what he really needs. Public librarians are used to this. A patron might ask a round-about question that meanders through several topics. In the end, the reference material he asks for isn't what he needs. Here's an example:

> "I'm painting my backporch but I have a baby at home and I'm worried about toxic paint because she spends so much time outside now and I know that a lot of paints are labeled non-toxic but I'm not sure if I can use them outside. Anyway, I was going to ask her doctor but you know how they are. I don't want to call and take a chance that the office will bill me. Besides, I come to the library every Tuesday and you have books on everything, so where would I find a good one on painting? Is there a home improvement section?"

This may seem like an exaggeration but people will tell you much more than you need to know. You'll often hear a lot of their opinion mixed in with the requested facts. A librarian could simply answer, "Yes, we have a home improvement section along the back wall." The patron will probably walk away thinking that his question has been answered.

But has his reference need been filled? No, what he really wanted to know is what paint he can use on his backporch that will hold up against the weather and be safe for his baby.

You have to learn to filter out interesting but extraneous information. You cannot plan a search until you know what you are looking for. There may be more than one component (safety and durability in the example), but there should still be an overall theme (in this case, paint). To learn more about how to streamline a request, see the following sidebar.

What Is the Best Place to Look for It?

Once you determine what is being sought, you need to decide on the best place to look. Think about the resources you have available to you and what their strengths are. For example, encyclopedias are great for historical summaries but are not a source for current statistics.

The Reference Interview

You will often seek out information someone else has requested of you. It's important that you understand what the person is asking for. Librarians learn the art of the reference interview in library school. Any researcher can put it to use, even for personal research.

Librarians are used to patrons who know what they want but don't know how to express it. They may be afraid of appearing ignorant or don't want to reveal too much. However, a researcher can't find the information if they don't know what is being sought.

Reference interviews should move from broad to specific. When conducting one, politely ignore irrelevant information and focus on the facts that the seeker is trying to find. Like a detective, you look for clues that lead you to the actual question. Ask questions that invite the seeker to expound on the request while staying on topic.

Avoid asking why they're looking for this information. First, it isn't necessary to delve into their personal reasons. Secondly, it could embarrass the person so that they don't seek out further help. (Bankruptcy, medical conditions, legal problems, and family relationships can all be sensitive issues. Also, there are certain professions where privacy can be an issue, such as a journalist who wants to protect a source.)

However, it is permissible to ask what the information will be used for if it seems appropriate and will help your research. For example, you might ask a student if this is for a class project and what grade level that would be. You have to use your judgment based on where you work and the clients you serve. You might do

In the earlier example of the painting patron, the home improvement section would not be the best place to look. There are many books and online sources that deal with child safety in the home.

research in an environment where people freely discuss what they're looking for and why.

A fifteen minute reference interview can save hours of research down the road. Every researcher has a story of finding pages worth of good information only to have the seeker look it over and say it wasn't what they were looking for. Here's an example reference interview between a librarian and patron:

> **Patron:** Do you know where I can find information on businesses?
>
> **Librarian:** We have many resources. Is there a particular company or industry you're looking for?
>
> **Patron:** Well, I'm thinking of opening up my own business. See, everyone tells me that my cakes are better than the professional bakers and that I should go into catering.
>
> **Librarian:** Then you would like information on how to open your own business?
>
> **Patron:** Sort of. I wanted to read about other caterers. Check out my competition first. Find out how much money they make. That kind of stuff.
>
> **Librarian:** Company profiles should be able to help you. Do you have a catering company in mind?
>
> **Patron:** I'm interested in local caterers.
>
> **Librarian:** Then you need a list of local caterers and their company profiles?
>
> **Patron:** Yes.

One of these could better answer his question. He could then move on to reference materials that deal with paint if he had more questions about how well a type of child-safe paint will hold up.

One of the first decisions you'll make is whether to go online. There are several points to consider. Is the sought after information current news? Is it unusual in any way (obscure, highly technical, specialized)? Do you want a lot of resources or will a few suffice? Can the question be answered with a simple reference source or today's newspaper?

Generally, if you want a high volume of resources and current information, going online is a good idea. If you're unlikely to find it in a book you have access to, try looking online. For example, I needed to know the Swahili word for apple. I was at home and didn't have an English-Swahili dictionary handy. I found in on the Web in about 15 minutes. If I had been in a library that had a language dictionary on the reference shelf, it might have been quicker to look there. Since I was at home, though, it was quicker to go online than to drive to a public library. As the Web grows, you will be looking online more and more frequently.

Do Offline Homework

After you decide to go online, you don't simply log in and begin searching. You need to confirm the facts you do know and figure out how they'll help you. The librarian who conducted the reference interview with the would-be caterer needs to compile a list of local caterers. The phone book would be the most immediate source. The Chamber of Commerce might be a more thorough one.

You can avoid simple mistakes. Make sure all keywords are spelled correctly. Be aware of correct capitalization and punctuation because some search engines are case-sensitive. Check for geographic locations when necessary. For example, if you're looking for a city, you'll need to know which state (or province) it's in to use an online directory. Any relevant statistics or dates should be verified. You might be able to do this simply with the person making the request or you might have to use a common reference material.

Researching the Web

Anyone can get on the Web, choose a hypertext link, and keep clicking on links until he stumbles across something interesting. If you have time, it can be amusing. That's why URouLette and similar sites thrive.

• •

URouLette is one of the most popular sites on the Web. You spin the wheel and get sent to a random link. The address is: **http://www.uroulette.com:8000**.

• •

However, to be useful for research, you need to find relevant facts in an efficient and timely manner. Many researchers (especially "traditional" librarians) have become overwhelmed and written off the Web as too unwieldy to be worth consulting.

The Web is the future of researching though. Many resources are already online; some are exclusively online. Although many of these sources have had their own databases to dial in to, the trend is to join the Internet community. People want to dial one number and be able to access many different services. Companies are responding to that demand.

Finding information on the Web is not a matter of luck. Although it can sometimes be intuitive, you can find what you're looking for with relative ease. Some searches are time-consuming but that is true no matter what medium you use. Once you learn how to effectively do research on the Web, you should be able to find most items in less than 15 minutes.

Choosing Tools

The easiest way to shorten your search time and ensure success is to choose the right Web tool. Which tool you choose will depend on the request. There are two factors to consider: what is being sought and what kind of results you want. Do you want a few quality resources? Or are you more interested in volume?

I have already covered the tools of Web research: indexes, libraries, search engines, and newsgroups. You'll be aided by an understanding of addresses and the hotlists you have already compiled. When you know what you're looking for, consider the best way to retrieve it.

For example, if you have a broad search request on a common topic (such as lots of information on volcanoes) you'll probably have the best success going to an index. If the topic is a bit more unusual (such as Norse mythological gods used in marketing campaigns) you will probably want to use a search engine that covers a large portion of the Web and allows for complex search requests.

Academic areas are best served by libraries and indexes. Some information lends itself to a directory style catalog, such as a listing of city home pages. Current news events are best tracked on newsgroups and LISTSERVs until Web pages can be created or updated.

When you have a direct, simple request, a search engine may be your best tool. I have made the mistake of using an index when a well-phrased keyword string put into a good search engine would have been the better choice. For example, I assumed Yahoo! would have a link to an English-Swahili dictionary in its vast index. It did not and I ended up having to go to Lycos and put in the phrase "Swahili dictionary" to find one.

If you're looking for a company, you might want to surmise the address. Because many companies register their corporate name as their domain name, you can make an educated guess. For example, if you're asked to find IBM's Web page, it's easy to guess that it's **http://www.ibm.com**. There's no reason to go to a search engine.

The harder search is when you must use a combination of tools. Perhaps you need a search engine to help you find an index. Maybe you have to read a newsgroup to find an URL. It's important to choose which tools you'll use and the order you'll use them in.

When to Follow the Links

Another important skill of Web research is determining when to follow someone else's hypertext link and when not to. Too many people keep clicking and clicking without really seeing anything relevant. Links can be like a siren's song, offering the promise of enlightenment just a Web page away.

When should you follow a link? Obviously, when it appears it will take you somewhere useful. If you're looking for biological resources and you're in a science index, you click on biology. It's point and click researching.

Keyword Connection

Researchers fall into the trap of clicking on any link that contains their keyword. (It's also easy to get sidetracked with "fun" links put there to amuse you.) If you're looking up French international businesses, you don't need to click on a link that's for French gourmet food. Sometimes frustrated when their server connection to a site times out, researches will click on "related" links. Sure, you can get through, but what's the point if it won't have what you're looking for?

I've seen researchers looking for Supreme Court "decisions" click on Supreme Court "biographies" of the justices. It gave them the immediate gratification of going somewhere, pulling something up on the screen. It did not, however, meet their research need. Another way researchers get sidetracked is a link that promises a picture. If you need the textual information, why waste the time loading an image? The Web is full of graphics as it is. You'll only add to your research time if you stop to admire the pretty pictures.

There are many legitimate reasons to follow a site's links. Obviously, if you're moving through an index, you'll be doing just that. What about links that are listed at a particular site? Ask yourself whether the Web page is answering your question? If so, why go anywhere else?

If it isn't answering your question, will the links on this page take you to a site that can? It can be difficult to determine based on the name of the link, but you can make a preliminary judgment. Sometimes a Webmaster will be kind enough to give you a description of what to expect.

A Link's Address—Where It Will Take You

If your browser lets you see the address, you can take that into consideration when deciding to follow a link. Are you looking for academic resources? You'll have better luck with a top-level domain of .edu than .com. Are you interested in your local government? Then addresses with the top-level domain .gov probably won't help you. If you want Canadian history, you may have better luck with a site that originates in Canada, so look for .ca in the URL. Of course, Canadian information could be on a server in the United Kingdom, but when faced with many sites to choose from, that can be a reasonable way to narrow your selections. Start with the obvious and then go to the others only if necessary.

You will learn to read addresses automatically and make decisions without realizing it. I have learned that .de is a German server. Often, their site will be in German, which I can't read. It doesn't automatically eliminate all sites with .de in the URL, but I look at one I know I can read first. In general, I try to avoid commercial sites that are giant ads. So I look at .com sites that have cute names with a wary eye. (For example, **http://www.icantbelieve.com** comes to mind. Do you really need to read about fake butter?)

Abundant Sources

Another reason to follow links is you may want several sources. Frequently, there are links to related sites. This is a helpful and appropriate use of hypertext. Keep in mind that commercial sources may not have pure motives for the links they provide you with. Sometimes commercial sources really strive to provide quality information. Other times, they are only giving you the equivalent of an online infomercial. In that case, their links usually go only to other companies they have business dealings with.

When to Start Over

If you have been looking for 15 or 20 minutes with no luck, it's time to rethink your strategy. Have you been clicking on link after link and not answering your question? Then it's time to start over. Look at your search strategy. Did you choose the right tool? Should you have used a search engine instead of an index, or the other way around? Is the subject your looking for too current or obscure to be on an index yet?

Another possibility is that you're using the right tool but the wrong keywords. Did you use a term that can mean different things? For example, you could do a search on the Alamo in San Antonio but pull up a long list of businesses that have the word "alamo" in their name.

If you have tried to put together an URL and are having no luck, go ahead and use a search engine. Surmising addresses is supposed to be a time saver, not a brain teaser. The problem could also be with the Boolean logic or other limiting factors you used. Be sure what you meant is being conveyed to the computer. Too many pluses, minuses, but's, and or's can get confusing.

Eureka!

All of your Web research has paid off and you have a resource that answers your questions. Maybe you found it immediately or maybe it took a little digging. Either way, you feel elated now because it's more interesting to read the answer than to wonder about it.

There are a few things you should do. First, you must evaluate the quality of the information you have found. If it's worth keeping, then you must take steps to preserve it.

Evaluating Your Find

There are two extreme views of online information. Neither of them are good approaches to Web research but unfortunately few people fall in the middle. Which view you sympathize with will affect the way you evaluate your Web discoveries.

Technophiles

On one end is the computer technophile. The technophile believes if it's online, it's golden. They faithfully trust anything found on a computer. Perhaps the technology gives the information stored on it credibility. Technophiles usually revel in the online information explosion. They're the ones who get sidetracked by the graphics, sound bites, and moving images the Web offers.

Technophobes

On the other end are the technophobes who don't trust anything found on a computer. Some go so far as to distrust people's motives for putting information online. They believe that if it's online, the information will be typed in incorrectly at best and purposely altered at worst. Technophobes reluctantly use the Web. They often look for reasons to discredit it.

Research Confidence

Be aware of how you feel about online information because it will bias how confident you are of its accuracy. I imagine that town criers first reacted to printed notices with a similar skepticism. "Unless you hear it from a person, how can you know it's accurate?" they probably mumbled.

Today we rely on "official" sources and we tend to discount information given to us by a lay person. While official resources are on the Web, much of it is put online by an ordinary person with an interest in spreading the news. If you limit your research to authoritative resources only, you might miss many useful sites.

That's not to say that everything on the Web is worthwhile or useful. So how can you judge what is accurate and relatively reliable? You use many of the same skills you use to evaluate a book.

There are many Web counterparts to printed sources: Supreme Court decisions, *Encyclopedia Britannica, Time* magazine, and so on. If you would trust the printed source, there's no reason to doubt the online version. In today's computer era, the story you see in print was originally done on a computer. They simply made it available to you in that form.

What about resources unique to the Web? Many of them have "about" files that explain to you exactly where the source originates from and who is responsible. (You'll also find disclaimers here.) You can often "speak" with the Webmaster via e-mail if you have further questions.

This is where understanding URLs can be invaluable. Having .edu in the address does indicate that the site is stored on a university server. But does the address end there? Is there a tilde and a person's name in the URL? Then it is likely to be someone's personal page and opinion, not the university's official statement.

If you visit a Web page that claims to be an official university site in the U.S. but doesn't have .edu in the address, be cautious. It's unlikely that a major university would go with a commercial provider when they have their own domain.

Tracking the source of a Web page through the URL can help you spot both fraud (rare but out there) and bias (much more likely). A site that offers information on tax reform might contain facts. But if the URL indicates it came from a conservative think tank, you'll probably find a "spin" on the advice given. Companies might give true information about a situation (crime statistics in major cities) but offer their product as the solution (their alarm system).

Despite the commercialization, the majority of the sites on the Web are there because a person really wanted to share information about a favorite topic. Most mistakes are honest ones. The majority of the information is valid, useful, and worth considering in your research.

So you've found a site that covers your topic, figured out who has made it available, and you want to put the data to good use. However, you're still worried about the quality. Evaluating the reliability is not different because it's on the Web.

When you receive a newsletter in the mail, how do you know if it's objective or political or a thinly-disguised ad? You tell by the content. A "vote-for-me" message is the same whether on the Web or in your junk mail. Have you ever received an ad for a book that will explain the mysteries of the stars for only $19.95? The only difference on the Web is that you can read more of the outlandish claims before moving on.

The more difficult calls are when someone in good faith publishes a Web page that deals with a worthwhile topic. A fan of Coretta Scott King decides to create a page dedicated to her. How well can you trust the information to be accurate? Chances are, much of it is correct. However, this fan would probably not post anything critical. If you're looking for the bad as well as the good, you would need more than one source. But that doesn't rule out the original King page.

Perhaps a gardener creates a Web page that tries to cover everything to do with roses. However, her method of treating aphids clashes with the advice you got from your local nursery. Does that invalidate her Web page or make online research suspect?

Not really. In the world of books and magazines, you'll find biographies written by devoted fans who never mention a negative word. You'll also find books that absolutely tear someone apart. Which one is right? You can find gardening books that disagree on a great many issues and the advice your grandfather gives you is different still. Why should Web pages be any more consistent?

Actually, Web research has a big advantage over regular book research. You can go from one related source to another quickly with hypertext links. You'll spend more time reading different points of view and less time looking up resources.

There are some things that are irrefutable facts. What is the periodic symbol for iron? If a Web site tells you anything other than FE, you need to look elsewhere. However, misspellings and miscalculations are honest mistakes that can happen in other forms of publishing too. If you find several mistakes at a site, don't continue to use it in your research.

It's true that someone can put a bunch of bogus statistics online to "prove" their point. Look for good citations to back up statistics. Did the Web page creator name the source? Is it a source you've heard of and could check on if you wanted to? If they claim to have done the survey themselves, do they explain their methodology or give raw data? You have to review it yourself instead of relying on another publication (such as a science journal) to make that decision for you.

Librarians already use these techniques on print sources. You can adapt them to Web resources with a great deal of success. Soon, it will become second nature to you. You will move from site to site, not realizing that you're evaluating while researching.

Bookmarking Sites

When you find a reliable, helpful site that you plan to use often, bookmark it! Don't assume that you'll be able to find it again or remember the address. (Chances are you could find it again but that's time consuming.) Don't rely on indexes to keep the link for you.

On the other hand, you don't need to bookmark every site you ever use. That will soon create an unwieldy bookmark list that you will have to sort through on a regular basis. If you will need to return to a site but only plan to use it for a short while, consider bookmarking it temporarily. When your research is done, delete that bookmark.

Retrieval Formats

Once you find that informational gem you've been searching for, you'll often need to get it from the Web to somewhere else. You don't want to have to log on every time you want to read it. Or you might be retrieving it for someone else and need to give them a copy.

You can print out the contents of a Web page. This is quick and you get what you see. If you simply need a bit of information that you will not use beyond that day, printing it out (or even jotting it down if it's a word or two) should be fine. Printing is also good for clients who want a hard copy.

If you think you will use this information often or if there is a lot of data, it would be wiser to save it to disk. You can simply transfer a copy to your hard drive. Once you have a copy on your computer, you can print it out as needed. Storing it on computer also allows you to manipulate it. Remember that what you save may be copyrighted material. Laws and ethics still apply, even in the more ethereal form of electronic storage.

Summary

A good search strategy will save you time and frustration. Once you learn how to formulate one, it will become second nature. From the minute you hear the search request, your mind will start considering research tools. Be careful to make a distinction between your preferences and knowledge of what's available. (Are you going on the Web when you could have used the almanac on your desk? Are you going to Yahoo! out of habit when a smaller index would be more appropriate?) Your search strategy will determine how successful you are in finding what you seek. The following chapters will cover research strategies for specific areas of research. They offer tips that will help you refine your searches.

8

Business and Finance

A ny bit of information can be used by a business in some manner. That's part of the reason why companies are flocking to the Web; they want to tap into the vast online resources.

However, there is a growing demand for information on the Web about businesses. Consumers want to know more about the corporations they're buying from. More than that, they want to know what the corporations are doing with consumers' money. The Web has some good business and finance resources for the business researcher.

Search Strategies

When people say they want business information, they often mean financial. The other big category in business information is facts about businesses themselves, such as company profiles. Other types of business information, such as travel advisories, salary calculators, and news updates, can be used for non-business reasons as well. You can find them grouped under a variety of categories, including business.

Thinking of relocating and want to keep the same standard of living in your new home? Visit the Salary Calculator at **http://www.homefair.com/homefair/cmr/salcalc.html**. It will tell you how much you need to make to maintain the same economic level you're at now.

Many sites are created or sponsored by large companies. They offer the business information in hopes that you'll use their services. Sometimes you have to go through pages of ads to get to actual data; other times, there's an ad on every page.

Finances

Business financial information is one area where bookmarks will come in handy. You'll probably find sites that you want to check often, perhaps daily. Once you settle on your preferences, there will be little reason to seek out new ones daily. Bookmark a good meta-index and check it on a regular basis (once a week is a good interval) for new business resources.

You might also participate in a LISTSERV or newsgroup that is related to your field. You'll see announcements from time to time about a new Web site. You can visit and evaluate it, and then bookmark it if it will be valuable. You might also find yourself on mailing lists as you become active in the Internet business community. You will probably be sent press releases extolling the virtue of a new financial Web site.

Once you do your initial research, financial information is relatively easy to find. You simply keep your bookmarks updated and check them as needed. This method is for people who use financial information on a regular basis, not the casual seeker.

Stock quotes are available online but often with a delay ranging from 3 to 20 minutes. You have to reload the page to get updated quotes, so you cannot simply go to a page and keep it running in the background. Other statistical business information available on the Web includes (but isn't limited to) currency exchange rates and mortgage interest rates.

How should you begin to look for financial information? A good index is the best way to start. Businesses want to be found and they try to get themselves listed in many places. For example, let's say you're interested in stocks and want to search for a comprehensive financial resource. You start your search by going to the meta-index Yahoo! at **http://www.yahoo.com** (see Figure 8.1).

You'll see "Business and Economy [Xtra!]" in large letters with "Directory, Investments, Classifieds, . . ." in smaller letters. To save a step, click on "Investments." The Yahoo! Markets and Investments page appears (see Figure 8.2).

Once there, you'll see the stocks category; select it. From the page that appears, you can choose from many categories. You know that

Figure 8.1
The Yahoo! Home Page has a business section to begin your search in.

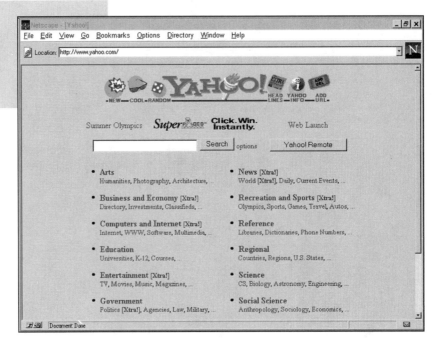

Figure 8.2
Yahoo!'s Markets and Investments page has a stocks category that helps narrow your search.

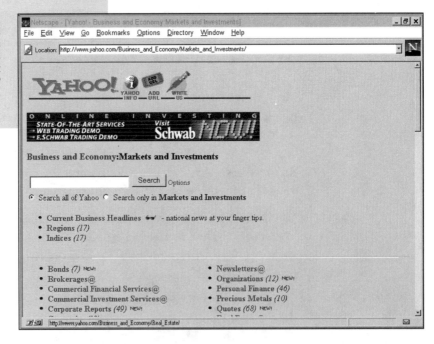

Figure 8.3
A Trader's
Financial
Resource Guide
is a good
Web business
resource.

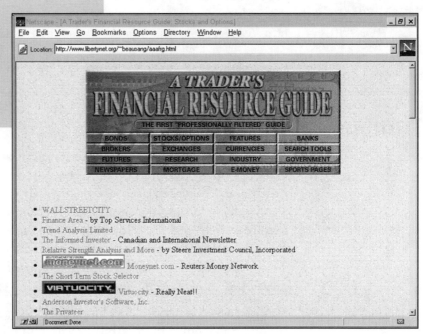

you want a source that covers several topics, so choose indices. You then see the Financial Resource Guide page (see Figure 8.3).

Here's your actual resource. To keep from having to go through all those screens again, bookmark this page. This site is an index specific to a subject area and will make a good launch point for more narrow searches for Web financial information, rather than using meta-indexes like Yahoo!.

If you find individual items within the index (such as Data Broadcasting Corporation to get stock quotes) that you use often, then bookmark that page. If you use the individual pages more often than the financial index page, then you can delete that bookmark. With use, you will learn which pages are worth keeping.

Check out information on retirement planning with BenefitsLink at **http://www.benefitslink. com**. The resources and services are free. You can read full-text articles about the many aspects of retirement finances.

Company Profiles

How do you begin a search when you want information about a particular company? An index might be able to help you, but probably isn't the best route for this type of search. If you know the name of a company, you can do a simple search at one of the more comprehensive search engines. However, if you have a company with a common name, you might get more hits than you can sort through. This is especially true for computer companies that naturally get mentioned in many online sources.

If all you want is a company's home page, the search and results are simple. You could go to AltaVista and put in the name of the company in the simple search form. For example, if you search for "Natural Bath Shop," you would receive thousands of entries. Fortunately, the internal ranking put the place you're looking for on the first page. A simple click and you get the page shown in Figure 8.4.

If you just need a company contact, this will do just fine. It's typical of most businesses on the Web—it tells about the company, offers some products for sale, and gives you a few related links.

If you want a more in-depth look at a company, you will have to search for more than the company name. Looking at another beauty company, let's say you try to find more information about Avon. So you do an advanced search at AltaVista. The search request is "Avon and (annual report)" with "Avon" as the ranking keyword. The first hit takes you to the page shown in Figure 8.5.

You'll get basic company information and stock quotes. It also gives you the address of Avon's Home Page. You'll notice that the annual report must be requested, so you won't be able to see it right away.

Figure 8.4
The Natural Bath
Shop Home Page
offers shoppers
the chance to
buy products
online and learn
a little about
the company.

Figure 8.4
The Natural Bath
Shop Home Page
offers shoppers
the chance to
buy products
online and learn
a little about
the company.

Figure 8.5
The Avon Home
Page contains
the company's
vital statistics.

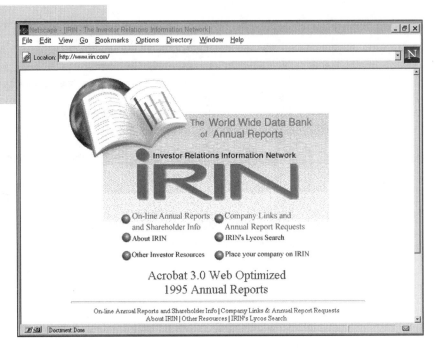

Since you can read the URL at the top of the Avon page, you can simply delete everything after the com/ and press return. By shortening the path, you'll be back at the main Web page (see Figure 8.6) of the Investor Relations Information Network (IRIN).

From this home page you can get a listing of every company whose annual report is available. If you need corporate information frequently, you can bookmark this page to come back to. Companies frequently choose to make their financial information available through a service, so you may find that many places you look up are associated with a larger database.

Some companies do make their financial information available at their home pages. An example is BancTec, Inc. which I found by entering the search request "BancTec" into Infoseek Guide. BancTec's Home Page (**http://www.banc-tec.com**) has links to the previous year and current quarter figures (see Figure 8.7).

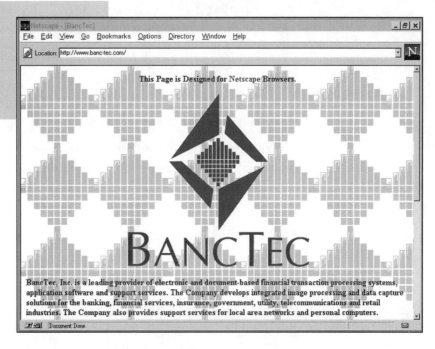

Figure 8.7
The BancTec Home Page has information about the company and offers links to its annual report.

Business and Finance Sites

Business sites are growing on the Web. Some are fee-based, so you have to decide how much you want the information. Unless you need it for professional research, you probably won't subscribe to a business database; especially when there are so many free ones. If you're not sure where to begin looking, one of the sites in the following section should get you started.

AT&T Business Network

http://www.bnet.att.com

"Welcome to a free goldmine of business information." This is the greeting at the AT&T Business Network Home Page. It might just be accurate too. This Web site has full-text articles, related links, and even a contest for coming up with the right Web source to a business problem. The home page is a little busy, but it's not difficult to get around.

Chamber of Commerce

http://chamber-of-commerce.com

This is the home page for the national organization with links to local Chambers of Commerce. Before making a trip to a Chamber of Commerce building, you can see if this online site answers your question.

Edgar Online

http://www.edgar-online.com

Edgar Online offers up-to-the-minute SEC electronic corporate filings. There is a fee for most services. However, if your business relies on this kind of information, Edgar Online might be a good resource.

Federal Reserve Bank of Chicago

http://www.frbchi.org

This Web site has information on the Federal Reserve and links to other reserve banks. There are special sections for bankers, educators, and the media. There's also an economic update and financial assessment of the Midwest region of the United States.

Hoover's Online

http://www.hoovers.com

Hoover's Online has company information. Some of it is free and some is fee-based. The corporate directory is free and a good place to conduct a quick search.

International Business Practices Guide

gopher://gopher.umsl.edu:70/11/library/govdocs/ibpa

This comprehensive site has a wealth of information to help "maneuver through the nuances of competing in global markets." It covers 117 countries. Anyone who deals with foreign markets should bookmark this page.

PC Quote

http://www.pcquote.com

PC Quote offers stock information. There is a difference in service between the free pages and the fee-based ones, but this is a good place for researchers to check on stocks.

Web Central Major Corporations

http://www.cio.com/WebMaster/competition.html

This is an alphabetical index of corporate Web pages. There are links to other corporation indexes.

World Exchange Rates

http://www.rubicon.com/passport/currency/currency.htm

This handy chart takes the source country and then computes the exchange rate for many other countries. World Exchange Rates is quick and easy to use.

Evaluation of Resources

Most business information on the Web is supplied by businesses themselves so you can assume it is accurate. Of course, you have to expect it to be favorable, or at least not detrimental to the company supplying the information. No company is going to advertise that

it's going bankrupt! If you follow business newsgroups, you'll probably hear rumors of business troubles there.

Your concern with business information on the Web is less with accuracy and more with bias. Major corporations are not going to risk their reputation with outlandish claims. You can judge Web resources with the same measures you use on printed business sources.

Education

The hype has been around for a long time. The hype that says computers are educational and students must have one to succeed. The hype that now says students must be on the Internet to do well academically. Some have counterreacted to the hype by attacking the Internet.

Past the hype, however, the Internet can be a valuable tool for teachers and students. The Internet won't do homework and won't replace trips to the library, but it will give students a whole world of facts, images, anecdotes, and data to expand their knowledge. The Web is perhaps the best part of all. It's easy to use and offers students and teachers a multimedia environment to learn in.

Search Strategies

How you look for education sites depends largely on what you're looking for. Just about any site can be educational in its own way. The term "education" covers a wide range of levels, from pre-school to graduate school.

Most people are referring to kindergarten through grade 12 when they say they want educational resources. They want something that their children can learn from. Children are comfortable using computers, sometimes more so than their parents. Teachers who want to make the Internet part of their curriculum look for sites that offer more than moving pictures and sound files.

Educational resources also refer to a teacher's tools. Many sites on the Web are created by teachers for other teachers to share advice and materials. The Internet has been around for a long time and educators were some of the earliest users. Many of their forums have been transferred to the Web from other types of Internet sites (gopher, ftp, and so on).

When looking for educational materials, you have to be sure of your search request before getting online. There are many resources available, so the narrower your request, the more likely you are to suc-

Teachers Helping Teachers was created by teachers for teachers. It is a forum for teachers around the world to share ideas and experiences. The address is **http://www.pacificnet.net/~mandel**.

ceed. You also have to decide if you're looking for a general index or library with many links, or if you want to search for a single subject.

If you want a "child-friendly" search engine, Magellan rates its sites and marks general audience ones. Among indexes, Yahoo! offers Yahooligans! for children. These are helpful tools that families appreciate. However, it only guarantees that you will most likely not be offended by the material your child links to. It does not mean all the links are educational.

If you're concerned about "child safe" sites, you can look for the SafeSurf label. It means that the site's content has been judged satisfactory for children. SafeSurf does not replace supervision by a parent or teacher. For more information, go to **http://www.safesurf.com/kidswave.htm**.

Even Kids Web, which was created specifically for school children, offers sports and entertainment links. After all, recess is important! Students can learn a lot from non-academic resources. If your student has to write a report on a famous gymnast or a legendary singer, these links can be useful.

In general, if you want broad indexes, you can find them by following the links of a meta-index. It's even feasible to rely on meta-indexes, as long as you bookmark sites you plan to use often. For example, the World Wide Web Virtual Library's Education section has thousands of links, organized efficiently in five ways:

- **Alphabetically**—lists every site in alphabetical order

- **Education level**—divided into primary, secondary, tertiary, and postgraduate

- **Resources provided**—divided into bibliographies, books, course details, databases, funding, lectures and tutorials, teaching methodologies, software, and educational technology

- **Type**—divided into general, regional, institutions, and clearinghouses

- **Country**—divided into dozens of countries and listed alphabetically

Every site listed has a description that can help you evaluate which links to follow. The Zooary, shown in Figure 9.1, shows a typical description.

Figure 9.1
This fact-oriented page has information about The Zooary. It also links the researcher to the Zooary site.

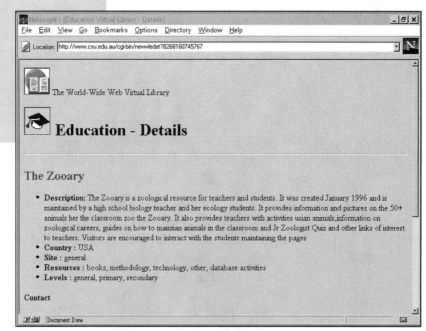

Educational Subjects

You can use an education index if you need information on a certain subject (such as a science fair, history paper, or book report). However, I have yet to find an education index that contains every possible link. There are just so many educational resources on the Web that one index cannot cover them all. I have found and used some thorough and well-planned education indexes. In every case, however, I've known of other resources that were not listed.

If you want to be sure of getting a complete list of resource options, you would be better off using a comprehensive search engine, such as Lycos. Most subjects will have information online but there are some exceptions. Local histories, such as a biography of your town's founders, will not be online unless someone from your town has taken the time to enter it. (This applies to smaller cities and towns. Larger cities like New York City and Chicago have well-documented histories.) Also, if your child is doing a report that students do every year, your local and school libraries will have built up a collection dealing with that subject. You might find information online, which can breathe new life into a report that a teacher has read hundreds of times, but don't forsake the local resources.

The Web can be a great place to start a school project, regardless of grade level. For example, say you need to find information on lizards for a eighth grade report. You start your search at Lycos. However, just entering "lizards" will get you more than you want to sort through. You choose to customize your search and get this search screen (see Figure 9.2).

Still wanting to be somewhat general, you put in the search request "lizard reptile" in the query box. Then select all terms (and) and strong match from the Search Options text boxes. You ask for the detailed listing because you anticipate a lot of matches and want enough information to narrow the search.

You get back three matches, although Lycos notes that there are 14,281 sites that contain the words lizard, lizards, reptile, and reptiles. You notice that selection number two (Lizards and Other Reptiles)

Figure 9.2
This Lycos search
screen lets you
narrow your
search request.

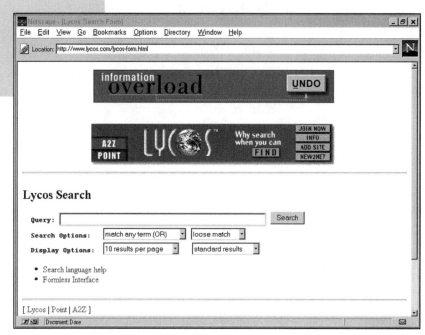

looks promising. It appears to be someone's personal page but has a
lot of information (see Figure 9.3). A click and then you find yourself
on the Lizards and Other Reptiles Home Page (see Figure 9.4).

The Lizards and Other Reptiles page turns out to be an index of
related resources. It's aim seems to be pet owners, but that doesn't
rule out its usefulness. If none of these links quite fulfills what you're
looking for, there's another listing you can read. Click on Herp Net
Resources FAQ. The Herp Internet Resources FAQ page appears
(see Figure 9.5).

You will most likely find several Web resources that can help a student write a report. This was much more efficient than entering
"lizard" by itself. That would have returned more than 4,000 results
with references to bands, personal Internet names, and even lounge
lizards. You can see why its important to limit your searches.

Figure 9.3
The Lycos search results on lizard reptile.

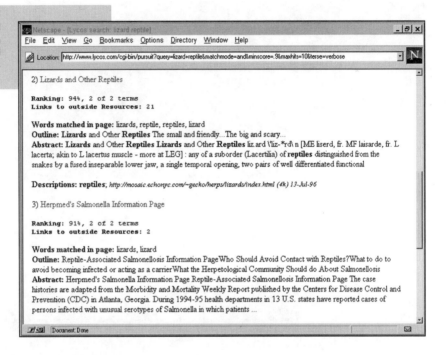

Figure 9.4
The Lizards and Other Reptiles Home Page starts with a definition and goes on to provide detailed information.

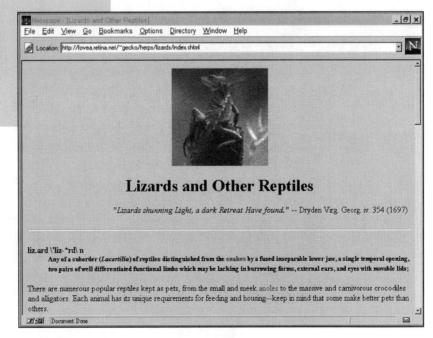

Figure 9.5
The Herp Net
Resources FAQ
Home Page has
many useful
links for those
studying lizards.

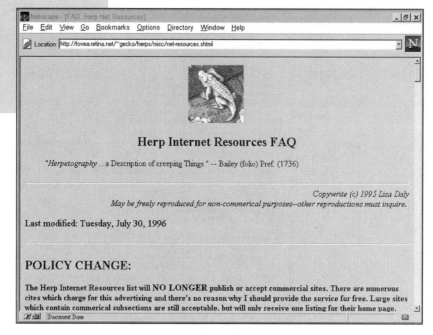

Education Resources for Teachers

Teachers have a lot of resources on the Internet. Lesson plans, curriculum guides, associations, and other education-related topics are all available in abundance on the Web. The most frequently cited one is the Educational Resources Information Center (ERIC), which is probably the most comprehensive teacher resource available. It was already an active database used by many educators before joining the Web. ERIC was created in 1966. It's supported by the U.S. Department of Education, Office of Educational Research and Improvement, and The National Library of Education. There are many links that lead to various ERIC services, such as the one shown in Figure 9.6. You can find an ERIC Frequently Asked Questions list at **http://aspensys3.aspensys.com/eric/faq.html#10**.

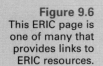

Figure 9.6
This ERIC page is one of many that provides links to ERIC resources.

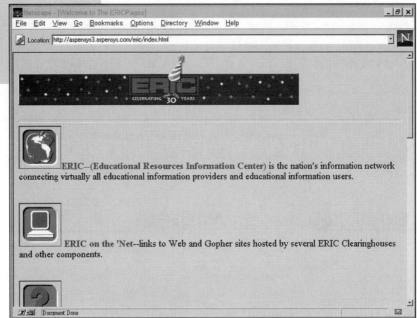

Not all teacher information is geared for K-12. Higher Education Processes is a Web resource for higher education. There are also individual resources specific to a subject. You can use a meta-index or a search engine to find some good teacher indexes. Bookmark them and any individual links you will use frequently. It's easy to get information overload, so once you do your research, stick to the ones you find the most useful. You can check on a regular basis for new indexes. However, chances are you will hear of them through newsgroups and links to indexes you already have bookmarked.

Education Sites

Almost any site can be called educational but some are specifically geared to students and teachers. Teachers will want to bookmark ones that are relevant to the classes they teach. Students can take advantage of the many learning tools that are available to them.

Armadillo's K-12 WWW Resources

http://chico.rice.edu/armadillo/Rice/K12resources.html

This is an index for teachers, students, and to a lesser extent, parents. It's divided into sections for easier browsing. Researchers are asked to rate the sites that Armadillo links to and send the rating back to it.

Busy Teachers' WebSite

http://www.ceismc.gatech.edu/BusyT

Busy Teachers' WebSite was created by a researcher for teachers to have a one-stop place to go on the Web. It covers many substantive links in an easy to follow format.

Educational Internet Resources

http://www.the-spa.com/guy.williams/main1.htm

Educational Internet Resources was created by Guy Williams, Education Consultant at the Department of Education. This page isn't an official Department of Education Web page though. His goal is to make educational resources on the Web accessible while eliminating redundant links.

ERIC

http://www.ericsp.org

This URL will take you to the ERIC Clearinghouse on Teaching and Teacher Education. The resources are about the profession of teaching.

HEPROC

http://rrpubs.com/heproc/index.shtml

HEPROC is a resource for higher education. It has related resources and discussions about the field of higher education. The goal is to provide collaborative, participatory discussion and research.

Kids Web

http://www.npac.syr.edu/textbook/kidsweb

Kids Web is an easy-to-use, icon-driven index for school children. Although it's aimed at children, researchers will find the resources it links to useful as well (especially when making lesson plans).

Teacher and Student Resources for Education

http://members.aol.com/Jimnastics/resource.html

This Web site is divided into five traditional school subjects with an Other category to cover everything else. Although not as large as other indexes, this is a good place to begin for new users who don't want to be overwhelmed.

The Teacher Resource Page

http://grove.ufl.edu/~klesyk

The Teacher Resource Page is divided into six general sections. It has a listing of schools on the Internet in addition to links for teachers and students.

Evaluation of Resources

Most education sites for teachers are created, maintained, and contributed to by teachers. You can trust them as much as you would trust a newsletter, conference, or other collaborative effort. A few indexes are created by librarians or others with an interest in education. Some, like ERIC, have become a standard.

When evaluating sites to be used for educational purposes (such as the lizard site example) you have to use the same techniques as you would for a printed source. Where did it come from? Is the source of the information documented? Is the person providing the information some kind of expert, either with a degree or by sheer virtue of working in the field? If you found the Web site through an education index, you can assume that the index creators thought this site had merit.

The more formal educational subjects and profession of teaching are well represented on the Web. Once you build your personal index of bookmarks, you will find the Web is a resource you turn to often.

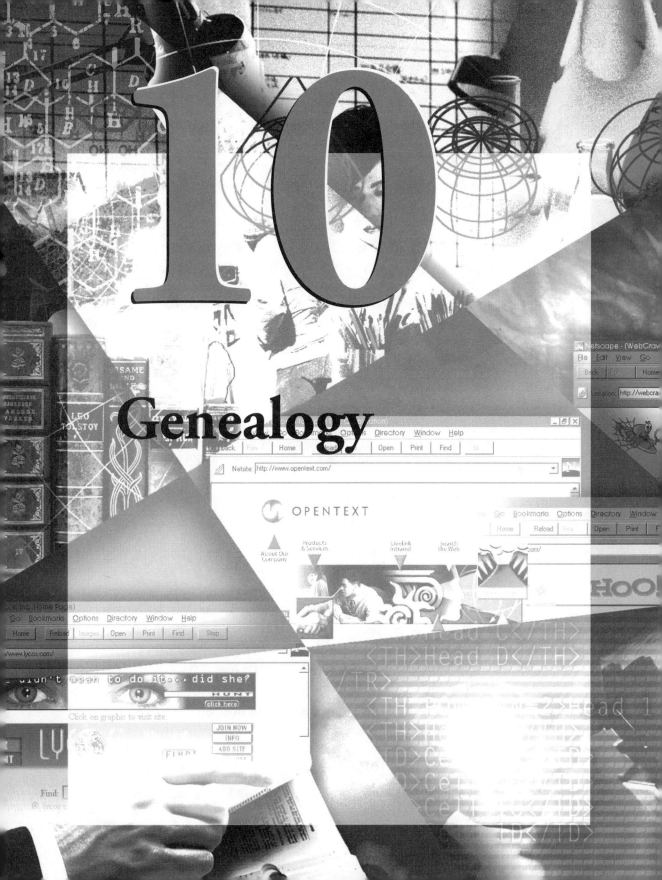

10
Genealogy

An ever-growing field, both among professionals and hobbyists, is genealogy. There have always been historical societies and people interested in preserving their family heritage. Computers have given genealogists a boost as families become more widespread. Computer databases have made organization easier while allowing more people access to historical information.

The cost of genealogical research prohibits many researchers. If your family hails from Maryland and you now live in Arizona, it can be expensive to take the kind of research trip necessary to fill in the family tree gaps. Of course, computer data cannot replace the satisfaction of returning home. It cannot let you walk through your grandmother's girlhood home, but it can make genealogical research easier than ever before.

Many genealogists have also made research deals so that a genealogist in a certain region would do research for another located somewhere else. In exchange, each one would expect their favor returned. This plan gives you a competent seeker looking where you cannot go physically. You can meet genealogists across the nation by getting online.

Search Strategies

The computer has been a huge aid to the field of genealogy. Databases can keep vital records. In fact, modern records are put on computers, so one day it will simply be a matter of releasing the information publicly. Many dedicated genealogists have even entered in records that pre-date the computer age.

A family history researcher looks forward to the day when all records will be available online. No more trips to city hall basements, searching for your great-great-grandparent's marriage certificate. You'd be able to look it up in a database and get immediate information.

Until that happens, you can take advantage of the resources that are on the Web. How do you find them? Meta-indexes can start you out, but shouldn't be used on a regular basis. Most genealogy sites link to related ones, so you can always continue your research that way. However, if you search for genealogical resources on a regular basis, you'll want to employ a more efficient method.

Building a personal index with bookmarks will be essential. You should keep them updated on a regular basis, at least once a month. If you are a serious genealogist, consider joining a LISTSERV. You can share information with fellow researchers and receive announcements of new Web sites. There are several different types of Web sites which can aid your research. Some pages center around names while others concentrate on nationality or historical documents. Consider which kind you'll need to answer your questions. For example, you'll only want to bookmark a family name page if it's part of your family tree.

Surname Web Pages

Genealogists have flocked to the Web. There have been many benefits to sharing information. Some have compiled huge databases of surnames which others can search. Many of these databases include links to others who are searching for the same name. In fact, it's common to see posts asking for contacts from other people with the family name a genealogist is researching. Some people have created entire Web pages that detail their family tree or describe their surname.

What does a surname Web page look like? They vary widely. Figure 10.1 shows an example of what you might expect if your family name has been given a place on the Web. In this case, it is the McDonald clan that is being touted.

National Web Pages

Some genealogy pages focus on region or nationality instead of surname. Filled with geography, history, and culture, these pages give a

Figure 10.1
The McDonald
Links Home Page
is designed to
unite people
around the world
who share the
same surname.

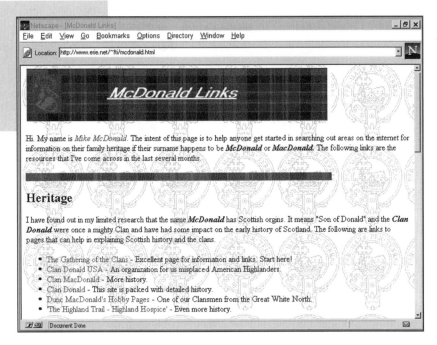

rich background in which to study your family ties. These pages may or may not originate in the country they represent. It's common for a U.S. citizen to do a page on Italy or Germany or whatever country his or her ancestors emigrated from. (These pages can also be good for researching a country's background, whether it's for a genealogical question or not.) Figure 10.2 shows the Italian Genealogy Home Page.

Research Web Pages

Other Web sites include historical records that genealogists (often in connection with genealogy societies) have painstakingly entered. Other helpful sites define genealogy terms, explain Soundex entries, and help you understand Census data. Heraldry pages are also fun

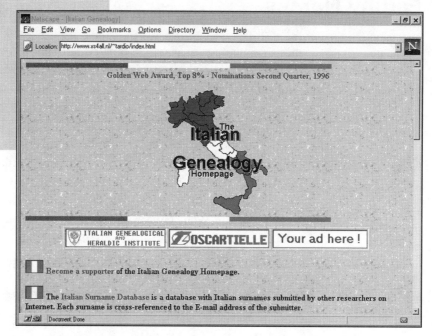

to visit. Many genealogy societies have Web pages and have made this information available through their home pages.

If you have a love of history, it's easy to get caught up in these sites. Genealogists have put a lot of work into making the information available in an efficient but agreeable manner. Newsgroups and Web sites often work in conjunction with references to each other.

How you research genealogy resources depends on what you're looking for and how deep your commitment to family research is. If you have only a passing curiosity, you might be able to satisfy yourself with material you can glean from meta-indexes. But this discipline is addictive! You may soon find yourself involved in the more in-depth research that a genealogist will want to do.

Family Names

One of the first things people want to know is if their family name has a home page or is in a database. Perhaps we all kind of hope that someone else has figured out our lineage and all we have to do is read and claim it. There's no easy way to find out if your family name has a genealogical page. Doing a search at any of the search engines will give you more results than you want. That's because names are everywhere on the Web. You'd get people's home pages that have nothing to do with genealogy. A lot of your results would simply be documents that contain the name you're searching on. Open Text has the power and search forms to do a precise search, but doesn't cover enough of the Web. Unless you have an extremely unusual name or a precise search request, search engines will consume your time and frustrate your search. (Even searching for general genealogical resources can be time-consuming when you go through search engines. Again, you must have a precise search request.)

This means you have to rely on indexes someone else has already created. The genealogical indexes are good, but finding them can take some diligence. Yahoo! has a fairly good section. Search engines tend to produce more hits than you can efficiently sort through. The good news is, once you find a site it tends to link to more.

When you do find a listing of surnames at an index, be sure you read what the particular listing means. Usually it refers to people who have registered their own name and are searching for others with the same one. A link on the index might even set you up to send e-mail to that seeker if you click on it. (Of course, you simply exit if you don't want to send e-mail.)

Does the difficulty in using search engines for genealogical research mean you should give up? Certainly not. There's a wealth of information on the Web—genealogy is just better suited for indexes. You can always use search engines for supplementary information, such as sites about your ancestor's country or historical events that shaped your ancestor's life.

Genealogy Sites

There are many wonderful genealogy sites on the Web but tracking them down can sometimes be difficult. Several individuals have created indexes that help researchers find what's available. This list will help you find indexes and other useful genealogical Web sites.

Cool Sites for Genealogists

http://www.cogensoc.org/cgs/cgs-cool.htm

Cool Sites for Genealogists is produced by the Colorado Genealogical Society. The chosen site has a description and link. An archive of previous cool sites is also available. This site is a good gauge of which Web references other genealogical researchers are using.

Cyndi's List of Genealogy Sites on the Internet

http://www.oz.net/~cyndihow/sites.htm

Cyndi has compiled a comprehensive list of genealogical resources on the Web—over 5,000 links. They're indexed alphabetically. This is a great place to begin when you want as many resources as you can find.

Genealogy Toolbox

http://genealogy.tbox.com/genealogy.html

The Genealogy Toolbox is a collection of links to genealogical resources on the Web. You can search the listing or browse through a family tree graphic.

Genealogy Online

http://genealogy.emcee.com

Genealogy Online has links to services and archives that are invaluable to the genealogist. From converting names to Soundex to a sampling of the 1880 census, this is the place to go for serious genealogical research.

GenWeb

http://sillyg.doit.com/genweb

GenWeb describes itself this way: "The GenWeb Database Index contains links to all known genealogical databases searchable through the Web. It is limited to searchable databases and does NOT include links to sites devoted to a family unless a database is available for searching." Despite the description, this is a good place to look if you're hoping someone else has already done the family name research for you.

Land Record Reference

http://www.ultranet.com/~deeds/landref.htm

Property records are one resource that all genealogical researchers will have to contend with. Land Record Reference explains how. It tells how land is acquired and how to read property records. It also defines common terms.

Searchable Genealogy Links

http://128.100.201.33/html/lo2.htm

This site is exactly what the title says; it is a list of genealogy sites that can be searched. One nice feature is that the list is divided into countries and nationalities.

Using the Census Soundex

http://www.familyhistory.com/faqs/narasdex.htm

This document is published by the National Archives and Records Administration to explain how the Soundex system works. Genealogists doing research in the U.S. will have to use Soundex to make effective use of Census records. Genealogical librarians should bookmark this site and share it with patrons.

Evaluation of Resources

Most genealogical information on the Web is put there by experienced researchers. Sites produced by individuals and societies tend to be more informative and better organized than ones produced by companies. Some of the family histories may be questionable (such as the woman who says she traced her lineage back to Adam and produces a family tree to prove it.) However, most people put the information on the Web in good faith.

The helpful sites (indexes, how to's, immigration history, and vital records) are trustworthy overall. Personal histories may be flourished, although many are honest and report the bad with the good. Some even enjoy it, such as the descendent of Jesse James who has tried to fill in as many generations as possible on the James family tree.

How can you evaluate a site for yourself? First, see where it comes from. Is it produced by a society? If it's an individual's page, is this person respected by the genealogical community? Perhaps the page has been given the Golden Web Award, which Web users vote on. (If millions of people say it's good, can they be wrong? Yes, but probably not!)

If you do a lot of research, you will pick up on certain trends. If you visit a Web page that doesn't seem to agree with all the others, you need to investigate. There may be a good reason, but it's usually a sign that the information on the page itself is wrong.

The Golden Web Award is given to genealogical Web pages that show "aptness to genealogy on the Internet, value as a research site, ease of use and accessibility, and for overall design and look." To vote, go to **http://www.gensource.com/GoldenWeb**.

You have no way of checking on vital records without retrieving hard copies of them yourself. If you happen to have copies, compare them to what's online. Chances are they'll match. If you don't have hard copies, you must rely on the integrity of the organization or person who has made the records available. Again, most genealogists put information on the Web as a service to others. Even on the vastness of the Web, genealogists have maintained a genteel friendliness.

11

Government
Information

Government information is a broad term that can apply to many areas. First, there's the matter of which government: federal, state, or local? And that's making the assumption that you're talking about the United States. Other countries produce information at all levels of bureaucracy and more of it is finding its way on the Web every day.

Search Strategies

The most frequently looked up government information is pending legislation, laws, rules, codes, and regulations. The government decides what we must do in many areas of our lives, so this is naturally what we're concerned with. Of course, many people want to look up what some other party has to do, according to the law.

However, government information does offer a lot more than rules and regulations. Topics range from the history of White House families to how to prepare for a hurricane. There are many agencies and most of them have a place on the Web. Sometimes you can even get information online before you can in printed form elsewhere. When you want government information, try to think of which level and agency would have produced it and start there. For example, if you want to know the allowable tax exemptions for the upcoming fiscal year, you will want to look at the federal level for the Internal Revenue Service.

A top-level domain of .gov lets you know that the site came from a government server (and more than likely is government information). However, government information can also reside on other servers (such as one located at a university). Furthermore, only U.S. federal government information has .gov in its address.

Federal Government

The U.S. federal government probably dominates the arena of government information. Some impressive sites have been created in the past few years. What's the best way to find an agency on the Web? Most of the time, you can simply determine its address. The federal government has kept its URLs wonderfully simple. Whenever possible, an address has been limited to the host machine and domain name. Usually, the domain name consists of the agency abbreviation and top-level domain of .gov.

For example, let's say you need information about the United States Department of Agriculture. You know the agency's abbreviation is USDA. So you type in **http://www.usda.gov** and you find yourself there (see Figure 11.1). You didn't have to use a search engine or index.

This will usually work but there are some exceptions. The Internal Revenue Service, for example, has the slightly longer address of

Figure 11.1
The USDA Home Page has an easy to remember address.

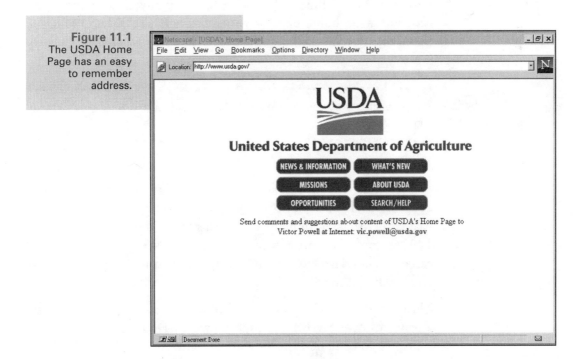

http://www.irs.ustreas.gov. You might be able to figure that out or use an index to find it. Search engines can be used, but tend to pull up a lot of extraneous sources that you have to sift through.

The IRS is actually part of the U.S. Treasury Department, so its address is logical. When surmising the addresses of government agencies, consider if the one you're looking for is part of a larger agency.

What if you're interested in legislation? Congress has established a Web site just for that. THOMAS, named for Thomas Jefferson, makes bills and other congressional information available for the public. These full-text documents include the Congressional Record, committee actions, historical documents, and an archive of previous bills (back to 1993). However, it is not the only Web resource. The Library of Congress has many links which you can find at its home page or going through THOMAS (which is maintained by the LC).

For more information on the Library of Congress, read the section describing it in Chapter 4.

For example, the University of Michigan Documents Center has congressional information organized specifically for research. Remember that, in most cases, actual records won't be earlier than 1993 (records were not put online until 1993). Key legislation from earlier years related to a current issue has inspired some people to type in the full text.

Most members of Congress have their own home pages, such as Senator Carol Moseley-Braun's page shown in Figure 11.2. One good source of information on individual members of Congress is Cap-

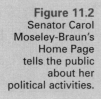

Figure 11.2
Senator Carol
Moseley-Braun's
Home Page
tells the public
about her
political activities.

Web. CapWeb was created by Capitol Hill staffers. Its goal is to provide information about Congress and links to related Internet resources on the Web.

The White House also has a home page that is a multimedia experience (see Figure 11.3). If you have the properly equipped browser, you will see flags flapping in the breeze of cyberspace; hear greetings from the President, First Lady, and Vice President; and take colorful tours of the White House grounds. The Web page creators have done a lovely job. They include a lot of historical and current information presented in an enjoyable manner. The home page graphics actually change with the time of day.

The judicial branch has been the least forthcoming in Web information, although that is changing. You can get Supreme Court decisions going back to 1990 from Cornell University. Cornell also has

Figure 11.3
This is the White House Home Page in the afternoon. You can see how it looks in the morning in Chapter 1.

the Code of Federal Regulations. The United States Federal Judiciary page has information on other federal courts' decisions and related judicial resources(see Figure 11.4).

So what is the best search strategy for government information? Why have I written more about sources and less on how to find them? In my experience, the best approach is to decide what resources you will use on a regular basis. Then spend an hour or so following the links, and bookmarking the ones to be used regularly. After that, you simply rely on your bookmarks.

Whenever you need to find something you do not have a bookmark for, either determine the address or follow a link on one of your bookmarked pages. I would not recommend this approach for most subject areas, but it really works in the area of government information. Also, whenever a new federal Web page appears, it seems to get

Figure 11.4
The U.S. Federal Courts' Home Page is a good resource for judicial information.

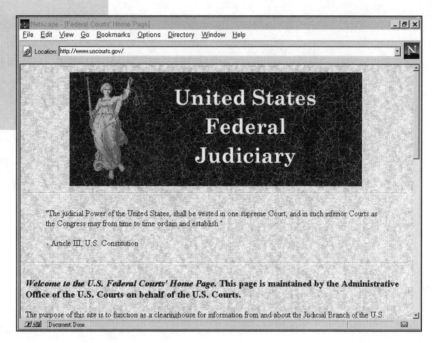

attention in the media as well as newsgroups. If you regularly read a newspaper, you will probably learn when new federal Web pages come online.

State and Local Government

Many states and cities have home pages on the Web. State agencies are also creating their own Web pages. City councils and state governments have put meeting notes and other news on their pages. One of the quickest ways to link to government information is going through one of the city networks, such as City.Net or USA CityLink.

For example, if you want to find out more about sales tax in the city of Austin, Texas, you can start your search at City.Net, shown in Figure 11.5.

Figure 11.5
The City.Net
Home Page has
links to places
around the world.

Figure 11.5
The City.Net
Home Page has
links to places
around the world.

You'll notice that Austin is listed as one of the Most Popular U.S. City Destinations. If you click on it, the link takes you to Austin's page, shown in Figure 11.6.

If you choose City Info, and then click on government, you go to the Austin City Connection link. Another click and you see the screen shown in Figure 11.7.

Depending on your browser, you have several ways to choose the next category. You can click in the links listed in the frame to the left or use the pull-down menu in the middle of the screen. Government makes the most sense, so another click and you're at the government page shown in Figure 11.8.

Nothing says sales tax but you notice the link titled "Fiscal Year 1995-96 Approved Budget Overview." There you find an outline of the budget with "Sales Tax" as an option (see Figure 11.9).

Figure 11.6
The City.Net
Austin page
gives a short
description of
the city and links
to find out more
information.

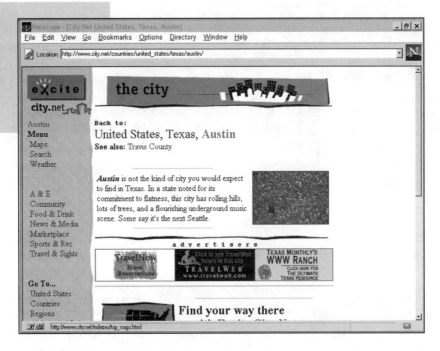

Figure 11.7
Austin City
Connection is
easy to use and
offers a wealth of
information about
the city.

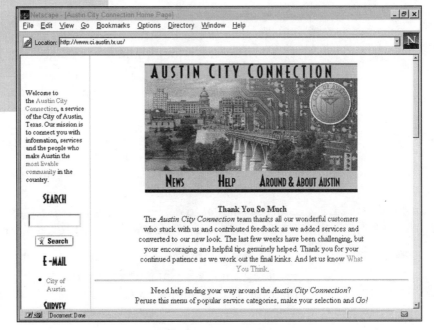

Figure 11.8
The Austin City
Connection
government page
is well-organized.

Finally, here is the information on sales tax in Austin (see Figure 11.10). This was a long route to take, but effective. If you research a particular city on a regular basis, you'll want to bookmark links to it. State government information can be found in much the same way. In fact, the Austin page has links to Texas ones.

Some state government addresses are relatively easy to figure out, such as the one for the Florida Supreme Court (**http://justice. courts.state.fl.us/courts/supct**). However, many agencies have their Web pages on university or commercial servers, making their addresses harder to determine. For example, the Florida State Attorney's Home Page has this address: **http://legal.firn.edu**.

If you want to use a search engine, be sure you have a specific search request. Simply searching on the state name will result in more links than you will have time to sort through.

Figure 11.9
The Austin City Connection Fiscal Year 1995-1996 Approved Budget page has a tax link.

Figure 11.10
The Austin City Connection Sales Tax page answers your questions.

Other Governments

One way to find links to other governments is through City.Net. You would search just as I did the Austin search. Both the Library of Congress and Yahoo! have government indexes, and don't forget to search for embassy home pages as well. Many embassies throughout the world have created home pages that represent their country. These pages often have explanations of how the government works for those who might not be familiar with that country's procedures. Be prepared for languages other than English, although many governments are thoughtful enough to provide English (and other languages) versions for those who cannot speak the native language.

You will probably have more success using a meta-index to choose a country and then government information rather than using a search engine. If you have a specific search request, a search engine might be able to help you. However, if you need facts about Japan's Upper House of Parliament, you'll probably be better off going to a Japanese index than trying to search on those terms.

Government Information Sites

There are many places to begin a search for government documents. Decide which level and branch of government you're looking for before starting your search. This is not a comprehensive list of Web sites; rather, these are good general sites to launch from.

CapWeb

http://policy.net/capweb/congress.html

CapWeb has information about the happenings at Capitol Hill. It contains many links to related sources and full-text documents. It also has practical advice for people who want to know more about the political process. CapWeb complements THOMAS nicely (although CapWeb was created first).

CIA World Factbook

http://www.odci.gov/cia/publications/95fact/index.html

This has been a popular reference on the Internet, even before the Web. Published annually, the CIA World Factbook is filled with information gleaned from around the world. It's good for research and trivia games.

City.Net

http://www.city.net

City.Net links the physical world to the virtual world of the Web. City.Net is a good place to find links to government information but offers much more than that. It covers all aspects about a city you would like to know: entertainment, lodging, maps, and so on.

Decisions of the U.S. Supreme Court

http://www.law.cornell.edu/supct/supct.table.html

This site offers the full-text decisions of the Supreme Court going back to 1990. It's indexed several ways and also offers a keyword search to aid your quest.

THOMAS

http://thomas.loc.gov

THOMAS was created specifically to make U.S. government information more accessible. Most people cannot afford to have the Congressional Record sent to their home, but they can read it online. Full-text legislation and other government resources can be found here.

United Nations

http://www.un.org

The United Nations Home Page offers information on publications, conferences, and news. Global Issues has links to hot topics in the United Nations, such as human rights, international peace, and economic development.

United States Federal Judiciary

http://www.uscourts.gov

This Web site offers information about the court system. It does not focus on court decisions but on how the court system works. This is a good reference for researchers trying to make sense of the judicial organization.

University of Michigan Documents Center

http://www.lib.umich.edu/libhome/Documents.center/legishis.html

This site was designed with students in mind. It offers both the full-text of legislation and many resources on how the legislative process works.

USA CityLink

http://usacitylink.com

USA CityLink brings the physical world to the Web. You can track down government information following the links. However, USA CityLink offers more than that; it's goal is to have links to all city Web resources for all the cities in the United States.

The White House

http://www.whitehouse.gov

This charming Web site offers more than a virtual tour of the White House. It has many interesting historical facts and modern day information. There's a children's version too.

Evaluation of Resources

Can you trust government-provided information on the Web? Can you trust the government? Your answer to the second question also answers the first. Web sites produced by the government will have the same information that's in public documents or that gets released to the media. Whether you believe it's accurate depends on your opinion of the source, not the medium it's on.

Should you be concerned about government information that is provided by interested parties but is not put out by the government? It depends on the source and motives. University-sponsored sites are no different than the government in terms of reliability. Political parties and partisan political action committees (PACs) might offer government information with a "spin" to it. If you think you are savvy enough to separate fact from propaganda, you can use a political resource. However, if a company is trying to sell government information, be wary. In the United States, government information is free, as long as you know the right agency to contact.

I f you do research on the Internet and those around you know it, it won't take long before this happens. Someone asks you, "What does http mean?" And you open your mouth to reply, maybe even say, "Oh, it means . . . " before you stop short. You've been using it for months or years now and you can't think of the answer.

You don't know the answer, of course, because it doesn't apply to your everyday work. You know that http is part of an URL and that is the method networked computers are using to pass along information. You know that when you see "http" your brain thinks "Web address," but you can't tell your friend that it stands for HyperText Transfer Protocol.

Maybe you did remember what http is, but I bet someday a non-computer user will come up with a term that you feel like you should know the answer to but don't. Where do you look up the answer?

Search Strategies

There are computer manuals, of course. If you were looking up how to set the margins in a software program you recently installed, a manual would make sense. There are Internet books as well. Obviously you're reading one right now! But if you're already online, or your computer is closer by than your manual, why not look it up on the Web? After all, you would be going to the source.

If your goal is to keep up with the latest Internet happenings, you should participate in the appropriate newsgroups. Things happen fast on the Internet and newsgroups and LISTSERVs are usually where you'll hear about them first. If you're reading posts on a regular basis, you'll find out new developments almost immediately.

Which newsgroup you follow depends on your area of interest. The news.announce groups will help you keep track of newsgroups themselves. Other newsgroups you'll want to follow are in the comp hierarchy. The following is a list of Web newsgroups:

comp.infosystems.www.advocacy

comp.infosystems.www.announce

comp.infosystems.www.authoring.cgi

comp.infosystems.www.authoring.html

comp.infosystems.www.authoring.images

comp.infosystems.www.authoring.misc

comp.infosystems.www.browsers.mac

comp.infosystems.www.browsers.misc

comp.infosystems.www.browsers.ms-windows

comp.infosystems.www.browsers.x

comp.infosystems.www.misc

comp.infosystems.www.servers.mac

comp.infosystems.www.servers.misc

comp.infosystems.www.servers.ms-windows

comp.infosystems.www.servers.unix

For your basic Internet reference questions, there are several Internet glossaries, histories, and guides. Some are aimed at "newbies" while others are written for the experienced user. Figure 12.1 shows a newbie Web page rendered by NetWelcome.

The Global Village gives interested parties a guided tour of the Internet (see Figure 12.2). If you're inundated with basic questions, you might want to send your patron or client on the tour or to one of the newbie sites.

If you don't like the term, "newbie" (someone who's new to the Internet and still learning how to use it), then you can opt for "just arrived netizen." A netizen is a member of the Internet community.

Figure 12.1
This Welcome
Newbie page
brings a friendly
handshake
to cyberspace.

Figure 12.2
Global Village's
Internet Tour
page is a good
place for a novice
Web user to visit.

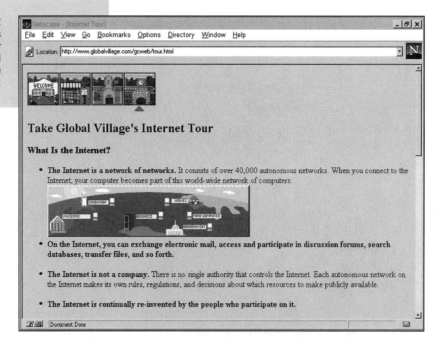

The Internet is thought of as the wave of the future, so it's hard to think of history and the Web in the same thought. However, you may find yourself wondering how the Internet and Web came into being. There are several wonderful references online, such as NetHistory (see Figure 12.3).

In addition to history and term definitions, you might need to know who's using the Internet and Web. Marketers want to know for business purposes, teachers for education reasons, hobbyists for curiosity's sake. There is an agency that tracks trends on the Internet and puts out current statistics. Matrix Information and Directory Services, Inc. (MIDS) makes some of its information available on the Web (see Figure 12.4).

Another excellent Web resource on Internet users can be found at PBS' Life on the Internet (see Figure 12.5). This site offers a timeline of the Internet. It also profiles different people online, from the Spiritual Surfer to the Digital Doctor. Life on the Internet includes Frequently Asked Questions (FAQs) and a trivia contest. It reminds

Figure 12.3
The NetHistory Home Page is the doorway to an interactive history of the Internet.

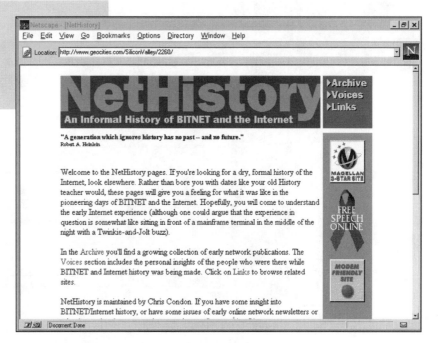

Figure 12.4
The MIDS Home
Page is the place
to go for Internet
statistics and
demographics.

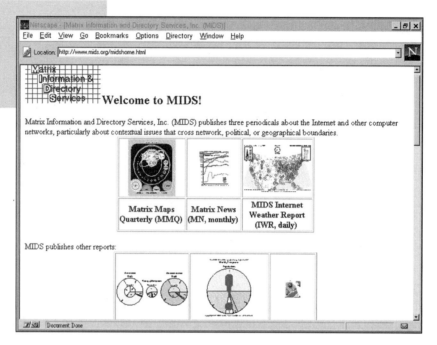

Figure 12.4
The MIDS Home
Page is the place
to go for Internet
statistics and
demographics.

Figure 12.5
The Life on
the Internet
Home Page
complements the
television series.

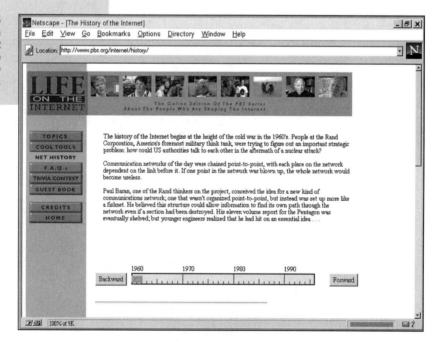

Figure 12.5
The Life on
the Internet
Home Page
complements the
television series.

you to watch the television version that adds to this site as well (or the other way around!).

So how do you find all of these sites? Search engines tend to return too many results; keywords like Internet, dictionary, history, and glossary are too common. Even meta-indexes tend to be a little skimpy in this area, with the possible exception of Yahoo!. (Although Yahoo! does not have all references.)

If you have a direct connection through an Internet Service Provider, the people running it may have already done the work for you. The ISP's home page will often have links to many tutorials and reference sites. They do get Internet questions often! Home pages of ISP's are often great places to start.

Of course, once you go to one site, it will lead you to another. Bookmark the sites you plan to use often. Consider saving the site's information to disk if it's long or if you think you will want to reference the information when offline. Again, if you read newsgroups or LISTSERVs, you will get tips there on the latest trends.

Internet Sites

Every site is a part of the Internet but some sites are dedicated to explaining the Internet. If you want to get to know the Internet better, consider visiting one of the online sources in the following sections before turning to manuals. If you plan to teach others how to use the Internet, keep several of these handy.

European Laboratory for Particle Physics

http://www.cern.ch

CERN is known as the birthplace of the Web. (For a brief history of the Web, go to Chapter 1.) Links from this page lead to both historical Web sites and ones concerned with the future of the Web. If you plan to create a home page and be part of the Web, you may want to visit for a little perspective.

Exploring the Internet

http://www.screen.com/understand/exploring.html

This is a handy little guide that touches on a little bit of everything. You can learn about netiquette or home page creation or e-mail all at the same starting point.

Global Village's Internet Tour

http://www.globalvillage.com/gcweb/tour.html

The Global Village explains the Internet in simple terms and offers a "tour" which takes the new user to Web pages stored on the Global Village's server. After the tour, the new user can link to the actual sites. There are also links to related sites.

Hobbes' Internet Timeline

http://info.isoc.org/guest/zakon/Internet/
History/HIT.html

Hobbes' Internet Timeline starts in 1957 and runs to the present. Each important event in the creation of the Internet as we know it today is noted. This site also has charts and graphs showing the growth of the Internet since its beginning in 1969.

ILC Copy of Internet Terms

http://www.matisse.net/files/glossary.html

Internet Literacy Consultants created this alphabetical list of Internet terms and their definitions.

Internet Glossary

http://www.marketing-coach.com/mh-guide/glossary.htm

McGraw-Hill makes this alphabetical list of Internet terms and their definitions available.

Life on the Internet

http://www.pbs.org/internet/history

PBS has created Life on the Internet to complement its television series. This is a must see site for an Internet junkie. If you're researching the culture of the Internet, this is a good starting place.

NetHistory

http://www.geocities.com/SiliconValley/2260

NetHistory is a museum of the Internet. In addition to the usual facts, this site has original publications from the early days and recollections from the people who shaped the Internet into what it is today.

NetWelcome

http://www.netwelcome.com/index.html

Newbies can hardly find a heartier welcome than the one from NetWelcome. It defines some basic terms, offers some guidelines, and tries to sell t-shirts to newbies.

News of the wURLd

http://www.isisnet.com/mlindsay/nindex.html

This is a collection of news of the wURLd newsletters. The site's motto is "Dedicated to the Beginner . . . there's no such thing as a stupid question," but the beginner in this case is the first time Web page creator.

World Wide Web FAQ

http://www.boutell.com/faq

This answers the basic Web questions. Even if you've been on the Web for a while, it might be worth the time to review it.

The World Wide Web: Origins and Beyond

http://www.seas.upenn.edu/~lzeltser/WWW

This page gives the history of the Web and offers some analysis of the Internet's most popular feature.

WWW Development

http://www.stars.com/Vlib

WWW Development is a collection of resources for Webmasters. This index is divided into general, server, and client so you can narrow your search for information immediately.

Zen and the Art of the Internet

http://www.cs.indiana.edu/docproject/zen/zen-1.0_toc.html

This is a traditional favorite Internet guide. It's been published in both electronic and print form. This site offers *Zen and the Art of the Internet, A Beginner's Guide to the Internet, First Edition*, in full-text.

Evaluation of Resources

With the exception of the PBS and MIDS sites, most Internet resources you find are written by a technophile with no official position. If you're concerned with authoritative sources, you might be dismayed at the lack of credentials. Both the academic world and the media look for experts when researching a topic. Experts are usually defined by academic and professional credentials.

However, many of these guides are written by people who are also writing the software that runs the Web. That alone should validate them as being accurate, reliable sources. After all, the people actually running the system are the true experts in what makes it tick. Some resources are put online as a service by a company hoping to

make money. It doesn't mean the information is wrong, just that you'll see many ads for their services.

So how do you know when to trust the information you're reading? Most people who take the time to write histories and guides do so out of a desire to help others. Unfortunately, some people publish online before they're completely informed themselves. It can get tricky. The best strategy is to use more than one resource and compare information.

When you're evaluating a site, does the address indicate it's a personal page? You know that a tilde in the URL can indicate a personal page. (It's not the technical definition of a tilde. However, you will find the most common reason you to see a tilde in an address is because that's how the server distinguished a user-created page.) If it's a personal page, it stands alone. If not, there's a good chance (but not 100 percent) that it's sponsored by an organization. An example would be an ISP that publishes a Web dictionary.

That doesn't mean personal pages aren't useful; simply there's just a different level of accountability. Companies usually have more people to work on a Web page and check each other's facts.

If you're active in the Internet community, you will learn the reputations of your colleagues. You might recognize the name of a Webmaster. Some people get reputations for being accurate and helpful; their sites get thousands of visits a day.

When you find a new Web page that you want to use but you're not sure of its accuracy, compare what you do know. Does it claim there are over a billion people on the Internet? Other facts might be off too since "a billion" is the wrong answer. If you would like, you can read about a Webmaster's background (if provided) or even correspond via e-mail.

The tone of the page will also tell you how experienced the Webmaster is. There seem to be three levels to Internet users. The newbies still have a "golly" attitude. They play all the WAV files they come across and wait for the moving ads to finish their cycle so they can see them. Then comes arrogance as the newbie becomes experienced. People in this stage are the most likely to flame others. Finally, the user reaches a stage where newbies aren't bothersome (usually) and arrogance seems silly. These people are the most likely to be helpful, and may reach out to new users.

So how does this affect the tone of a site? And how can you hear tone on a computer screen anyway? You can tell by their choice of words and style. Is the style sincere or sarcastic? Is the writer comfortable using appropriate terms? You can even try reading the words out loud and see where the emphasis naturally falls. Has the Webmaster thrown in a bunch of special effects that add nothing to the information being presented? Even seasoned Webmasters give into cool graphics, but a gratuitous number of colorful graphics does not make up for lack of content.

If the information presented matches up with what you do know and the Webmaster seems to be sincerely interested in a topic, the Web resource is reliable. Any inaccuracies are honest mistakes. Some of these pages are remnants from the hacker culture that seems to be in remission on the Internet. You can count on Internet informational pages to be written by people in the trenches, the ones who actually work with the Web every day.

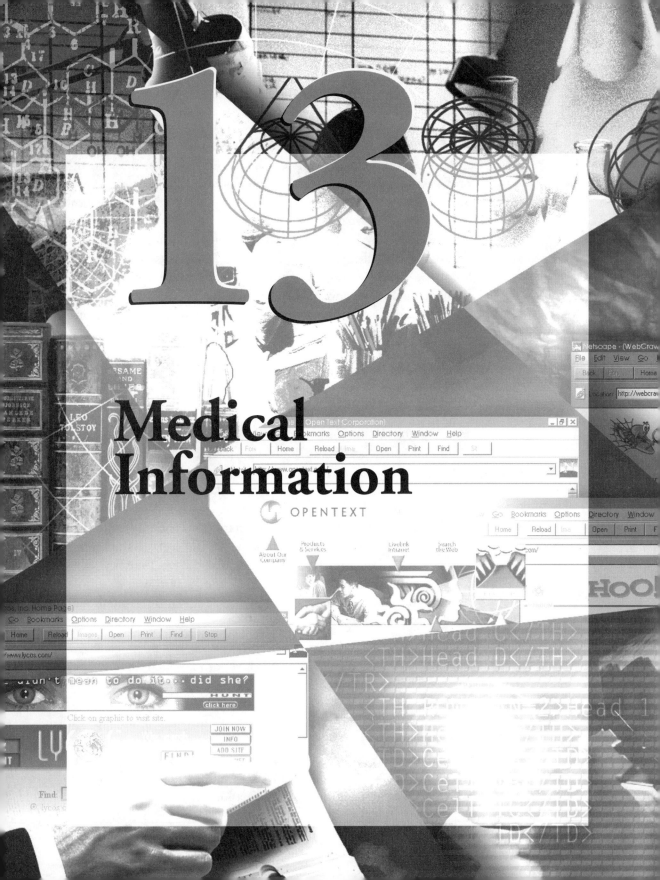

13

Medical Information

Medical information abounds on the Internet. Perhaps it's because medicine can be a high-tech field and those in the profession are drawn to the Internet. More likely, it's because everyone can relate to health issues. There are many types of medical information. University clinics and large hospitals have home pages that include everything from pharmacy hours to insurance information to tips for fighting the common cold. Medical associations have home pages filled with treatment information and pleas for funding. Individual ailments have their own sites. LISTSERVs are especially popular; those who share a condition talk with one another and offer mutual support.

Search Strategies

Medical information is a big umbrella term for several different areas of interest. There are health concerns—people who are healthy and want to stay healthy. They're interested in sites that deal with nutrition, exercise, and normal conditions like pregnancy. Medicine, both conventional and alternative, has thousands of Web sites. Also illnesses have their own Web sites as doctors and patients try to find cures. What you find on the Web can be helpful and reassuring, but it does not replace a doctor's diagnosis. If you have a medical condition that needs treatment, you can use the Web to find out more information, even alternative treatment methods, but you should still be attended to by a doctor.

Medical indexes make it easier to find resources than putting a vague search request like "health" or "therapy" into a search engine. Specific search requests might yield results from a search engine. However, because there is so much available, you will probably have to search often to keep up with the latest news. If you're in the medical research field you will want to build a personal index of trusted sites. For the occasional medical question—your own or someone you're trying to help—you can do well with a well-organized index or even a meta-index entry on medical information.

Health

The "go for the burn" fad of exercise has passed and many people are seeking ways to comfortably fit exercise and eating right into their lifestyles. The Web has many pages created by both medical professionals and those with an interest in health. You can use search engines for specific search requests, but a medical index might work just as well. If you use an index, you'll probably have to start general and work your way to a specific topic. With search engines, of course, the more explicit the keywords, the better chance you have of finding your topic. If you have to use several keywords, use a search engine that allows for complex searches.

For example, say you or your client want to know which kind of exercise burns the most calories. You go to Open Text and click on power search. You then enter the search string "exercise within summary near calories within summary" (see Figure 13.1). You get eight results (see Figure 13.2).

Figure 13.1
Open Text power search request for calories burned in exercise.

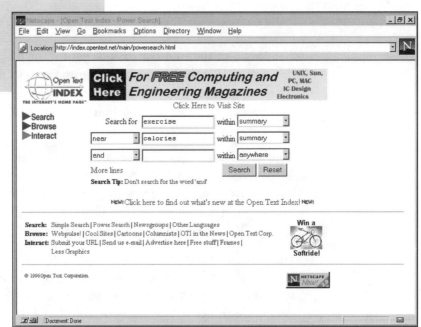

Figure 13.2
Open Text power
search results for
"exercise within
summary near
calories within
summary."

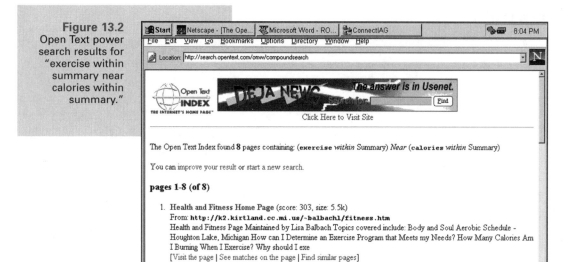

Number one and number six look promising based on the summary description. Neither of them are commercial, so they probably won't try to sell you exercise equipment or their fitness program. You click on number one and see that you're at the Health and Fitness Page (see Figure 13.3).

You see a similar question to your original one. A link reads "How Many Calories Am I Burning When I Exercise?" You click on it. That leads you to a page with an excellent description of calorie burning and several tables. The writer has cited her sources of information. You can read about her on the previous page.

You now have an outstanding resource but you're still curious about number six on your original results list. Your browser should have a way to let you go back to previous pages. You return to the list and click on number six. It leads you to a Gopher menu and there you

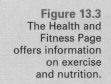

Figure 13.3
The Health and
Fitness Page
offers information
on exercise
and nutrition.

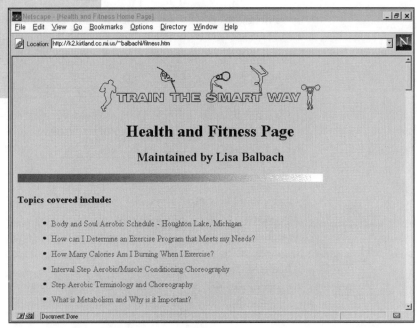

click on the calories link. Even though this site has more to do with counting calories than exercise, it does give a nice formula for calculating how many calories you need to burn to lose weight. Your client may be interested in that as well, but it does not answer the original question of which exercise burns the most.

Medicine and Illness

When searching for medical information, you have to balance time with reliability. You don't want to spend a lot of time going through indexes or long lists of search results. However, because the topic can be literally a matter of life or death, you want to be careful which Web resources you depend on. More and more people are turning to the Web to see if their doctor's advice meshes with what other

doctors in the field are saying. When doctors recommend surgery or medication, patients have not only gotten second opinions from the Web, they've read thirds, fourths, and fifths! Medical information on the Web does not replace being treated by a competent physician. However, the Web is helping people be able to ask more informed questions about their treatments. Some do the research on their own; others turn to professionals. If you do medical research with any frequency, you'll want to bookmark good ones to save on your search time in the future.

There's a lot of patient-support information on the Web. Dr. Frank Boehm reminds Web researchers that Doctors Cry, Too. His page offers essays on topics that affect doctors as well as patients. The address is **http://dr-boehm.com/dr_cry2.htm**.

You can begin with an index that will gradually narrow until you reach your answer. For example, if you're searching for information on Chronic Fatigue Syndrome, you might begin with the Essential Links to Medicine index (see Figure 13.4). Because you know that Chronic Fatigue Syndrome is a chronic condition, you choose ChronicIllNet to begin your search (see Figure 13.5).

There, you immediately see an icon for Chronic Fatigue Syndrome. Another click and you have materials and other Chronic Fatigue Syndrome links on the Web. This search started with a medical index. How do you find medical indexes? Essential Links is one you could start with, but there are many more. Meta-indexes and simple searches can lead you to medical indexes as well. Many universities have links to medical information on the Web from their home pages. It's there for the benefit of their students, but you can use it as well.

If your interest is in alternative medicine, you might start your search at the graphic-intensive AltMed Web (see Figure 13.6). It has

Figure 13.4
The Essential Links to Medicine page is a good place to begin medical research.

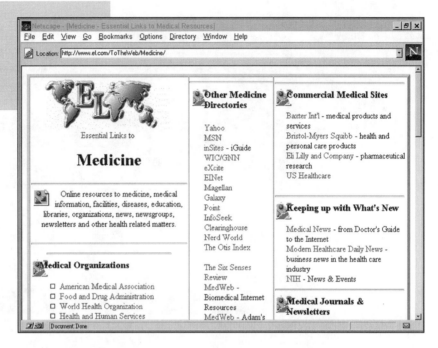

Figure 13.5
The ChronicIllNet Home Page links to many different informative pages, including one for Chronic Fatigue Syndrome.

Figure 13.6
The AltMed Web
Home Page is a
useful research
site for those
interested in
alternatives to
modern medicine.

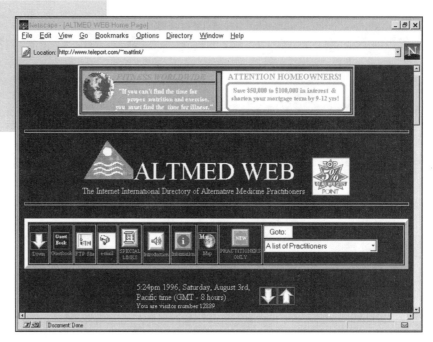

Figure 13.6
The AltMed Web Home Page is a useful research site for those interested in alternatives to modern medicine.

a listing of doctors who practice alternative medicine. There are also many links to related Internet resources. The Alternative Medicine Home Page is also a good starting place.

Physician-Oriented Materials

Patients have often wished they had the same medical information that the doctor does. The Web has many sites geared toward physicians which medical researchers can take advantage of as well. The Doctor's Guide to the Internet has the goal of saving the doctor time by gathering links to medical resources on the Web (see Figure 13.7). It covers everything from conferences to new drugs on the market. Med Nexus is another Web site that covers the health care

Figure 13.7
The Doctor's
Guide to the
Internet Home
Page offers
resources for
physicians, but
can be useful
to anyone
interested in the
medical field.

system in a colorful way. It has information for the nursing profession as well as doctors.

Medical Sites

Anyone can put up a home page and anyone can offer medical advice. If you're going through an index, see if that index has a development policy or if the goal is simply to link any related Web resource. If you frequently deal with the same medical topics, you might want to follow a LISTSERV or newsgroup. You can get mutual support and tips on good Web sites. Some things have easy answers—what's the leg bone called? However, on questions of diagnostics and treatments, be sure you're aware of the source of information. The sites in the following section can give your medical research a boost.

The Alternative Medicine Home Page

http://www.pitt.edu/~cbw/altm.html

The Alternative Medicine Home Page is best described in its own words. "This page is a jumpstation for sources of information on unconventional, unorthodox, unproven, or alternative, complementary, innovative, integrative therapies."

AltMed Web

http://www.teleport.com/~mattlmt

AltMed Web is an international directory of alternative medicine practitioners. Graphical and easy to use, it includes links to related sites.

ChronicIllNet

http://www.calypte.com

ChronicIllNet has information about ongoing medical conditions, such as heart disease or cancer. It also includes links to frequently overlooked conditions, such as Persian Gulf War Syndrome. This is a good site to begin research on chronic conditions.

CyberDoc

http://www.cybermedic.org/medspace

A doctor in the United Kingdom will answer questions submitted by Web researchers. Cyberdoc is meant to be informative, not diagnostic. This site also has related medical links.

Doctor's Guide to the Internet

http://www.pslgroup.com/docguide.htm

The Doctor's Guide to the Internet is a large index of medical information available online. It's goal is to do the research for doctors, so they'll only need to go to this site.

Essential Links to Medicine

http://www.el.com/ToTheWeb/Medicine

This is a comprehensive listing of what the Web has to offer in the field of medicine. This is a good place to begin a search when you aren't sure where to start or how to narrow the search request.

Health and Fitness Page

http://k2.kirtland.cc.mi.us/~balbachl/fitness.htm

The Health and Fitness Page has information on nutrition and exercise, especially aerobics. This page is designed to help someone determine a personal exercise program.

The Longevity Game

http://www.northwesternmutual.com/games/longevity/longevity-main.html

Want to know how long you will live? The Longevity Game calculates how much time you have left based on your answers to a questionnaire.

Med Nexus

http://www.mednexus.com

Med Nexus covers many aspects of the health care system. It requires (free) registration.

MedWeb

http://www.cc.emory.edu/WHSCL/medweb.html

MedWeb has links to a variety of medical subjects, from Aerospace Medicine to Virtual Reality in Medicine. It's indexed several different ways for convenient searching.

Evaluation of Resources

How do you evaluate medical information? This is one area where verifying credentials may be essential. An incorrect definition in a genealogical dictionary online is annoying but not life altering. If you receive bad medical information and act on it, it can be dangerous.

Many doctors answer questions online. Most list their background; a few do not. You should use some of the same guidelines you would use for a new book you have read on medical facts. Is the doctor a credible source? Is the information written by a doctor or medical facility personnel? That does not mean they have to create or maintain the Web page. It means the information needed to start in a reputable place.

Some medical references, such as the *Physician's Desk Reference*, have Web counterparts. If you're familiar with the print source of the information, there should be no reason to doubt the online version. Even when you're uncertain of the accuracy, the Web's medical pages can be a good springboard. Patients can go into doctors' offices with informed questions. Medical reporters will know what the latest trend is and better be able to interview medical professionals.

Of course, personal accounts (such as birth stories) are anecdotal. Therefore, they are neither true or false but simply one person's experience. It can be helpful to know what someone else has gone through because it gives you the perspective of a patient.

14
Music

The Web is not a quiet place. One of the purest forms of communication thrives online. Music lyrics and sound files are two of the most sought after items on the Internet. Much of the research is done for personal edification; however, many businesses have found that they need music facts for various reasons. All music types are represented on the Web. Bands and individual singers have home pages—either of their own doing or a fan created one. Music history, genres, instruments, and all things lyrical have found a home on the Web.

Search Strategies

Music can be a universal language. It's the words that confuse us. Most families have a story about a child's misunderstanding of the words of a well-known song. (My mother tells people how I sang "bringing in the sheep" rather than "bringing in the sheaves.") Adults do it too. There is actually a whole series of books and articles that list wrong lyrics people have sung along to.

Early in the Internet's history, users tried to help each other out. They would type in the words of famous and not so famous songs. When you found yourself asking, "Did he really sing that?," you could look it up. Most of these song and lyric listings were at FTP sites. List maintainers tried to make them available through Gopher sites, but these sites often crashed from the amount of traffic and data.

Now there are many lyric sites on the Web and you're not limited to reading the words. You can listen to popular songs in online listening booths. Some of these music samples are a few seconds long, but others are the entire song.

Although a viable archive of music lyrics has been a goal for many researchers, lots of other music resources enhance the Web. (Music librarians have a wider range of materials to look for, of course.) The best way to find your music resource depends on the kind of resource you're seeking. Are you looking for a general reference on a particular genre of music, such as classical? Are you more interested in a specific artist or composer? If you're searching for music genres or the instruments that make music, there are several indexes that can help. The object of your search will influence how you try to find it.

Lyrics

Searching for music can be tricky. It depends on what you think of when you say you want a music resource. Most search requests I receive for music are really for the words put to music. Lyrics can be difficult to find only because lyric sites typically crash from too many users. With the advent of the Web and corporations supplying the hardware, some seem to be surviving. Search engines can help you find lyrical sites. Once you find a lyrics site you like, bookmark it, but realize that it might not last long.

There are many lyric archives. Some are centered around a theme, such as all the songs from a television series. Others try to include every song possible. You often get more than the lyrics. You might get information about the performer, song writer, album, and date of publication. Some archivists will give variations that were sung on different dates. Songs from television series will often be divided into episodes and you'll learn about the series that way. Songs from movies are also popular.

Do professionals put these lyrics online? Many times no. They're inputted by a dedicated fan. Whenever possible, they use an official source, such as the lyrics included with an album. Often, though, they're relying on their own ears, literally transcribing what they hear. These archivists do a remarkable job. Nevertheless, discrepancies creep in. It's something to consider in the evaluation of resources.

If you want to hear music on the Web, go to MusicLink's Music on the Internet at **http://toltec.lib.utk.edu/~music/wwwzipp.html**. It has links to all types of music.

How do you find a good lyrics archive? The original FTP archive sites are still good ones. Gopher sites had a hard time handling the traffic and amount of data generated by a lyrics site. Fortunately, the Web has been able to handle the traffic better than Gopherspace. If you use the Web to access an FTP music lyrics archive, what you'll see is straightforward, with no graphics or dazzling fonts. It can be slow, however, you will find a large selection of songs and performers. These FTP archives are organized alphabetically by artist, so you must know the name of the singer or group.

However, less cumbersome ones are available on the Web now. The Lyrics Page is one popular resource that allows users to browse or search for the desired song (see Figure 14.1). One nice feature is that you can also put in a phrase from a song for a full-text search. Ever spent a day singing a tune and you can't remember who sang it originally? This site will help you cure that vexing problem. Almost all the lyrics are sent in by Internet users.

Figure 14.1
The Lyrics Page will help you put words to the music you can't quit humming.

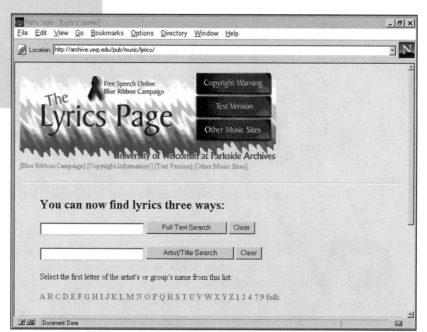

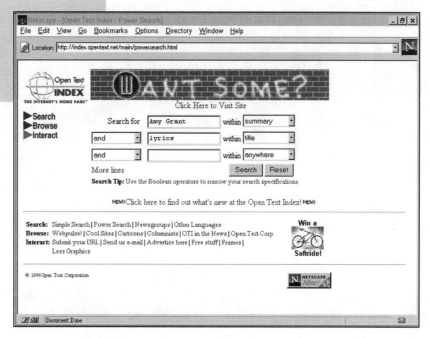

Figure 14.2
This Open Text
power search
screen is filled in
for an Amy Grant
lyrics search.

You can look for lyric Web sites with search engines, but you'll get a long results list. For large lyric sites, you should use an index or links from a related site. Once you find one you like, bookmark it. You will probably have more success using search engines to find a specific singer's song lyrics. Depending on how well-known the singer is, you can enter a name alone or add a name with other keywords. The more detailed your search request, the better your chances of finding what you're looking for. For example, you could use an Open Text power search to look for "Amy Grant within summary and lyrics within title" (see Figure 14.2).

You get back only seven results, which is easy to sort through (see Figure 14.3). In fact, you will notice that most of them have the same address. The sixth site looks promising, so you click on number six, Lyrics for Amy Grant Songs.

Figure 14.3
Results of the
Amy Grant lyrics
search using
Open Text.

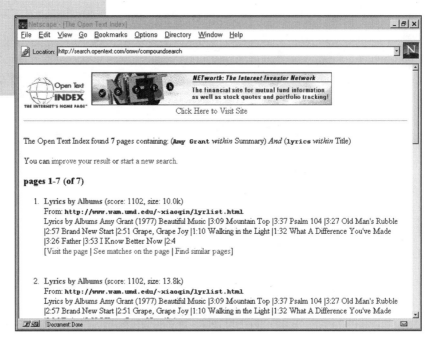

You find a song listing that was last updated in December of 1995 (see Figure 14.4). That's OK though, because it includes almost all Amy Grant songs produced. This page also tells you who's responsible for the archive. You could probably find whatever song you're looking for by following the links, but what if you would like to check it against other sources for accuracy? You could do another search using a different engine.

However, there's probably a simpler way. At the bottom of this page you can click to return to the home page. You do so and find yourself at the introduction. At the bottom of that page you have the option of going to the starting page. Another click and you have an index of resources. You choose Other Resources on WWW. There you see other Web pages and even a lyrics archive. It won't take you long to find out all you need to know.

Figure 14.4
The Lyrics page for Amy Grant has the words of most of her songs.

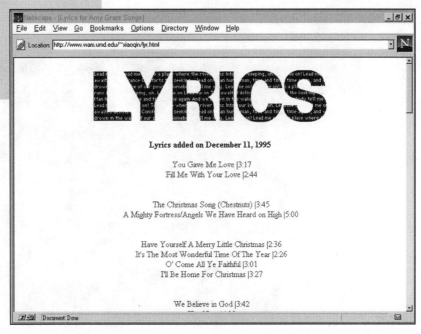

If you have no luck on the Web, you can always try a newsgroup dedicated to music lyrics. One group to try is **alt.music.lyrics**. People post lyrics that interest them and queries about ones they want to know. You can post the song and ask for the words. Or, if you remember the words and not the singer, you can get help with that too.

Singers, Bands, and Musicians

Maybe you're interested in more than the lyrics. You want to know about the performer. You have a favorite band that you want to learn more about. Just as there are large indexes of lyrics, there are also ones for those who perform the songs. You might find what you're looking for on The Ultimate Band List (see Figure 14.5). If you're

Figure 14.5
The Ultimate
Band List
Home Page has
information
on many
popular bands.

searching for a band using a search engine, remember to use limiting factors. Names like Genesis and Red Hot Chili Peppers can pull up topics you're not interested in.

Genres

Perhaps your interest in music goes beyond artists to a certain type of music. Indexes are probably your best resource for research because entering "country music" into a search engine would get you thousands of hits. Meta-indexes like Yahoo! are a good source. Music specific to a country would be searched for the same way. A music site that strives to have links for every type of music is Aardvark's Archive of Genres (see Figure 14.6). It's a long hypertext list filled with genres from around the world.

Figure 14.6
Aardvark's
Archive of Genres
Home Page has a
global outlook
on music.

Pure Music

Have you been reading up to now in frustration? This is just a bunch of bands and pop songs! Where's the music? Yes, there are plenty of sites that remember the instruments and the musicians who put them to good use. Some Web sites are dedicated to a single instrument, such as the Piano Page (see Figure 14.7). Others are dedicated to the composers who bring the instruments to life, such as the Catalogue of Classical Composers Home Page shown in Figure 14.8. There are even music scores so you can play the music yourself (see Figure 14.9).

How do you find this information? For instruments, a meta-index is your best choice; a search engine would pull up too many results for words like piano, flute, and trumpet. Music sites tend to link to

Figure 14.7
The Piano Page
celebrates and
educates about
the popular
instrument.

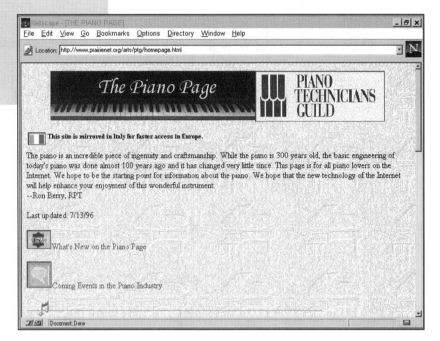

Figure 14.7 The Piano Page celebrates and educates about the popular instrument.

Figure 14.8
The Catalogue
of Classical
Composers Home
Page brings the
old musicmakers
into the new
medium of
the Web.

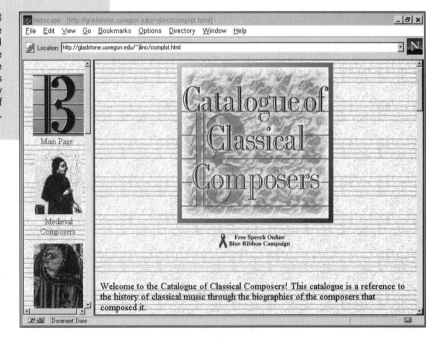

Figure 14.8 The Catalogue of Classical Composers Home Page brings the old musicmakers into the new medium of the Web.

Figure 14.9
The Music
Archive: Scores
page allows
researchers to
print out music.

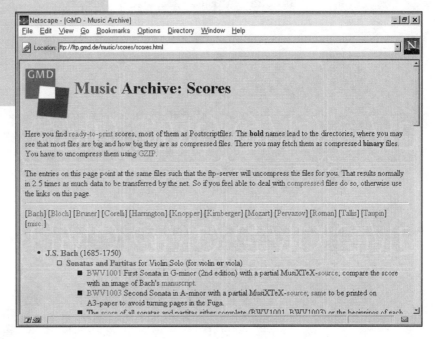

one another, so you can also count on one resource having links to more. There are also newsgroups and e-zines you might want to read if you're interested in a particular instrument. The newsgroup will lead you to Web sites. You can find composers through search engines when they have unique names, such as Heiter Villa-Lobos. His distinct name makes it easy to run a search and find what you're looking for. But what do you do when the name is John Williams? You'll get thousands of irrelevant hits in your search results. One option is to add more to the name if you know it (such as John Towner Williams). However, you might miss Web sites that don't include his middle name in the searched area. You can add limiting keywords, such as musician or composer.

Using a search engine to find composers can be a good strategy. You might have just as much luck answering your question going through a music index. It depends on how much information you want to collect on a subject.

Music Sites

The Web can be as musical as you want it to be. Of course, if you have the multimedia capabilities, you can listen to a lot of what you find. Even if you're confined to words on a screen, you can still hear the music in your mind with these sites. After all, can anyone simply speak the words, "The hills are alive with the sound of music?"

Aardvark's Archive of Genres

http://stl-music.com/gen.html

Aardvark's Archive of Genres promises that you can find anything musical with its search form. It bills itself as having "HUNDREDS upon HUNDREDS of links listed alphabetically, each linking to BILLIONS and BILLIONS of other sites. Well, close anyway." If you have no idea where to begin a music information search, start here.

All-Music Guide

http://www.allmusic.com/amg/music_root.html

The All-Music Guide has an easy to use search form for finding whatever you want to know about music performers, especially contemporary ones.

Catalogue of Classical Composers

http://gladstone.uoregon.edu/~jlinc/complst.html

This beautiful site tries to list all the composers of the classical genre. Biographies of many of the composers and a music dictionary are a highlight of this resource.

Digital Tradition Folk Song Database

http://pubweb.parc.xerox.com/digitrad

This site offers a thorough search engine of the Digital Tradition Folk Song Database. There are more than 5,000 songs and several ways to search for them, including full-text.

LEO

ftp://ftp.informatik.tu-muenchen.de/pub/rec/music/vocal/lyrics/uwp

LEO stands for Link Everything Online. This site includes an FTP music lyric archive that you can access through the Web. If you're in North America, be warned that it comes from Germany and can be slow. It also has one of the largest collections online.

The Lyrics Page

http://archive.uwp.edu/pub/music/lyrics

The Lyrics Page is a quick, easy to use site that offers three ways to find the song lyric of your choice. A text version of this site is also available.

Music Archive: Scores

ftp://ftp.gmd.de/music/scores/scores.html

This site offers well-known musical scores that you can print out. Browse through an alphabetical list of composers to make a selection.

The Piano Page

http://www.prairienet.org/arts/ptg/homepage.html

The Piano Page approaches this popular instrument from every angle. You can learn about the industry, find a buying guide, or link to related Internet sites from here. It's mirrored in Italy to make it faster for European Web researchers.

The Ultimate Band List

http://american.recordings.com/wwwofmusic/ubl/ubl.shtml

The Ultimate Band List has links and information about bands, even the newest ones. If you need to track down a band's home page, this is the place to start.

Evaluation of Resources

Evaluating music resources on the Web can be difficult. If you need to publish lyrics to a song, you can often find them on the Internet. However, you have to trust that they were entered correctly. You may or may not know the site's source of information. Copyright can even become a concern in some cases. (A lawyer would better answer copyright questions than a librarian.)

Well-established lyric sites tell you where the lyrics come from. Even if they're contributed by other Internet users, you can think of them as a good resource. You have to judge their trustworthiness in part by what you're using them for. Are you looking up the words to settle a bet? Are you publishing them in a news magazine? Sometimes one Web page simply copied the lyrics listed at another. You have to go to the original Web page to determine the source. Web pages created by individuals with just a few songs (usually their favorites) listed might be reliable. I recommend checking other resources, just in case the site creators have made a mistake (unless they name their source and you think it's accurate). If that's the only place you can find the lyrics, however, you might have to go with it.

Web pages created to promote a singer or band are most likely accurate, just biased in which information was chosen to be distributed. Many of these efforts are done with a fan's devotion, so the attention to detail is quite good. Much of what is written on instruments and music genres is done by those in the academic field or experts—the ones actually playing the instruments on a regular basis. Sites get reputations. If you participate in a LISTSERV or newsgroup, you'll learn which ones are recommended by people in the field. You'll have to look at the credentials of the source to decide how reliable the information is. Most of what's on the Web concerning music is commendable.

15

News

The Web is news. But once you're on the Web, how do you find out news? You often hear of people finding out about events on the Internet before they're reported in the media. It happens all the time. The most vivid example I can think of was during the Persian Gulf War. I learned that Iraq had bombarded Israel with missiles before television reporters went on the air with the news.

However, most of this communication takes place on newsgroups and LISTSERVs. It was through a chat session that I learned about Israel during the war. News travels fast through word of mouth and the Internet has given people the tool to make it travel faster (and farther) still.

That doesn't mean news isn't on the Web. Not since the printing press has there been such a change in communication. The printing press allowed information to be widely distributed. Those who controlled the press literally controlled what was known. The fourth estate rose up, controlling television and radio as well as printed materials.

The Internet combines the power of the press with the ease of a telephone. If you need to call a friend, you don't wait for a designated time. You pick up the phone and call. When you see your neighbor, you chat about local happenings. You can find that same quality on the Web. You have news and you can publish instantly.

Search Strategies

Being able to spread news on the Web (and the Internet in general) has been a boon in communication. For example, say you move away from your hometown. You can't get the local paper or tune into the local television and radio stations anymore. But if someone puts up a Web page featuring your town, you can still keep up. Or maybe you don't want to subscribe to your local newspaper; an alternative one can be published on the Web for you and other dissatisfied customers to read. Best of all, you can often select which articles to read without even glancing at ones that aren't interesting to you.

The media figured out that it was being cut out of the loop. Why turn on the television and listen to a 30 minute broadcast for a two minute report you're interested in? You can go online and read (and often hear and see) about events from the people actually experiencing them.

So, the media started going online. Many were already on computer databases that were sold to corporations. With a lot of hoopla and some shaky starts, the press found its way on the Web. You have a choice of sources now. You can go with the professional ones that have corresponding print sources (newspapers, television, and radio news services) or the strictly online ones. Some professional sources try to charge for their service or offer limited service with the hopes that you'll pay for more. For the most part, you can avoid these fee-based news sites and still satisfy your need to know.

Most professional news organizations that have gone on the Web have supported themselves the same way they support their non-virtual products: they sell advertising. In order to charge advertisers for the privilege of filling advertisement space, these online publications must attract a lot of readers. Typically, they track readers two ways. First, they can count the number of hits their home page and related pages receive. Second, they ask readers to subscribe or register. There isn't a monetary cost, just the loss of anonymity. The news organization gets demographics to show the advertisers and you get a free newspaper.

News sources are easy to find on the Web. The danger isn't being unable to find what you want; it's being unable to sort through all that's out there. It's extremely easy to get sidetracked from your original goal, especially when news organizations are starting to offer a good selection of comics and editorial cartoons.

The best way to find news on the Web is through an index. However, you often can discern the URL without even looking it up. The search strategy for the actual seeking is pretty straightforward. You think of which source you need and then find it in a good news index. The hard part is finding the actual article once you have the newspaper or other news source pulled up on your monitor.

Newspapers

The professional press coming online has actually been a boon to newshounds. Thanks to the computer, you can read today's edition one minute after midnight in many cases. If you're up until 2 A.M., you can read the headlines and articles before your morning paper arrives or the morning news shows come on.

Major newspapers have sites on the Web that offer full-text stories and graphics. Many add features unique to the Internet such as sound files and links to related sources. Newspapers often are limited by space because they can only print so much in the available newsprint. On the Internet, they can often offer related texts that they may not have had room to print in their physical newspaper. For example, the mayor's speech in its entirety instead of key remarks.

Newspapers try to use easy to remember addresses, such as **http://www.csmonitor.com** for the *Christian Science Monitor*. There are thousands of newspapers online. Some, such as *The Nando Times*, have created impressive Internet publications that stand on their own. Many Web newspaper sites ask you to register before being able to access the full content.

How do you find a newspaper? If you don't know the address and it isn't obvious, you'll have the best luck going through an index. This is especially true if you're looking for a certain region but you don't the exact name of the newspaper. For example, if you're looking for the newspaper in Jacksonville, Florida you would not think of *The Florida Times-Union*.

For another example, say you need to find a newspaper in Utah. You can look in the *Editor & Publisher International Yearbook* to get a listing of Utah newspapers. However, that won't tell you which ones are on the Web. Furthermore, you might not have a copy of the E&P handy. (Although you could visit the online E&P site which has a searchable index of online newspapers.) You do have your computer and Internet connection, so you get online and go to a newspaper index. You choose News and Newspapers Online (see

Figure 15.1). You then choose North America and go to the page shown in Figure 15.2.

You choose United States, then scroll to Utah. There are two selections, both from Salt Lake City. You click on the first one, *Deseret News,* and see what their home page has to offer (see Figure 15.3). After a quick look, you return to your index to click on the second choice, *Salt Lake Tribune* (see Figure 15.4). Both Web resources look good and fulfill your search request. If you need Utah news sources on a regular basis, you could bookmark both of them.

You should bookmark (and subscribe to if necessary) newspapers you plan to read frequently. For occasional searches, you can rely on indexes. (Just bookmark a good index.) There are enough news indexes on the Web to be a fail-safe if your favorite index disappears or drops a link. In fact, if you rely on news sources often, you'll want to keep track of several good news indexes.

Figure 15.1
The News and Newspapers Online Home Page has links to resources from around the world.

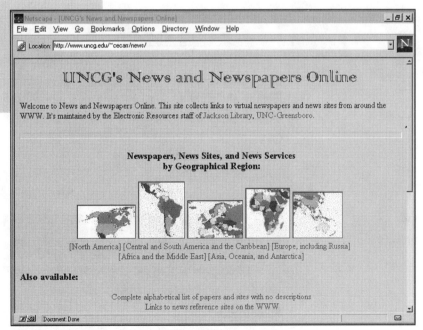

Figure 15.2
The News and Newspapers Online North America page helps narrow your search.

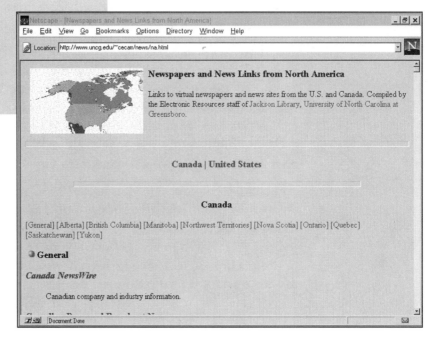

Figure 15.3
Deseret News is one of the Utah newspapers listed.

Figure 15.4
The Salt Lake Tribune is the other Utah newspaper found in the search.

Major Papers

Some newspapers grow so big in scope they become more like national (or international) newspapers than local ones. These newspapers are the most frequently searched ones. News librarians have a special category for them; they're called major papers. Many online services that supply the full text of newspapers to companies (and especially other newspapers) allow for major paper searches. It allows news librarians to look through the text of several of these large newspapers at once.

So far, there isn't a service on the Web that does a major papers search. This will probably change soon. Until then, you can still look at (and often search) most major papers on the Web.

What are the major papers? Opinions vary, but there are some core ones. They're typically associated with large cities and have bureaus (or smaller newspapers that are part of their chain) across the country. Major papers are not always the best resource. When I was a news librarian, reporters often would ask me for an article from *The New York Times* only to be disappointed to learn that what they really wanted was in *The Gainesville Sun* or the *Roanoke Times & World News*. A newspaper with a smaller circulation than a major paper doesn't mean less news necessarily.

However, major papers do provide a national record and will probably continue to have a certain prestige about them. If you want to keep up with the major papers, you only need to bookmark their sites. Major papers with a Web presence are *The New York Times, The Christian Science Monitor, USA Today, The Washington Post, Chicago Tribune, Houston Chronicle, Los Angeles Times,* and *The Miami Herald.* Popular newspapers outside the U.S. are *The Toronto Sun* and *The Times* (London). Although they're on the Web, some are better than others at providing news. Figures 15.5 through 15.14 show a short gallery of the home pages of major papers.

Figure 15.5
The Christian Science Monitor Home Page lets researchers read news and interact with each other.

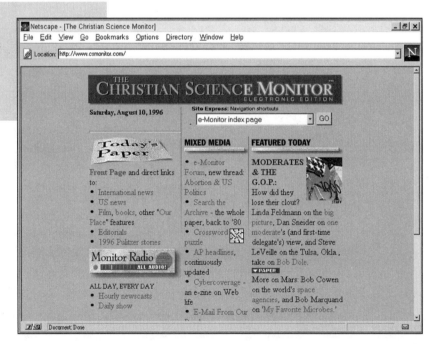

Figure 15.6
The *USA Today*
Home Page
features the same
accessibility as
the print version.

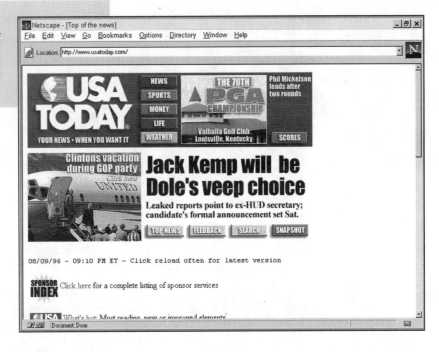

Figure 15.7
The *Chicago
Tribune* Home
Page offers
readers the
chance to
comment on
the news.

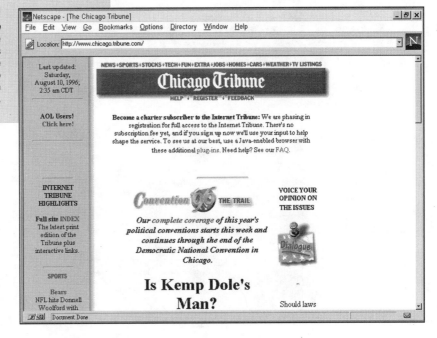

Figure 15.8
The *Houston Chronicle* Home Page offers news from the print version and features specific to the online version.

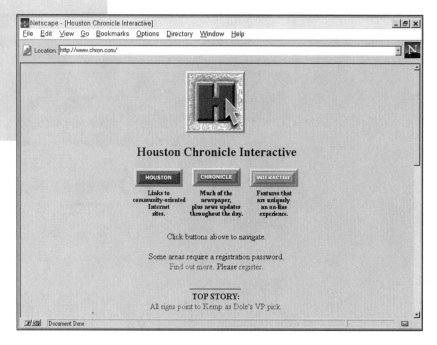

Figure 15.9
The *Los Angeles Times* Home Page looks less like a newspaper and more like a typical Web site.

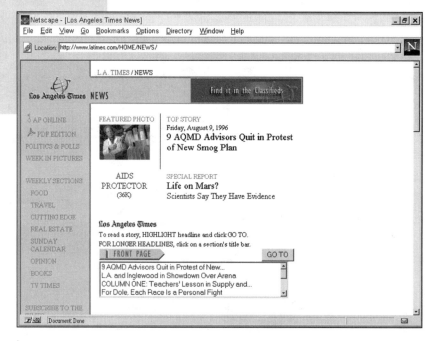

Figure 15.10
The Miami Herald Home Page is easy to read because it has successfully created Web versions of traditional newspaper features.

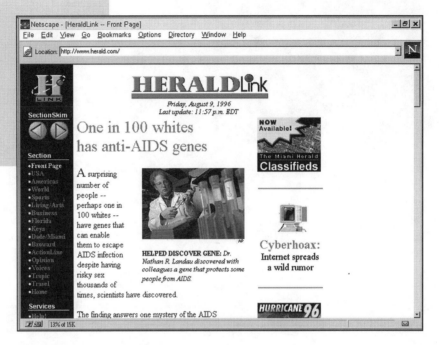

Figure 15.11
The New York Times Home Page is more colorful and innovative than the print version.

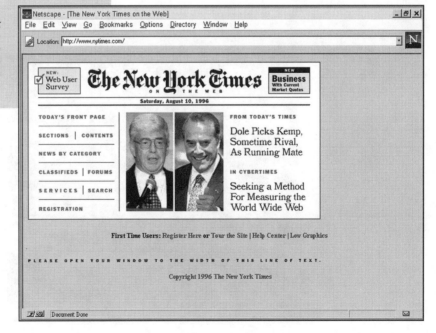

Figure 15.12
The Washington Post Home Page combines Web search options with a traditional-looking newspaper.

Figure 15.13
The Times Home Page requires registration before reading the news.

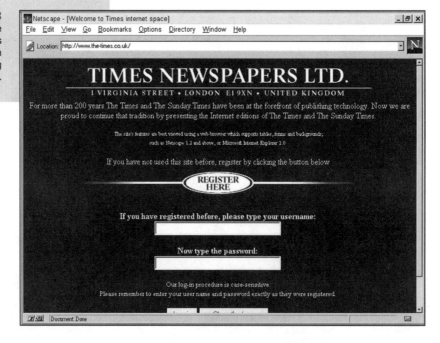

Figure 15.14
The Toronto Sun Home Page turns traditional newspaper sections into clickable icons.

Television and Radio Stations

Newspapers may be the oldest form of mass media but they are no longer the only option. Many people rely on broadcast news to meet their information needs without glancing at a newspaper. However, the Web has pulled more people away from television than it has from newspapers. Both television and radio station owners have noticed the shift and they have established Web presences as well.

Television networks don't just inform, their priority is to entertain. Nevertheless, the major networks have Web sites that offer some amount of news. NBC and CNN have done the most thorough jobs. You usually can find television networks simply by constructing an address based on the network's abbreviation. For example, CBS is **http://www.cbs.com** on the Web. Once on the Web, televi-

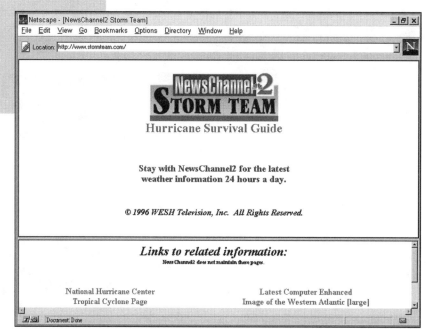

sion news and newspapers don't look different. Both rely on fonts, pictures, and moving objects to attract and hold a reader's attention.

Many local stations have gone on the Web as well. They offer local news and guides that are relevant to the area. For example, WESH, a channel in Orlando, has set up a Hurricane Survival Guide on the Web (see Figure 15.15).

Radios stations are also setting up Web sites. Often meant to entertain, some are news-oriented. One of the best known radio programs is *Voice of America*. The broadcasts are not copyrighted so they put them online for anyone to read. As VOA is intended to be broadcast outside of the United States, Internet sites may be the only way Americans can follow the programs outside of the United States.

News Services

If your interest is national and international news, you might think of the newspaper as the go between. Most national and international news you see in your newspaper came from a wire service. Thanks to the Internet, you can read many of the same wire services that newspapers, television, and radio stations receive. You're still getting your news from a reporter; however, you read what the wire actually put out without the editing (and frequent cuts) done by your local newspaper.

There are only so many wire services, so research is easier once you bookmark the ones you want to follow. They are free to Web users since the provider works out an agreement with the wire service. Yahoo! has an agreement with Reuters, that news stories will be supplied and updated every hour. You can read a headline list and then click on whatever interests you. There's an archive of recent stories. The Associated Press is available via *The Boston Globe*. Articles are updated every half hour. You can find a good collection of international news services at News Sources On The 'Net (see Figure 15.16).

Other News Sources

News magazines, such as *U.S. News* and *Time*, are also on the Web. You can find them in the same way you find newspapers. Others have taken a different approach to news gathering and reporting. They have organized pages with the same sections a newspaper or magazine traditionally have: features, hard news, and so on, while related sites are linked. You get more than traditional sources this way. Figure 15.17 shows news on the net, and an example of this approach.

News Sites

There are many wonderful indexes and news sources on the Web. If you feel overwhelmed by the choices, choose one of the sites in the

Figure 15.16
The News
Sources On The
'Net Home Page
leads to global
news resources.

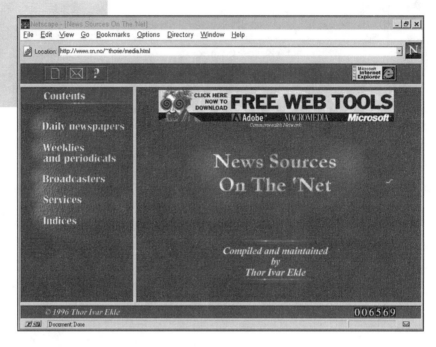

Figure 15.17
The news on the
net Home Page
offers several
different news
resources
grouped
by subject.

following sections for your first venture into Web news. This is not a comprehensive list but can help you begin.

The Alpha Complete News Index

http://www.select-ware.com/news

This site offers news sources from around the world. Only publications that do not charge a fee are listed, but there are still plenty to choose from. This is a good site for international news.

Associated Press

http://www.globe.com/globe/cgi-bin/globe.cgi?ap/apnat.htm

This is the Associated Press wire unchanged by editors. You read what a journalist at a newspaper would be reading. It's updated every half hour, so you can expect current news.

The Best News on the Net

http://www.NovPapyrus.com/news

If you're more interested in quality than quantity, this site is the place to begin your news resource search. News sites are chosen because they represent the best, although the best is not clearly defined. There are many easy-to-follow categories to help narrow your search.

CNN Interactive

http://www.cnn.com

CNN offers the same news your hear on TV on the Web. You choose the subject area and then the story. If you like CNN on cable, you'll like the Web site too.

Editor & Publisher Interactive

http://www.mediainfo.com

This is a Web version of *Editor & Publisher*. In addition to the media listings, there are articles about issues of concern to journalists. Journalists can debate issues in an interactive forum as well. This Web version lists media on the Web, rather than being a duplicate of the Yearbook.

Electronic Newsstand

http://www.image.dk/~knud-sor/en

The Electronic Newsstand is exactly what the title says, except you don't have to pay for materials you find here. Links are divided into subjects to aid your search. You'll find all the categories that you normally do in a newspaper (for example, weather or sports). This resource has been around for a while and many researchers still reference it.

MSNBC

http://www.msnbc.com

This online news service is a joint venture of the National Broadcasting Company and Microsoft. It covers all of NBC's news offerings, from network television to cable to news sources created just for the Web. It can be a little confusing where the story you're reading originated from, but the news is there and easy to read.

NeWo: News Resource

http://newo.com/news

This site has news sources from around the world. You click on the map to choose the region you want to read news from.

News and Newspapers Online

http://www.uncg.edu/~cecarr/news

This is a comprehensive listing of world wide news sources divided into geographic areas. It's easy to use and find the source you're looking for.

News on the Net

http://www.reporter.org/news

Organized into sections you see in a newspaper, this site doesn't rely on one news source. Rather, each section can have articles from several sources. If you want a good mixture of news sources that deals with current events, this is the site to go to.

The News Page

http://www.arastar.net/news

The News Page is an easy to use collection of news sources that are organized by region and specialty. It's a good collection of Web resources.

News Sources On The 'Net

http://www.sn.no/~thorie/media.html

This is a well-organized index of international news sources. It includes some sites that other indexes don't list. This is a good place to go if you're looking for a news source that isn't well-known.

The Virtual Daily News

http://www.infi.net/~opfer/daily.htm

This news source is aimed primarily at the U.S. but can be used by anyone. It is icon driven, and offers news in subject areas. Neither this index nor the sites that it links to require registration or fee payments. If you want a guarantee that you can use the source you link to, this is a good index to start with.

Evaluation of Resources

Evaluating news sources on the Web is not difficult. If it comes from a professional service, it's as trustworthy as any print product. A file on the Web is certainly less ephemeral than a sound bite on the airwaves. News sources are easy to find. There are many indexes and links from other people's home pages. Your Internet Service Provider might have links to news resources on its home page.

One thing to look for in a news resource is an archive. Those with archives will be valuable to you in the long run because you can look up events after they have happened. If your news source does not have an archive, you might have to start saving stories you plan to refer to again.

It becomes a little more difficult when the news item is written especially for Internet publication. Compare Web exclusive sites to professional ones. (Some would say that Web specific ones are professional. The distinction will be less pronounced as Web publications are less of a novelty and more mainstream.) If they're consistent on similar stories, then chances are they will be accurate on others as well. Remember to check the credentials of the Webmaster and original writer if you have questions.

For the latest gossip, you'll have to hang out in the newsgroups. But if you want fast, accurate news about the world's happenings, you can find them on the Web.

16

Reference
and Literature

The word flourishes on the Internet. All you know of a person is the words they choose to put on the screen. People who would not write a letter to send through regular mail might write page after page of computer screens, either for e-mail or their Web page. Writing and reading what others have written is the main reason people are online. Sound files and moving graphics are only an extension of the communication. Without the words, there would be no Internet culture.

Perhaps because the written word is so important to Internet users, literature has prospered on the Internet. We not only share our ideas, we share the ideas and words of those we agree with. Thousands of people have typed or scanned in stories from all areas. You can find a good book online just as easily as in a library. (However, you might have a hard time carrying it with you to your favorite reading spot.)

Along the same lines, reference works are abundant on the Web. If we're going to communicate with words, we need to share the same vocabulary. However, reference materials go beyond the simple dictionary. Encyclopedias, specialized dictionaries, conversion tables, and fact files all have homes on the Web. The computer is an excellent storage facility of data and the Web has become the means to distribute it.

Search Strategies

It seems like literature and reference works would be easy to find on the Web. In fact, one could easily make the case that all information found on the Web is a reference of some kind. However, this chapter refers to typical resources you would find in a ready reference collection. "Ready references" earned their name because librarians found these sources to be the quickest and easiest way to give an accurate answer to a quick question. These books are often on a bookshelf near a librarian's desk.

Finding ready references isn't as easy on the Internet. A few sites have appropriated the phrase as the name of their site but don't offer a comprehensive collection. Reference sources have actually been slow to come on the Internet. Many of the earlier ones were cumbersome. Perhaps it's because the people putting information online assumed researchers would continue to rely on books for quick questions. However, there is an emerging need for references online, especially unique reference materials. A lot of reference materials are on the Web now but can still be hard to track down.

If you plan to use Web references on a regular basis, build your own ready reference collection. Name a bookmark file "ready reference" or some other phrase you'll remember. When you find a site you'll use frequently, bookmark it under that name.

Literature, on the other hand, is relatively easy to find. You'll have a bigger problem sorting through everything than you will finding it. Popular books in the public domain are almost certainly on the Web (or retrievable from the Web) in some manner. Even books and articles still under copyright law can be found on the Web as more and more publishers are choosing to publish on the Web and in print at the same time.

A growing area of literature on the Web is interactive books. There are many varieties. Some allow you to pick a character and follow this character throughout a story. You will read a different story than the person who chooses another character because you only read about what your character experiences. Other forms of interactive books allow the readers themselves to write the story. In essence, the reader is both author and audience.

To find a literature source, you will probably rely on an index. Which index you choose depends on your topic, from classics to contemporary. Usually, you can find the book you're looking for within a few minutes of searching. Articles might take longer, depending on your topic.

Reference Materials

It seems that reference materials would be the ideal candidate for indexes. Yet I've found that I've had better luck using search engines to pinpoint the exact tool I need rather than relying on an index to have the link to the reference material I'm searching for. There are so many reference materials on the Web that few indexes make an attempt to link to them all. An index might be useful. If you're at a site anyway, you might check their listing. However, don't spend a lot of time going from index to index in hopes of finding what you need.

When looking for reference materials, which search engine you choose will affect your results. Search engines with smaller databases might not include more unusual resources. Also, you'll want to use a search engine that allows you to narrow your search. Simply entering "encyclopedia" or "dictionary" into a search field would yield far too many results to sort through. A search engine that balances a large database with many limiting factors is your best tool.

Search engines that allow you to enter detailed requests are the best for finding Web reference resources. You'll want to specify not only the reference type you're looking for (such as almanac) but also the subject matter of that reference (such as sports). AltaVista and Open Text have forms for exact search requests. However, AltaVista has the wider database. Excite allows for Boolean logic and other limiting factors but does not try to cover the whole Web. You can find reference resources (especially the common ones) with any of the search engines. The consideration is how many relevant ones you will find.

Part of effective searching is knowing when to use the search engine and when to look on the bookshelf. For ordinary dictionaries, you'll

probably use the one on your desk. Whatever your language, it's simply easier. (You might also rely on a spell checker or dictionary program. That's easier than looking on the Web for a resource that will not tell you anything new.) What you will go online for are dictionaries that cover subjects you don't regularly delve into.

For example, you might need the Italian word for "book." However, you don't have an Italian/English dictionary in your office. So you go to AltaVista to do an advanced search. The search request would be "(Italian near English) and dictionary" with ranking criteria being "dictionary, Italian" (see Figure 16.1).

Figure 16.2 shows the results list. You choose the third one which reads "English-to-Italian Dictionary." Figure 16.3 shows you the page that appears after you click that listing.

Figure 16.1
This AltaVista search form is filled out for an Italian/English dictionary.

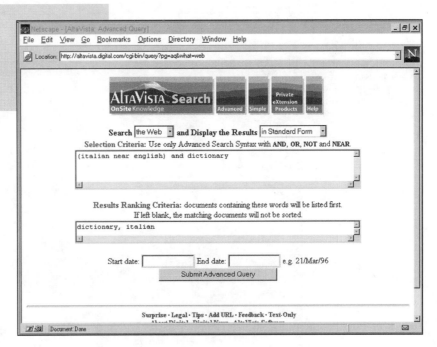

Figure 16.2
This shows the search results from AltaVista for an Italian/English dictionary.

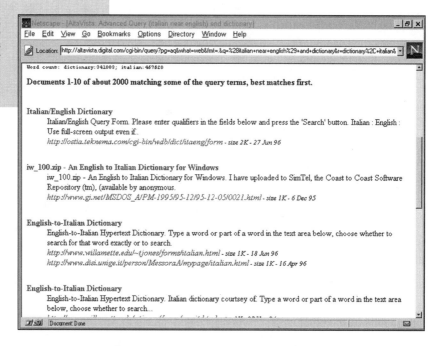

Figure 16.3
The English-to-Italian Hypertext Dictionary Home Page is a good resource and satisfies the first part of the search request.

This site lacks flashy graphics; indeed it is simply a search form. However, it does everything you need it to do. Type in the English word **book** and click the Search button. Figure 16.4 shows the results.

Not only does it tell you the word-to-word translation of "libro," it gives you other words and phrases which use the word "book." If you would need to look up a lot of words, you could bookmark the home page.

If you look up words in many different languages, you might want to bookmark a few indexes. Remember that no index covers every resource available. However, one of the more thorough ones is On-line Dictionaries (see Figure 16.5). It has links to dozen of language dictionaries, as well as specialized dictionaries (such as a synonym dictionary).

Encyclopedias are another popular resource. Don't get hung up on the word "encyclopedia." There are many Web pages that cover a

Figure 16.4
This list of Italian translations for "book" answers the second part of the search request.

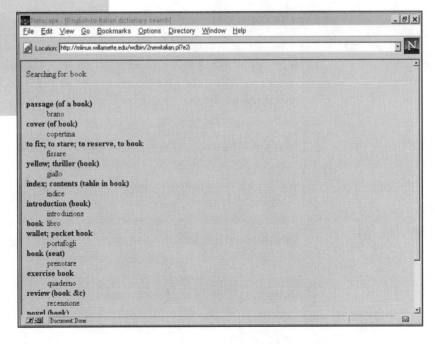

Figure 16.5
The On-line
Dictionaries
Home Page
links to many
different types
of dictionaries
and would be a
great addition to
a personal index
of reference
materials.

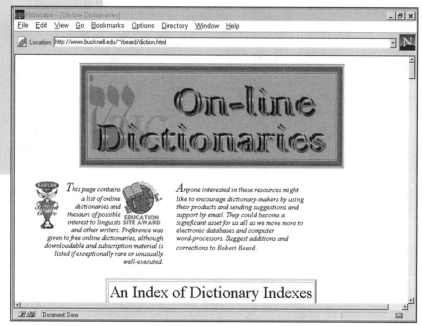

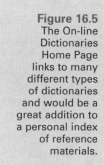

topic more thoroughly than an encyclopedia would but don't have the word "encyclopedia" in the title because the site is limited to a few subjects. Even Britannica Online doesn't have the word "encyclopedia" in the title.

Many online encyclopedias do not have separate entries written for the publication. Rather, they're more like indexes that have been organized like encyclopedias. Each entry is really a link to another Web site that covers the subject you clicked on. This arrangement is better than an index because it ensures that you will only have to look through informative sources. If you like encyclopedias, it may be easier for you to use a reference that is set up like one. Some even use macropedia and micropedia headings. If the link isn't working though, you can't read about that subject. Also, you may be able to find the site yourself without having to go through an encyclopedia.

If you want an encyclopedia where all the entries originate from one source, you may have to go with one that charges a fee.

Often, you won't find traditional reference words in the titles of sites. For example, one site is simply called Rulers. It lists world leaders for countries and organizations, such as the United Nations. It gives the birth date, death date, and term served for each leader. Is this an almanac, dictionary, encyclopedia, or biographical source? If it answers your question, does it matter to you what it's classified as? The point is when you're searching for a resource, you may not find it on the Web in a neat category as you would in an actual library. Indexes and online libraries can help. Often, however, you will have to look for the reference source yourself, especially if you want a unique one.

Online libraries can help because a librarian has compiled a list of sites under what they are, not what their titles says. For example, the Internet Public Library lists Native Hawaiian Data Book under almanacs even though the title does not suggest it is an almanac. That's because the librarian has already gone to that site and evaluated the resource. The Native Hawaiian Data Book has the statistical charts and brief facts that are hallmarks of an almanac. Unfortunately, there are more reference resources than there are librarians evaluating them.

There are good indexes on the Web if you really want to bookmark an online starting point. My Virtual Reference Desk is one of the most comprehensive and easy to use. It's divided into "my" categories. You can go to Virtual Facts on File, My Virtual Encyclopedia, My Virtual Newspaper, and My Search Engines. The Virtual Facts on File most closely resembles a ready reference section. My Virtual Encyclopedia is more of a topical index. You can reach many reference resources within a few screen clicks.

Another site with a similar name, Virtual Reference Desk (maintained by the Libraries of Purdue University), is a good one. As you can see, using library terms is popular. It's easy to get the sites confused. Part of the reason library terms are used is to give the Web researcher a clue as to what the site offers. Many Webmasters want

researchers to realize that they offer the same material that can be found on a reference shelf of a library.

Literature

There are so many stories that the Web can tell you. You can find everything from classics to modern day offerings of fellow Web researchers. Literature, unlike reference sources, is best found through an index. There are many well-constructed ones. Some are general; many focus on a particular area of literature.

Online Books

If you're simply trying to remember your favorite Shakespeare quote, you may want to go to a quotation site. Bartlett's, shown in Figure 16.6, is online but it's not the only place to find a phrase

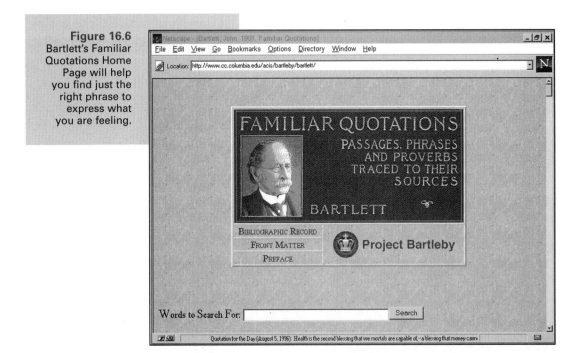

Figure 16.6
Bartlett's Familiar Quotations Home Page will help you find just the right phrase to express what you are feeling.

you're looking for. In addition to the usual classic, Biblical, and presidential quotes, you can find many sites dedicated to less formal sources. You can read pearls of wisdom from Star Trek, supermodels, fortune cookies, *Mad Magazine*, and various movies.

William Shakespeare, Mary Shelley, Mark Twain, Emily Dickinson, and many others have their writings showcased on the Web. In general, if you're looking for a famous, well-known author, you should look under the name in an index. How do you determine how well-known an author is? For authors of previous eras, do high school students study their works in English class? If so, then they probably have their own entry and possibly a Web page or two. For contemporary authors, ask yourself if their books regularly make the bestseller lists.

Other ways to find authors and their books is to look under the title of the work, genre, or era. Collections are frequently built around a theme, such as women writers of the 19th century. You can do a search via your favorite search engine on the author's name. However, going to a well-constructed index is probably the more expedient way to find a particular book.

You can find literature indexes through the meta-indexes, such as Yahoo!, WWW Virtual Library, and My Virtual Encyclopedia. Once you find literary sites you want to visit again, simply bookmark them to begin your own Web library. Another good starting point is Literary Resources on the Net, which allows you to browse through the many categories or do a simple one-word search.

Probably the most famous Internet literary resource is Project Gutenberg (see Figure 16.7). It began long before the Web, tracing its roots back to 1971. It's goal is "to make information, books, and other materials available to the general public in forms a vast majority of the computers, programs, and people can easily read, use, quote, and search." Most of the work is done by volunteers. They have a LISTSERV just to keep up with each other and avoid duplicating work. There is also an explanation of copyright dates and laws because Project Gutenberg relies on works in the public domain. This is a good place to get a simple and clear explanation of copy-

Figure 16.7
This Project
Gutenberg page
is a Web gateway
to the thousands
of books online.

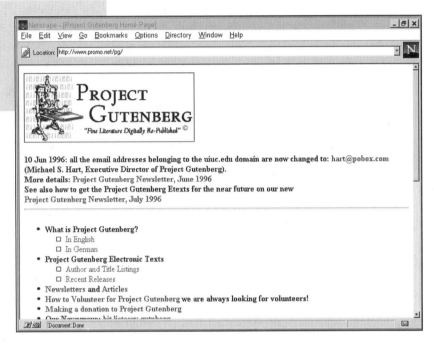

Figure 16.7
This Project
Gutenberg page
is a Web gateway
to the thousands
of books online.

right protection in the United States. It also touches on copyright laws in other countries. Because the Gutenberg Project uses ASCII text, you won't see color pictures or moving graphics but you will get the full text of the book you're looking for. Of course, authors think the words are the most important part!

Literary Magazines

Literary magazines are probably the most bountiful form of literature on the Web. Many of us enjoyed writing for a literary magazine in high school or college. More on the edge than books, they can delight or offend with their offbeat perspectives. A lot of what makes its way into these magazines is forgettable, as authors seem to dwell on the same subjects of death and love. It often seems they equate depressing with profound.

However, there are some gems out there. You might read a short story by a future best-selling author. On the Web, they're known as *e-zines*, which stands for electronic magazines. Many indexes and online libraries have links to them. There are so many, that one index probably wouldn't cover them all. You probably won't use literary magazines in your research that often. Just remember that these literary e-zines are on the Web in case they come in handy in the future. (They can be useful for tracking trends; are people reading more mysteries? Romance? Science fiction? Also, a newspaper may want to do an article on Web fiction.) Of course, you might want to read one and contribute if you have literary impulses.

Interactive Fiction

Interactive fiction may not have as much research value as the classics; however, there's a growing trend to offer stories in a multitude of formats (compact discs, videos, and books dealing with the same story are often released at the same time to the public). This is most commonly seen with large movies, which spawn CDs, toys, novels, t-shirts, and anything else marketers can think of. Already, there are movies that allow the audience to determine the course of action. Quietly developing on the Web (and in other Internet mediums before that) is a growing community of readers who want a little input into a storyline. The audience can both read and write a story (or at least vote on the plot's direction). Figure 16.8 shows the beginning of one popular interactive book.

Interactive novels can be a little more difficult to track down than the classic ones because some literary indexes don't acknowledge them. Sometimes they're classified as role-playing games rather than online books. There are cases where this is true; it's a fine line that you will probably have to judge for yourself. Yahoo! is probably your best chance among the meta-indexes. If you know the name of an interactive novel you're trying to find, you might want to use a search engine. However, if the name is something like "Thread" or "Media Secrets" you might have a hard time narrowing it down.

Figure 16.8
This Interactive
Novel page takes
readers into a
mutli-level story.

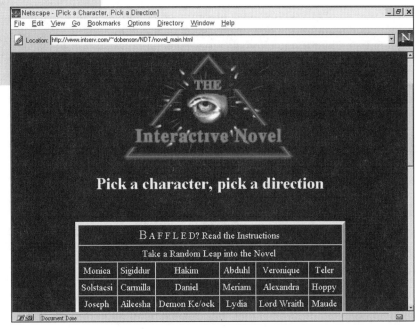

Reference and Literature Sites

Sometimes the hardest part of research is knowing where to start. The following sections list several sites that can get you going. Some of them have already been discussed in this chapter. This is not a comprehensive list of all the reference and literature sites that are available. Some reference sources, such as Britannica Online, charge a fee for information. However, most are put together by other researchers who believe that information and ideas should be shared.

ARTFL Project: ROGET'S Thesaurus Search Form

http://humanities.uchicago.edu/forms_unrest/ROGET.html

This site is exactly what the title says. It offers two forms: one for searching the full text, the other for searching headwords. Truncation is allowed. This is *Roget's Thesaurus* version 1.02, which has been released into the public domain.

Britannica Online

http://www.eb.com

Britannica Online is an online version of the print encyclopedia. There is a fee for using it, although some items are available free of charge. Britannica's Lives is an especially useful feature because it allows researchers to look up a date and read about who was born on that day. It also offers classic entries, such as Albert Einstein's Space-Time article.

The Complete Works of William Shakespeare

http://the-tech.mit.edu/Shakespeare

This Shakespeare site is one of the best literary sites I've seen on the Web. Whatever you want to know about the bard's work, it's probably here. It allows you to search or simply read the plays and poetry of Shakespeare. Some history of the literature is given and the glossary can help students. This site is about William Shakespeare's literary work; it does not include biographical information about the man himself.

ECHO—EURODICAUTOM

http://www.uni-frankfurt.de/~kurlanda/eurodicautom.html

This site is a dictionary that covers many European languages. You choose the source language and the language you want the word translated into. Then you input the word and wait for a response. This site is thorough but can be slow, especially for Web users in North America.

Electronic Children's Books

gopher://lib.nmsu.edu/11/.subjects/Education/
.childlit/.childbooks

Electronic Children's Books is a collection of children's books in the public domain that are available at a Gopher site. This site is essentially the index. It allows simple searches of the text. This is a good place to begin when searching for children's literature because it's already been narrowed to a certain topic.

Encyclopedia Smithsonian

http://www.si.edu/welcome/faq/start.htm

The Smithsonian receives many questions from the public. This is a compilation of the most frequently asked ones and the museum's answers. Some of the entries have illustrations and all are thorough. This is a good place to look for historical information, especially topics in vertebrate zoology. For information about the museum itself, you have to click on the icon that takes you to the Smithsonian Home Page.

Foreign Languages for Travelers

http://www.travlang.com/languages

This is a fun and informative site. You select the language you speak, and then click on the flag of the language you want to learn. There are many to choose from. You then get information about the language and forms for online dictionaries. You choose a word grouping, such as Shopping/Dining. You get a list of words in your source language and the one you want to learn. Click on a word to hear how it's pronounced. This language site focuses on a practical vocabulary rather than a comprehensive one.

Free Internet Encyclopedia

http://clever.net/cam/encyclopedia.html

The Free Internet Encyclopedia, divided into macropedia and micropedia, is composed of information available on the Internet. It is designed for people in the United States. Created by librarians, this is a good place to begin a search for a topic you would expect to be covered in a print encyclopedia.

An Incomplete Collection of World Flags

http://www.adfa.oz.au/CS/flg

This site's name does it an injustice. It is one of the most complete flag sites I've found on the Web. It allows you to approach the topic in a variety of ways, from geographic location to name of the nation/organization the flag represents.

Literary Resources on the Net

http://www.english.upenn.edu/~jlynch/Lit

This literary index allows you to browse through genres or to search for a word. It has many links and is a good starting place for literature sources on the Web.

My Virtual Reference Desk

http://www.refdesk.com

My Virtual Reference Desk has a cute name and full contents. This is one of the most comprehensive Web resources on reference material available. This is a good place to start if you want a reference Web site. It gets to many links (and to the actual site with the information) in a minimum number of links.

The On-line Books Page

http://www.cs.cmu.edu/Web/books.html

This Web site offers more than 2,000 free books in English. It allows the reader to search by title, author, or subject. Links to other online book sources are also included. This is a good place to begin a book search on the Web. If this site doesn't have it, it can probably point you in the direction of one that does.

On-line Dictionaries

http://www.bucknell.edu/~rbeard/diction.html

On-line Dictionaries covers a variety of languages and specialized dictionaries. It has links to other dictionary indexes as well. On-line Dictionaries is comprehensive and easy to use. It's a good place to begin no matter what kind of dictionary you're looking for.

Project Gutenberg

http://www.promo.net/pg

Project Gutenberg is an ambitious plan to make books available to as many people as possible. The books are in plain text and are inputted by volunteers. Project Gutenberg is also one of the oldest efforts to put literature online. Many sites that advertise they have books online simply point to Gutenberg.

Rulers

http://www.geocities.com/Athens/1058/rulers.html

This site has information about rulers of the world both past and present. If you want a vital statistic on a leader, this is the site to go to.

The Skeptic's Dictionary

http://wheel.ucdavis.edu/~btcarrol/skeptic/dictcont.html

From alien abductions to witches, this Web site explains (or more accurately explains away) occult beliefs. Definitions include bibliographies so you can go to an author's source. Although there is bias (the goal is to debunk a belief) the facts are accurate. Most definitions simply give a straightforward presentation and allow the reader to make a reasonable conclusion from the facts.

Virtual Reference Desk

http://infoshare1.princeton.edu:2003/vlib/erefdesk/Eref3.html

This is a collection of reference sources on the Web. This is a good place to begin if you don't want to wade through a long list and want a quick answer.

The Virtual Reference Desk

http://thorplus.lib.purdue.edu/reference/index.html

This is a well put together collection of reference resources on the Web. It includes links to other reference collections as well. The Virtual Reference Desk is easy to use.

The WorldWideWeb Acronym and Abbreviation Server

http://www.ucc.ie/info/net/acronyms/index.html

This is a collection of acronyms and abbreviations and what they stand for. You can search by the acronym/abbreviation or by one of the words in the acronym/abbreviation. The site also records acronyms that are not found in its database in the hopes that someone will fill in the blank one day. This is a good site to combat all the jargon you encounter in government, military, and computer documents. This site will let you look up an acronym or abbreviation that was obvious to the writer but not to you.

Evaluation of Resources

Most reference material is made available by people in the information business. They use references every day and want to provide accurate ones for others to use. Reference materials are hard to put a spin on. That's why most originate with one interested individual or educational institution.

As with reference materials, literary sources are put online by people with a love of books. Their desire is to spread literacy and the love of reading. (They do not want to replace books with online versions, but only offer more options so that everyone has access.) They are not likely to deliberately post something with an error in it.

Allow for honest mistakes and incomplete information. Realize that the source the Webmaster worked from might not have been accurate. You still shouldn't trust that everything you read is correct. However, you can count on most reference materials as long as you are aware of obvious problems (bias, incorrect on common knowledge items, and so on).

If there is a non-virtual world counterpart (which probably came first) you have no reason to doubt the online version. People don't write whole new dictionaries—they simply enter existing ones. Encyclopedias have the same information, whether digital or paper. Most books are created on computers now. To insist it's only accurate once it has been printed places medium over content.

17

Science

What about science? That's the question Dreamfinder asks Figment in Disney's *Journey Into Imagination*. The question is repeated over and over later in the ride as the characters explore all the fun and imaginative things that can be done with science.

The characters just as easily could have been exploring the Web. Webmasters have gone out of their way to create science Web pages that make the subject interesting, even exciting, to the public. Scientists were some of the early users of computers by nature of their profession and have naturally gravitated to the Internet. There are many science references on the Web, from the elementary level to advanced.

Search Strategies

The different sciences can be divided into groups many ways. There's physical and biological; applied and theoretical. There are more elaborate schemes with biology on one end and psychology on the other. However, the Web is so vast that it allows for much more precise divisions. You can find Web pages that deal with molecular cell biology. Whatever area of science you need information on, there is probably a Web resource to help you.

So how do you find it? The method depends on the the resource sought. Search engines allow you to go directly to a site, provided that it is able to find precisely the site you're looking for. That's the problem with searching for such a broad topic. Simply entering "chemistry" into the search request field of a search engine probably will give you too many results to make sense of.

If you can't find your science subject in an index's list, consider what branch of science it's a part of. For example, you might not see an entry for geology on the first page but one for earth science. That entry should lead you to a list with geology in it.

The best approach for general scientific topics is to look at the meta-indexes for more specific indexes which then lead to the actual resource. Web sites usually offer links to related sites, so you can learn about other resources that way as well. This approach is fine for the casual researcher in science fact. If you research science topics on a regular basis, you will want to build a personal index of trusted science Web sites and update them periodically. You can do this by checking the indexes regularly and following related science newsgroups.

Physical Sciences

Let's say your patron wants a simple explanation of recent developments in superconductivity. Using a search engine, you would pull up thousands of resources. Without some other factor to narrow the search, you could not reasonably find the Web resource. So you start with the meta-index Yahoo! (see Figure 17.1).

Figure 17.1
This search for a superconductivity resource begins with the Yahoo! Home Page.

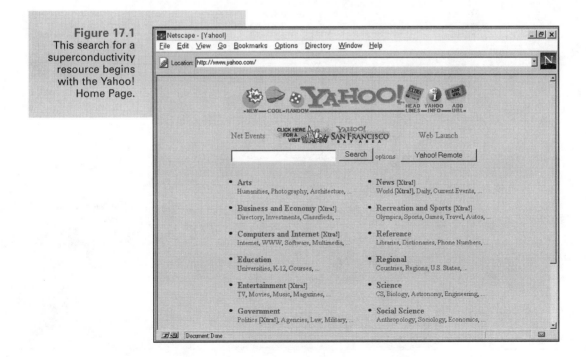

From the home page, you choose science. That provides you a list of topics (see Figure 17.2). There's a category for physics, which you choose because superconductivity falls in the category of physics (see Figure 17.3).

On the Yahoo! physics page, you see a category for superconductivity. That's what you're looking for information on, so you choose it (see Figure 17.4). There's a link titled "An Introduction to High Temperature Superconductivity" which sounds promising; you click on it (see Figure 17.5).

This Web site will answer your patron's question in an easy to understand article. Notice that the majority of the search was going through Yahoo!'s hierarchy of topics. This strategy found the Web resource fairly quickly. For general topics it will work well. If you need to research physics on a regular basis, you should bookmark an index, such as the Physics Internet Resources (see Figure 17.6).

Figure 17.2
The Yahoo!
science page
offers links to
many branches
of science.

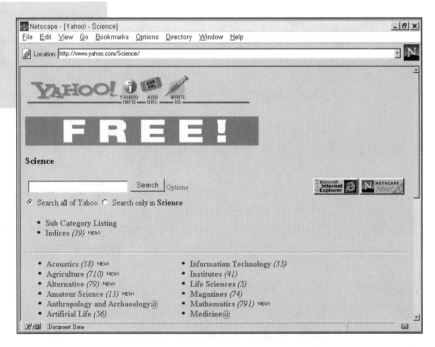

Figure 17.3
The Yahoo!
physics page has
a link to super-
conductivity
resources.

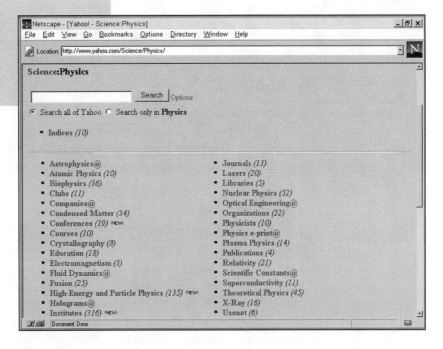

Figure 17.3
The Yahoo!
physics page has
a link to super-
conductivity
resources.

Figure 17.4
The search has
finally been
narrowed to the
Yahoo! super-
conductivity
page.

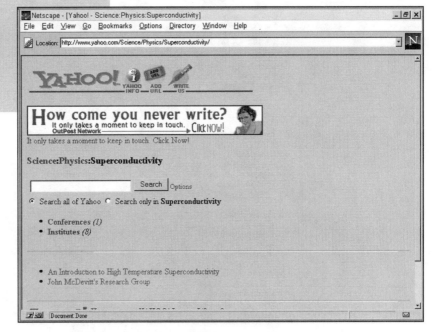

Figure 17.5
The Introduction to HTS page has clearly written information about superconductivity.

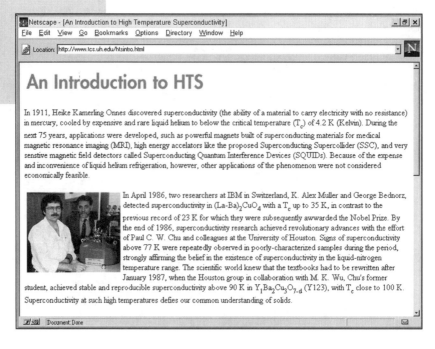

Figure 17.6
The Physics Internet Resources Home Page is a good launching point for physics research on the Web.

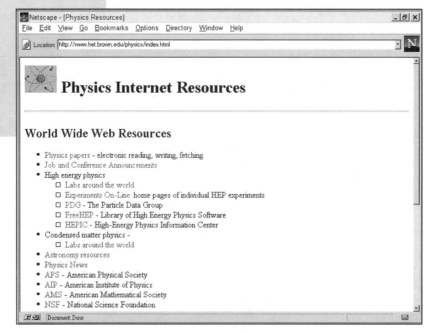

Biological Sciences

Biology may not seem to mesh with the technology of the Web but the two have complemented one another nicely. The media made it impossible to miss the premier of The Visible Human Project. This project's goal is to make "a complete, anatomically-detailed, three-dimensional representations of the male and female human body" (see Figure 17.7). However, it is not the only anatomical computer model on the Web, nor is human the only species being studied.

Of course, most people's experience with dissection is in junior high school when they're required to cut up a frog. In recent years, students and teachers have looked for alternatives. The Web has several pages that offer computer alternatives to the classroom assignment of frog dissection. Students can now dissect a virtual frog. One site that offers this is The Interactive Frog Dissection. Another is the Whole Frog Project. Both are set up for classroom use but anyone interested in anatomy can learn from them.

Figure 17.7
The Visible Human Project Home Page tells how the anatomical computer model of a man and woman was created. Researchers can also get information on how to obtain a copy for study.

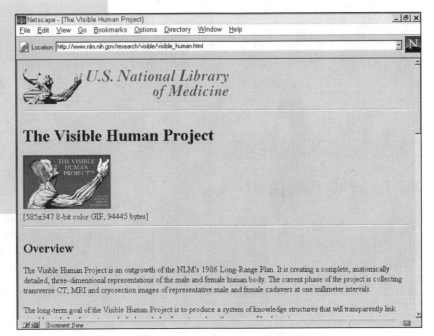

Figure 17.8
The Heart
Preview Gallery
page lets
researchers tour
the human heart
in a multimedia
environment.

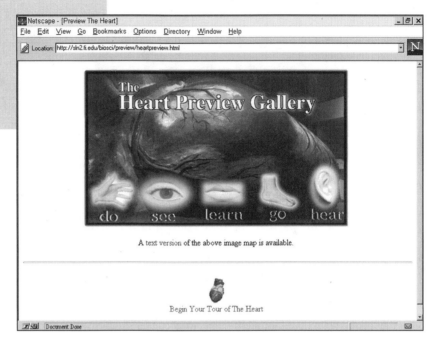

If you prefer to stick with your own species, The Heart Preview Gallery is a must see. This thorough site allows you to travel through the heart. You can listen to and watch the heart beat. There's a glossary and links to related sites but much of what you're looking for concerning cardiac information can probably be answered here.

Science Projects

One topic I get a lot of requests for is science projects. It seems that we all have to do one at some time. Like most students, I dreaded doing mine when in school. I wish the Web was available back then. Webmasters with a yen for science manage to make science projects look fun. In fact, many sites are designed not for the school science

fair but simply to be activities that anyone with an interest can do. Researchers can glean a lot of basic science facts from these pages.

How do you find these sites? I've yet to find an index that covers them all. Web libraries, with their emphasis on education, seem to be the best method of tracking these science sites down. For example, let's begin a search at the Internet Public Library (see Figure 17.9).

From there let's choose Youth because science projects are normally geared for students (see Figure 17.10). In the Youth section, there is a category called Dr. Internet; let's choose it (see Figure 17.11).

There is a category for science projects on the Dr. Internet page; click on it. That takes us to a page that has experiments and links to other sites that have science project information, shown in Figures 17.12 and 17.13.

Figure 17.9
The Internet Public Library Home Page is a good resource for student research.

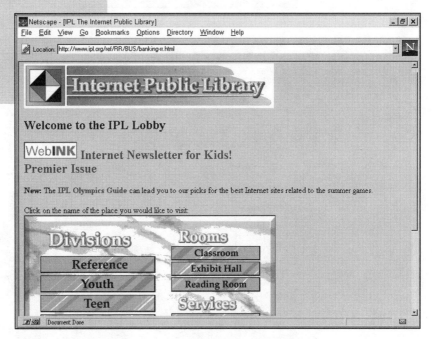

Figure 17.10
The Internet
Public Library
Youth page
has links to
educational
materials.

Figure 17.11
The Internet
Public Library Dr.
Internet page
offers helpful
links for students.

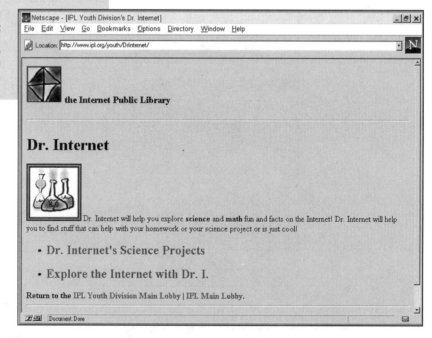

Figure 17.12
The Internet
Public Library
Dr.Internet's
Science Projects
page tells
students about
experiments they
can do at home.

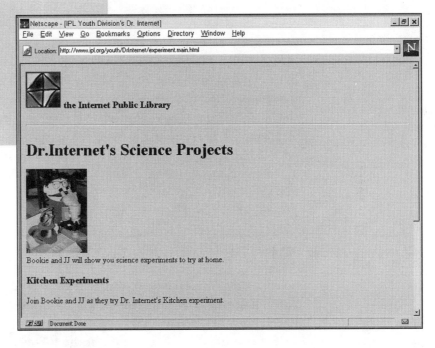

Figure 17.13
The Internet
Public Library
Dr. Internet
Finds Other
Experiments
page links
students to other
science resources
on the Web.

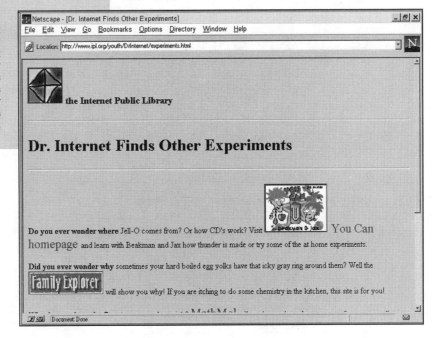

The best science project page I've found on the Web is the Super Science Site. Designed to encourage students, teachers, and parents to conduct experiments, it offers explicit and easy to understand directions on how to do a science fair project. However, students don't have to wait until the science fair to start experimenting. There's a section on every day experiments that can be done around the house. Students can take part in an ongoing experiment, usually a survey. Teachers can apply for $500 science grants to finance science equipment in the classroom. Even children who normally avoid anything sounding scientific will find something to enjoy at this site.

Science Sites

Science sites are plentiful on the Web and easy to find. The difficult part is finding the one that answers the question you're searching for. Indexes can help narrow down a search but no one index will have all the resources listed. The sites in the following sections can help you get started in your science search.

Biotechnology Dictionary

http://biotech.chem.indiana.edu/pages/dictionary.html

The Biotechnology Dictionary is a searchable listing of terms in the fields of genetics, biochemistry, general biology, chemistry, pharmacology, toxicology, and medicine. Some of the entries are illustrated.

Chemicool Periodic Table

http://the-tech.mit.edu/Chemicool

Chemicool has a cute name, rather than a stuffy scientific sounding one, but don't discount it. It's an excellent resource for the elements. It even makes the periodic table easy to read.

Chemistry on the WWW

http://badger.ac.brocku.ca/~gt95ab/chem/chem1.html

Chemistry on the WWW is an index of chemistry on the Web. This Web site is a good beginning for chemical searches. It's also bookmark-worthy for those who frequently deal with chemistry topics.

The Heart Preview Gallery

http://sln2.fi.edu/biosci/preview/heartpreview.html

This complete site offers information on all aspects of the human heart. You can see and hear a heart. The Heart Preview Gallery is the best place to look for cardiac information.

The Interactive Frog Dissection

http://teach.virginia.edu/go/frog

The Interactive Frog Dissection is designed to help students learn the anatomy of a frog. It gives still and motion visuals of frogs with explanatory text. It's an alternative to actual dissection.

MendelWeb

http://www.netspace.org/MendelWeb

MendelWeb is designed for teachers and students. It includes classical genetics, introductory data, analysis, and elementary plant science. It also has Gregor Mendel's 1865 paper, "Versuche über Pflanzen-Hybriden," and a revised version of the English translation.

Physics Internet Resources

http://www.het.brown.edu/physics/index.html

Physics Internet Resources Web page is an index of physic resources on the Web, in Gopherspace, and via FTP. This is one starting place when looking for physics resources.

Science Hobbyist

http://www.eskimo.com/~billb/index.html

If you're passion is science, visit this page. It touches on everything —education, demos, museums, and even science myths. This is an excellent resource if you research science topics on a regular basis.

Space Link

http://spacelink.msfc.nasa.gov:80

Space Link is the site to go to for NASA information. Most of the material at this site is educational and accessible. For space research, this is the first place to look on the Web.

Super Science Site

http://www.superscience.com/home.html

Super Science Site's goal is to encourage students and adults to have fun with science and learn in the process. This is the first place to look when researching science projects.

The Structure of the DNA Molecule

http://outcast.gene.com/ae/AE/AEC/CC/DNA_structure.html

This Web site offers a thorough explanation of DNA and genetics in easy to understand language. It includes graphics, a glossary, and both print and Web resources. (The Web resources are linked.) This is a good site to start a search on DNA.

UCMP Glossary

http://www.ucmp.berkeley.edu/glossary/glossary.html

This glossary covers a variety of science topics on a technical level. It's written for those in the science field or familiar with science topics.

The Visible Human Project

http://www.nlm.nih.gov/research/visible/visible_human.html

The U.S. National Library of Medicine has worked on The Visible Human Project for years. It's goal is to produce a three-dimensional image of a female and male, with the image transparently linked to the corresponding information. This site tells about the project, what stage it's in and how to see what has been done so far.

Whole Frog Project

http://www-itg.lbl.gov/ITG.hm.pg.docs/Whole.Frog/Whole.Frog.html

The purpose of the Whole Frog Project is "to provide high school biology classes the ability to explore the anatomy of a frog by using data from high resolution MRI imaging and from mechanical sectioning, together with 3D surface and volume rendering software to visualize the anatomical structures of the intact animal. Ultimately we intend to be able to 'enter the heart and fly down blood vessels, poking our head out at any point to see the structure of the surrounding anatomy.'" It's an alternative to actual dissection.

Evaluation of Resources

Science sources can be difficult to evaluate. Part of the problem is that what one scientist says is valid and factual another will refute. However, most of what you will look up will be facts that the science community agree on.

If the source of the Web site is a university or science agency, it's most likely accurate. The information might even be more up-to-date than what you'd find in a textbook. In some cases, scientists publish findings online faster than they can in the traditional print sources. (For example, scientists publish facts about a recent earthquake on the Web before it can be published in a journal.)

Most of what you find on the Web is reliable and will tell you where the information comes from. Would you trust the source if you were reading the information in a journal or book? Then you can also count on the Web source being accurate.

PART III
Appendixes

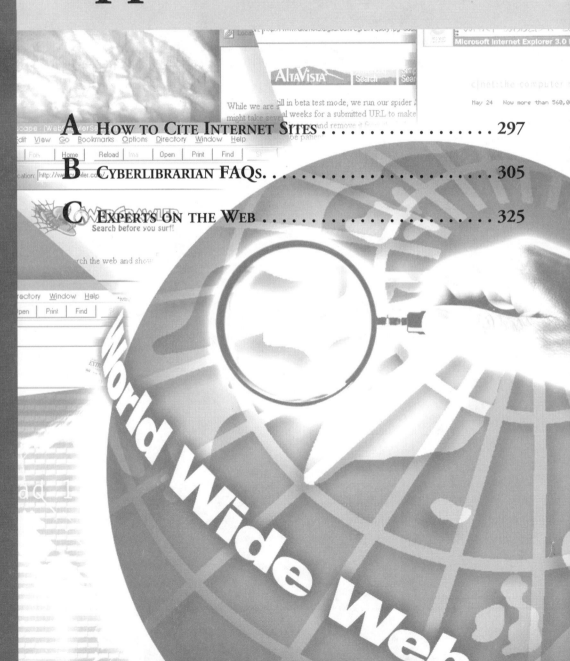

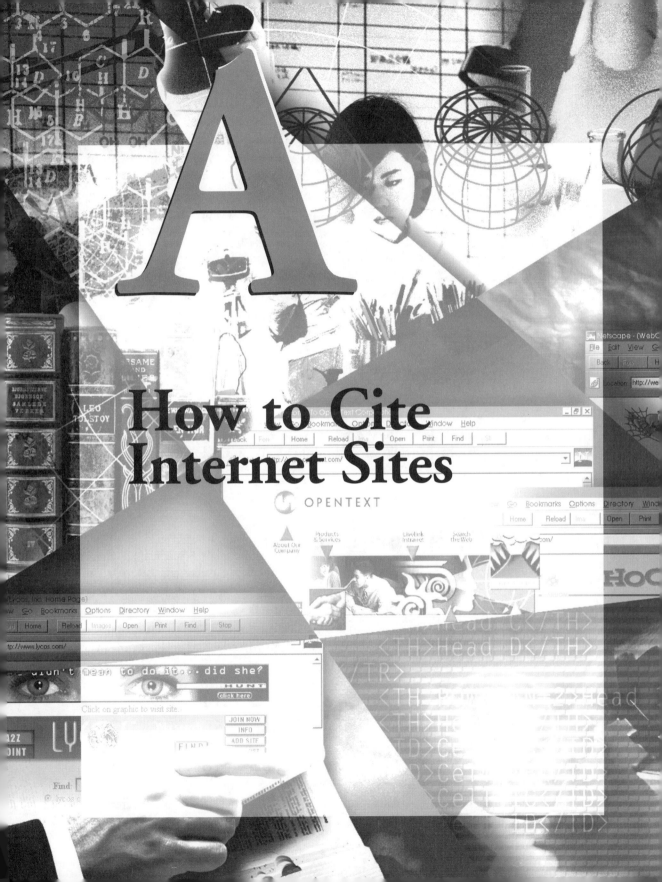

After finding the perfect site on the Internet that has every fact you were looking for, you want to share your findings with the world. You might have to write a paper for your job or class. Then comes the dilemma. You need to note your sources, usually through a bibliography. But how do you list an Internet source?

Even with books, there's a lot of inconsistency in how citations should read. How you list your sources for a term paper in high school will be different than how you list them in college and probably still different than how you would for a business proposal. The academic world has different standards in the various areas of study, and professors often enforce their own preferences. When I was in college, each of my teachers would alter the standard citations just enough that I felt like I was learning how to compile a bibliography all over again.

So if book citations can't even be consistent, how can the untamed Internet be distilled down into an easy to understand source bibliography? It really isn't that difficult if you use logical elements that are part of every site.

Internet Citation Elements

Many people make the mistake of trying to make the Internet site citation match a book citation. What's in a normal book citation? There are variations, but most citations consist of the author, title, edition, publisher, date of publication, and page the information was found on. Those who look at an Internet site and agonize over what the edition is or who the publisher is are probably wasting their time. Teachers who require that Internet and book citations match element to element don't have a good understanding of the nature of the Internet.

Before you can do a citation, you have to identify the important elements of an Internet site. The elements can change depending on the type of Internet site you're listing: Web, FTP, Gopher, Telnet, e-mail, newsgroup, or LISTSERV. (You might also reference

Internet Relay Chats or even discussions you have on an Internet phone. However, that is more like using a conversation as a source and should be noted as such.)

Online publications that have print counterparts can be cited just as the print version would be with the exception that you need to include the Internet address. Newspapers and magazines that make their articles available online are organized the same way as the print version as far as the elements of a citation are concerned: publisher, author, and so on. E-zines may exist in the virtual world only but often have the same elements of print versions.

Web, FTP, Gopher, and Telnet sites can be treated like books or some similar source in bibliographies. E-mail, newsgroups, and LISTSERVs are more like letters, lectures, and other forms of communication. Both can be valid sources but the communicative ones are more fleeting. Chances are that your readers will not find the same information when they visit a newsgroup or LISTSERV. There may be an archive of the conversation, but that is not where you found the facts so you would not cite an archive. You can, however, include archive information in a citation if you want to be complete. If you cite e-mail, it's much like using a letter sent to you through regular mail. You can tell your readers how to get in touch with the same person you corresponded with but the only way they'll see the same information you did is to make the e-mail message available.

No matter what your Internet source, the one thing they all have in common is that each source has an address. The best way for readers of your bibliography to find the source is to have the address. When looking for a book, one needs the author. Knowing the publisher is important too. If you're looking for it in a store, the ISBN number is often necessary and in a library you would need the call number. Of course, those numbers are not put into a citation often. With Internet sources, the URL is crucial. Without it, there is little chance your reader will find the source.

So how do you incorporate the usual elements of a citation into an Internet listing? Who is the author of an Internet site? It is the person (or persons) responsible for the content of the page. Whoever wrote the words, organized the information, and chose the graphics would be considered the author. On the Web, the author is often the Webmaster, especially in the case of pages made by individuals. The name is often at the bottom of the home page and nowhere else. However, Web pages can be designed and maintained by companies for an organization. Sometimes you might only find the author's Internet name (for example, jamcat instead of James-Catalano, Cynthia N.) Corporate pages may not include an author's name. In that case, it is appropriate to use the company name (for example, list the site under AT&T). If no author is given, you would list the site under its title.

Newsgroups, LISTSERVs, and e-mail messages are fairly simple to determine the author because it's whoever posts or sends the message. Be careful of anonymous postings. They can look like a name is in the header but it really isn't the writer. These sources will also be prone to Internet names being used without the real name being included. If the message is about a sensitive topic (a rape victim, for example) you might want to exclude the writer's name.

The title of a site is also easy to figure out: it's at the top of the page. Follow the usual rules of dropping "the," "an," and "a" when alphabetizing. The Internet does have a much wider range of punctuation than the print world. Use the name capitalization and punctuation the author does. Yahoo!, NetHistory, and news of the wURLd wouldn't win grammar (or spelling) contests but those are their proper names.

There really is no edition for an Internet site. Sites are constantly updated and changed. If you're citing an e-zine or other online publication, you can put in an edition number for the publication. Otherwise, there isn't a counterpart in the online world.

The publisher is another book carryover that doesn't apply to Internet sources. Like the edition, the publisher only becomes an issue for e-zines and online publications with print counterparts.

Publication date will probably be the date the site went online—that's because it is the only date available many times. Besides, that is when most of the information at a site is made available. Some Gopher and Web sites might put individual publication dates (they might be called copyright dates) on each article or file. In that case, use the publication date given. Several dates may be listed at a site (usually when the author includes every year the site has been online). Since you have no way of knowing when the page you're citing was created, use the date range given. E-mail, newsgroup, and LISTSERV messages would use the date they were sent or posted.

The page number is not the same for an Internet source as a book. Although some sites choose to number their pages, most do not have page numbers in the traditional sense. However each page has a unique address and title so a page number becomes moot.

There are elements to an Internet citation that you do not have in the traditional bibliography. As noted before, an URL is an important part of the citation. You also need to note the type of Internet source you accessed (e-mail, Web site, and so on). This is often called the *medium*. You might want to include archive information for a newsgroup or LISTSERV. (Is the archive stored at one site? Many use a three-step process through e-mail that would be difficult to include in a citation.) You can use the subject line in place of a title for e-mail messages.

Internet Citation Examples

Punctuation is a difficulty in citations. Some methods are quite complex, with the title being in quotes and the date in parentheses, and so on. There are many books that explain exactly how to punctuate a bibliography citation but not all the books agree. Teachers will have their own preferred method and catalogers will use their own system that doesn't translate into bibliographic form well.

The Internet is a product of a more streamlined world than traditional academia. It allows people to go to the source rather than through the filter of print media. The Internet is also a less formal arena for conversation. Titles such as professor and doctor often get left off of correspondence. Certainly things are done on the Internet simply because they "look cool." However, no one wants to create more work for themselves.

An Internet citation should reflect this simpler spirit. Punctuation should be used to set the elements apart. Other than that, it serves no purpose. Get all the relevant information into an Internet citation in a form that makes sense. Anything else is superfluous.

The following examples are some of the information presentations you will find on the Internet and how to cite them in a bibliography. The examples won't cover every case. Definitely, as the Internet changes new tools and ways of communicating will emerge. (How will you cite an Internet phone conversation, for example?) However, you can adapt these guidelines and apply them to many different forms of online information.

The Web is the fastest growing area of the Internet. You will probably find most of your resources there. It's one of the easiest to use methods of sharing information online. Not surprisingly, it's one of the easiest to cite as well. A Web citation should have these components: Author. *Title.* Date. Medium type. Address. Here are some examples:

Freeman, Elisabeth and Hupfer, Susanne. *Past Notable Women of Computing.* 1994-1996. World Wide Web.
http://www.cs.yale.edu/HTML/YALE/CS/HyPlans/tap/past -women.html

Mikkelson, David P. *Urban Legends Reference Page: Disney.* 1995-1996. World Wide Web.
http://www.best.com/~snopes/disney/disney.htm

Gopher sites flourished because they provided the chance to instantly see information online. They're limited to text but the bulk of information comes from text anyway. Many Gopher sites offer a wealth of information. They can be cited much like a Web page, with the same components: Author. *Title.* Date. Medium type. Address and path. Since the paths can be long, the citation can look complicated. It's actually easy to follow. Here are some examples:

larris. *Climate.* November 8, 1992. Gopher. **ecosys.drdr.viginia.edu Library/Atmosphere/Climate**

Thoen, Bill. *Internet Resources for Earth Sciences.* May 1992. **dewey.lib.ncsu.edu** NCSU's "Library Without Walls"/Study Carrels/Earth Sciences

FTP and Telnet sites are cited just as Gopher sites are. Here are some examples:

Jenkins, John H. *List of Asimov's Books.* May 14, 1993. FTP. **wiretap.spies.com Library/Media/Books/asimov.lis**

Braukus, Michael. *NASA Delays Launch of Space Shuttle.* July 12, 1996. Telnet. **spacelink.msfc.nasa.gov Spacelink.Hot.Topics/Future.Shuttle.Mission/Launch-Landing.Information**

The communication tools of the Internet are slightly different than the informational ones but the citations are similar. The author of an e-mail message is the writer of the message. It is common practice to list both the sender and the recipient's address in the citation. The subject line is the title and the date is the one from the message's header. The following are the elements: Message writer (Writer's address). *Subject.* Date. Medium Type. Recipient's name (Recipient's address). The following is an example of how to cite e-mail:

James-Catalano, Cynthia (jamcat@iag.net). *Virtual Shell Dictionary.* August 3, 1996. E-mail. Betty L. James (beach@gate.net).

A newsgroup citation has the following elements:

Post writer. *Subject.* Date. Medium type. Newsgroup address. Archive address.

The archive address is optional. A newsgroup may or may not have an archive. You may not have the full name of the author. Use the Internet name if that is all you have. If you don't know the poster's name, list the title first. The following are newsgroup citation examples:

Garcia, Paul. *Age Dating Gasoline.* August 1, 1996.
Newsgroup. **sci.chem.analytical**

Smith, Donna. Babylon 5 FAQ. August 7, 1996.
Newsgroup. **rec.arts.sf.tv.babylon5.info** Archive:
http://ivory.ora.com/rastb5

LISTSERV citations follow the same pattern as newsgroups. However, a LISTSERV has two addresses: the one to subsribe to and the one to post to. If your reader is going to get involved in the conversation, they will have to have the subscription address. A more complete citation has both. A LISTSERV often has a name that is different than the address. If the LISTSERV you are citing does, then include it. The elements are: Message writer. Subject. Date. Medium type. LISTSERV name. LISTSERV subscription address LISTSERV posting address. The following is an example of a LISTSERV citation:

Patel, Sarah. *Digital Clippings Collection.* August 6, 1996.
LISTSERV. NewsLib. Subscribe: **istproc@ripken.oit.unc.edu**
Post: **newslib@ripken.oit.unc.edu**

Soon after my first cyberlibrarian column first appeared in *Internet World*, I began receiving e-mail. A few messages were full of praise and sent by well-wishers wanting to tell me "job well done." However, the majority wrote me to ask for my help. Some requests were polite, others imperious, and a few were a little frantic. It started as a trickle of one or two messages a week and then my e-mail grew into flood proportions. It wasn't long before I was spending twelve to fifteen hours a week answering e-mail. I enjoy helping people but it was becoming clear that this was too much for one person to handle. Maybe if my full-time job was answering e-mail I could keep up; but I am working full-time as a news librarian, writing for *Internet World*, and taking care of my baby daughter.

I noticed some trends in the questions I received and in those that continue to fill my e-mail box. The most obvious trend is that the same questions are being asked over and over. Another trend is the frustration that Internet searchers are feeling. They can't find what they're looking for and they want someone to ask, "Who's responsible for this Internet anyway?" Because of my title, many people assume I'm some sort of authority figure who is accountable for their inability to find what they're looking for. By far the majority of searchers who write to me are pleasant. However, a few have demanded I give them what they're looking for immediately. I've received scorching letters from those who feel that I haven't answered them quickly or completely enough. I have been tempted to reply to these writers that I am not employed to answer their questions and any aid they receive comes from my willingness to help them. I don't send those letters (usually) because I understand that these queries are coming from people who know the fact they're looking for is online and eluding them.

An additional trend is that people need the information fairly soon. Often, by the time I can answer an e-mail message it's too late. Frequently, people write to me after they've already searched themselves and only have a day or two left to find the information. Even those with a longer time table might have forgotten the original question by the time I get a chance to answer them.

I still read every message that comes in and I appreciate the feedback. The conclusion I've reached is that people are frustrated because they don't know how to do research on the Internet. Most new users are trying to navigate the Web right now. The Web can be mind-boggling! This book, while written more for the professional researcher, can still teach anyone how to do research on the Web.

In this appendix, I have included the most frequently asked questions I receive. Chances are, you're wondering about a few of them yourselves. This FAQ is divided into sections that group similar questions together.

Web Basics

Do I need an Internet Service Provider? What's the difference between direct access and an online service?

If you want to experience the entire Internet, you will need to get direct access. Sometimes this is provided from your employer or university (for college students). If not, you will need to choose an Internet Service Provider. You will get an account that offers access for a monthly fee. Types of accounts and cost vary; you'll have to find out what's available in your area.

An online service is a company (for example, America Online or CompuServe) that produces its own network that you log in to. From that network you'll probably have some form of Internet access but might be limited to just e-mail or Web browsing. If you need Internet access but not the other features an online service provides, getting direct access through an ISP is much cheaper.

Who runs the Web?

Like the Internet itself, there's no central authority over the Web. The Web was developed at CERN but the laboratory is not in charge of it. (Although CERN does provide marvelous support and resources.)

Does someone keep track of the sites I visit on the Web?

Yes. It's not one central unit keeping track, but lots of individual Webmasters. Every time you visit a site, the Webmaster can record your e-mail address and often more. Sometimes they will subscribe you to mailing lists or send you advertisements. These tactics are unpopular with Web users but haven't died down. If you do not want the Webmaster to be able to read your account information, you can go to an anonymous site first. (The Center for Democracy and Technology at **http://www.13x.com/cgi-bin/cdt/snoop.pl** will explain how anonymous searching works and let you move on to other sites. Keep in mind the anonymous site will know who you are.) By linking from the anonymous site, you'll disguise your account but in exchange, your browsing will be slowed down a little.

Who pays for the Web?

We all do indirectly. You pay for it in fees to your ISP. The ISP must buy equipment and pay fees to larger companies (usually phone companies) for access to the physical lines that connect the computers.

What is the difference between the Internet and Information Superhighway?

The Information Superhighway is larger than the Internet. It includes all forms of technical communication. Online services are part of the Information Superhighway, as are such things as direct TV. The Internet is part of the Information Superhighway.

Why should I use the Internet when I can call a reference librarian at my local library?

Which is quicker? Actually, that should not be the main criteria considered. If you are unwilling to learn how to use the Web then you should call that reference librarian and wait your turn. If you would like to do the research yourself, see all the resources and decide what is relevant to your question, then learn to do Web research. Also, some resources may be available online that the local library doesn't have and the Web is always open for business.

Will the Internet, especially the Web, replace libraries?

I doubt it. Libraries play a role in our psychological development as well as intellectual. Libraries are more than buildings. They're often community centers, with story hours, local art displays, and club meetings filling the buildings. The Web cannot replace the feeling of holding a book or the quiet of a reading room. Even aside from that, there will still be research needs that are better met in an actual library than virtual one. For example, students pouring over large maps will appreciate a library, where the maps can be spread out one after another and studied. Children's books are still best leafed through, not clicked through. There's still something satisfying about physically browsing the bookshelves and pulling out a book to look at before moving on.

I tried to go to the site you mentioned in your column but it didn't work. Why?

There are many reasons a site might not work. My column is written about four months before it appears in *Internet World*. More than once, a site I have written about has closed down or moved without leaving a forwarding address. It could be that the site is simply busy and won't let you in until it slows down. Sometimes you'll see the horrible "file not found" message. It's possible that some aspect of the address' path changed so that the computer can't find the site. Don't give up on an address until you've tried it at least twice at different times of day.

I tried to link to a Web site from the home page of my Internet Service Provider but it said that it was not available. I saw it on Yahoo! and was able to link to it without any problems. Why?

I often have that happen to me as well. Another twist on this situation is when a link won't work but typing in the address to go straight there will. It could just be that when you tried to connect from your ISP's home page it was busy but when you tried later from Yahoo! it was not. Another possibility is that your ISP home page has an old address for the site that isn't working any longer.

Physical location and how the computers are networked can play a role in connecting to sites as well.

I tried to link to a Web site but it said I wasn't authorized. Why would there be a link to it if I can't go to it? Why is it on the Web at all?

Companies have sites on the Web for their employees and customers. To get the information at one of these sites, you have to have a password. It's on the Web so that employees and customers can get to it anywhere in the world. A Webmaster might create a link without realizing that a password will be required.

Why can't I get information that is stored on America Online? The TV show I watched this morning said I could find out more and gave me an AOL address. The announcer said it was on the Internet.

It started a little over a year ago. You'd be watching a morning talk show and a scrumptious recipe was being demonstrated. You'd start frantically writing down the ingredients when the host would say, "The recipe is on the Internet. We'll give you the address at the end of the show." You stopped scribbling and waited until the end of the show. Then an AOL address would be put on the screen. This trend seems to be fading as more morning talk show hosts learn about the online world. However, I still get questions about this from time to time.

The Internet and AOL are not the same thing. AOL is an online service that produces its own database. AOL users have some Internet access. Internet users can send e-mail to AOL users. However, they cannot get into the AOL database to retrieve information, such as the aforementioned recipe.

Why do announcers continually use the word Internet when they are really talking about America Online? I think most of it stems from ignorance of what the two are. I've noticed less gaffs as more time passes.

I only have e-mail access. How can I get to the information on the Web?

Many Web pages are set up so that you can send e-mail to get the content of a site. (It will likely be text, not graphics, from a site.) If you are interested in accessing the Web through e-mail, send a message to WebGate at **webgate@vancouver-webpages.com**.

I don't have an account but want to get information on the Web for my job. Can I do that?

Every now and then, I hear from people claiming they don't have an account or even a computer but they want to get information that's on the Web because they think it'll be useful for their job. Since they send me e-mail to ask me how they can go about it, I'm often confused by the request. One person did explain that he had an account and used his computer at home, but he didn't have Internet access at work and wanted to show his co-workers what's online.

His co-workers are in luck now. Makers of CD-ROMs are starting to put the content of Web pages on CDs which can be purchased. I have only seen press releases advertising the coming service, not an actual CD so I cannot give an accurate evaluation of this product. Overall, the best route to take is getting direct access. The Web changes much faster than CD makers can keep up.

Doesn't a search engine cover the entire Web? Do I have to use more than one?

No search engine covers the entire Web. Different search engines will result in different results. If you want to be as thorough as possible, you will have to use more than one. However, most research does not have to be that meticulous. For more on search engines, read Chapter 5.

I did a search with AltaVista and then another one with Infoseek Guide and got different results. Why?

Search engines look through their own databases, which have been created with different criteria. Also, search engines will rank results differently. From your point of view, a search engine can seem to give wildly different results to the same search request. (Although some search requests will have similar results regardless of the search engine used. The more specific your search, the more likely you are to get similar results.)

I did a search in Lycos and it said that the site was a 100 percent match. But I went there and it wasn't what I was looking for at all. Why?

The percentage shows how closely the Lycos search engine exactly matched your keywords. But it doesn't judge content, only how well the words match up. For example, you can enter in "Kuwait flag" hoping to get a graphic and description of the country's symbol. Lycos searches every word in a Web document. It might find an article which reads "The soldiers marched into Kuwait. Their spirit would not flag!" This site could get a 100 percent from Lycos but not answer your question at all. Other search engines that use ranking systems have similar problems. They can match words but not meaning.

What is netiquette?

Netiquette is etiquette on the Internet. There are guides on the Web if you wish to read one, but the basic principal is as simple as the Golden Rule. You don't appreciate unsolicited e-mail, flames, and inappropriate posts, so don't do it yourself. You'd like help from time to time, so offer it when you can. If you want a more detailed list of dos an don'ts, go to The Net: User Guidelines and Netiquette at **http://www.fau.edu/rinaldi/netiquette.html**.

How can I advertise my business on the Web?

Many Net users would just as soon you didn't. But Web advertising seems to be here to stay. If you decide to take the plunge, use prudence. Web sites that are blatant advertisements will not be accessed more than once by a user. Banner advertising is an acceptable form if you want to advertise on someone else's site. If you provide an information service, you might want to offer a free sample of your work. Be cautious of offering something for free and then trying to charge for it later when the customer is "hooked." Many Web researchers resent that and simply find other ways to obtain information. (If you start out saying there is a charge but you will give a free trial, your business will fair better.)

If you have a product that you think will be popular, I suggest setting up a Web site that includes related information. For example, if you sell solar panels, offer free information on how solar energy works. If you make your site valuable to researchers, they will come back.

How do I advertise my new Web site?

The best way to get publicity for your Web site is to send notices to meta-indexes and asked to be included in the listing. Meta-indexes have a backlog of requests and might not be able to include your site right away. If you're eager for immediate visitors, post an announcement to appropriate newsgroups and LISTSERVs you participate in. It won't take long before you're registering hits, especially if you have created an appealing and useful site.

Can I keep my child from seeing obscene material on the Web?

You're a parent. You've heard it before and I'll say it here. Nothing replaces parental supervision. I have a simple guideline for parents. If you had a TV with complete satellite access—you could get any channel in the world—would you hand the remote to your child and say, "Go ahead, watch whatever you want" and then walk away? If your answer is no, then don't give your child unlimited Web access.

There are ways to supervise without standing there every minute watching every click. There's software available that helps you monitor and block out offensive sites. You can also look for "kid safe" sites that sport a Safe Surf logo or have earned a green light from Magellan. There are many indexes and Web sites created just for children. They're easy to find and you can bookmark sites you deem appropriate. Instruct your child to stay with those and ask for your permission before linking to a site that might be inappropriate.

Nothing can replace you talking with your child about what you consider to be inappropriate for his or her age. Explain what is off limits and why. Children on the Web really aren't exposed to anything different than the rest of the world. There are TV shows you don't want your child to watch, radio programs you wish your neighbor wouldn't play so loud, and billboards that scream messages you would just as soon your child not see. Chances are, your child will be more likely to find and read something educational on the Web than watching something educational on television.

Another fear is that children will meet a pervert who will somehow lure him or her into danger. Have you taught your child not to talk to strangers? Are you aware of pen pals he or she has through regular mail? Then apply those same precautions to the Web. If your child says he has been talking with someone online, then ask who that person is. There are many adults online who are willing to help children with homework and serve as mentors. These adults would have no problem with you writing them if you are concerned.

There are so many wonderful sites on the Web. This is an exciting time to be involved with the Internet community. It's educational, fun and possibly even a form of job training for children. It would be a shame to deny a child the benefits of the Web because of fear. When your child enters the Web community, take the same precautions you would if your child was entering a physical place. Then relax and enjoy exploring the Web together.

Web References

How do I know that a Web resource is accurate?

How do you know a book resource is accurate? A television show? A newspaper? The ability to evaluate a resource doesn't change much because the medium does. However, there are key points to check for. Chapter 7 covers evaluation of Web resources and each subject chapter also has a section on how to evaluate the sites you find.

Don't people pay to put information on the Web? How can I trust it?

Some people view the Web as a giant advertisement thanks to all the hype that surrounds it. Do people pay to put information on the Web? Yes and no. People pay to put Web pages online. Sometimes they create them, other times they pay a company specializing in Web design to create the sites. Companies pay to advertise their products. The most obvious presence is the banner advertisements that run across the tops and bottoms of many sites. However, the content of Web sites is not dictated by the companies advertising on them. It's a little like television. Rarely do commercials on television determine the content of a station's programming. Yes, some Web sites are created simply to advertise a product but they are as easy to spot as an infomercial on TV. A majority of Web sites are created by people who want to share their knowledge and talents.

I read about some great resources in your column but I want a more specific one. Can you tell me about some other ones you know of?

The question above sounds vague, but I get variations on it regularly. For example, I write a column about history sites. Soon I receive e-mail from a professor praising my column but could I possibly tell him where he can a find a site on the War of 1812? I write about Chronic Fatigue Syndrome and receive a question for a Web resource on Epstein Barr. Sometimes people even ask me for advice on a situation they're facing.

You can be reasonably sure that I wrote about every relevant site that I knew of and considered worth citing. It's possible I learned of a site after writing the column (there is a time lag between when I write it and when it gets published). However, the only way I can answer the question is to do the research myself. I'm willing to help others, but if you want the answer in a timely fashion, it would be best to look yourself. This book will tell you about the research tools you need and how to use them.

I like the sites you listed in your column. Can you tell me about related newsgroups and LISTSERVs I can read?

There are thousands of newsgroups and LISTSERVs. I read less than a dozen on a regular basis. Occasionally I'll get a request from a reader that I subscribe him or her to a LISTSERV. I cannot subscribe anyone other than myself to a LISTSERV (at least not ethically). You can use the Web sites referenced in Chapter 6 to find a newsgroup or LISTSERV. Your news reader will have a way to look up newsgroups also. You'll have to choose a newsgroup based on the name in many cases but you can tell if it's the one you're looking for in your first visit to it.

Where can I find full-text resources, especially those with print counterparts?

The best way to find full-text resources is to browse a library's collection. Web libraries put full-text documents in their collection. If there is a specific publication you are looking for, you can look for it via a search engine. However, common words can make title searches difficult. (A search on the word "Time" for the popular magazine would give you more results than you want.) Besides, many indexes, from Yahoo! to the Electronic Newsstand offer links to well-known resources.

Can I cancel my subscription and read my favorite newspaper/magazine on the Web?

It's kind of hard to drag your computer to all the places you take a newspaper! If your habit is to read the paper over breakfast or a news magazine on the train to work then don't cancel just yet. Also, your local newspaper might not be on the Web yet. However, there is a wealth of news resources on the Web. You can even do a crossword. Chapter 15 tells you how to find them.

Can I look up a book in my local library's catalog?

There's a good possibility of it if you live in a mid-to-large city. Many libraries have put their catalogs online. Ask at your local library; the librarian can give you the Web address. University students will also be able to look up resources before heading to the library. Even if your library's catalog is not on the Web, you can use the catalogs that are online to answer some of your questions. Who is the publisher of the book? How is the author's name spelled? If your library doesn't have the book you're looking for, you can track down a library that does. When your local library does make their catalog available on the Web you can save a lot of time if you do your searches at home before going to the library.

Why don't you write about the Online Computer Library Center (OCLC)?

Catalog librarians are the ones most likely to ask me this. More than 22,000 libraries in the United States and other countries are connected. Librarians share catalog records in the world's largest bibliographic database. However, it's not accessible to the public and many special librarians do not have access either. Most Web researchers do not need catalog records but full-text resources. OCLC has started an Internet project called InterCAT (**http://www.oclc.org:6990**) which might be useful to Web researchers.

I'm looking for my old college roommate. Can I find her using the Internet?

Probably not. Many databases advertise that you can find long-lost friends using their services. However, the pull their information from phone books, city directories, and other listings that are available. There are many reasons why your roommate would not be listed. She may have opted for an unlisted phone number or listed the phone in a relative's name. Even if you do find a listing, there's no guarantee that the information will be correct. She could have moved since the database was compiled. Sometimes ISPs will sell their list to one of these services. You might be able to track down an Internet address if your roommate is online and her ISP sold their list. These services also ask for voluntary registration. If she wants to be found, she may have listed her name with one of them.

However, there are many to choose from and millions of names. If your old roommate had a common name, such as Jennifer Jones, you'll go through many entries. If you have an idea where she might be, you can narrow your search a little. For the most part, the only people these services are able to track down are people who have lived in the same place for a long time. An old college roommate probably won't fall into that category.

I've tested several of these "people finder" services running my own name. Only one service ever pulled up a listing for me—and it got my e-mail address wrong. Considering that my e-mail address appears in a magazine every month, that's pretty incredible.

Are adoption/birth records available on the Web? What about credit reports, criminal histories, driving records, and other vital statistics?

This kind of information is stored in computer databases. It's frightening what can be found out about a person through a well-done computer search. However, these databases are not open to the public or on the Web. Adoption and birth records are going to be the most difficult to find because they are sealed by law in many places. If you're trying to track down the birth of a person for genealogy research, looking in the appropriate newspaper for a birth announcement might be a more fruitful pursuit.

Other types of personal information is easy to track down if you have access to the right database. Employment histories, insurance policies, land records, criminal records, previous addresses, credit reports, and driving records can all be obtained through computer databases. Laws about what can be put online vary from country to country and in the U.S. from state to state. In Florida, it's relatively easy to obtain someone's social security number and most of the other records I've listed. In California, which has anti-stalking laws, it's much harder.

Who has access to these databases? Usually it's a company, such as a newspaper or insurance company, or a government agency, such as the police department, that use these databases. However, anyone with enough money can buy access into a lot of these databases. These databases can be expensive—most ask for large deposits and charge by the minute. If you need to find someone, a private detective might have access to a database that can track the person down.

Can I look for a job on the Web? Can I look up a prospective employer and find out about the company?

There are many "classifieds" on the Web that you can use to look for a job. America's Job Bank at **http://www.ajb.dni.us** is one of many that let you search for a job by occupation, location, salary, and other factors. CareerPath.com at **http://www.careerpath.com** promises classifieds from major city newspapers. Before the advent of the Web, people were exchanging job offers via newsgroups and you might have luck there as well. Some of these sites offer company information. You can also look for the company on the Web to see if their profile is online. (Chapter 8 covers how to find company reports.) What about the word-of-mouth information from employees already there who can give you the inside scoop? Cultivating friends on newsgroups and LISTSERVs, and then initiating a private e-mail conversation would be the best approach.

My high school reunion is coming up and I'd like to put together a list of facts from the year we graduated—popular songs, price of bread, top news stories, etc. Where can I go on the Web to get this information?

You can track down this information on the Web. Some sites, such as Britannica's Lives (**http://www.eb.com/cgi-bin/bio.pl**) or This Day in History (**http://www.historychannel.com/today**) can help. I don't like to discourage eager Web researchers, but this question is more easily answered in the mundane world. Several computer programs are available at a fairly inexpensive price that are designed specifically for these anniversary-type questions. If you don't want to invest in a program, consider going to a card shop that sells printed sheets for birthdays and anniversaries. These sheets have facts from the year and day you choose on them. There are also entire books that cover a year. Created as a series, each book details the same subjects: fashion, music, vital statistics, etc. You pick out the year you're interested in. These resources will help you answer your question more quickly than a Web search.

How do I cite a Web site in my bibliography?

I probably get this question once a week now. I have written my guideline on how to cite Internet sites, which you can read in Appendix A. My guidelines might differ from other versions you'll see. Naturally, I think my version is the most logical!

Cyberlibrarian Profession

What's the difference between a cyberlibrarian and a cybrarian?

In Chapter 4, I explained a little about the cyberlibrarian profession. There is no difference between the words "cyberlibrarian" and "cybrarian." Cybrarian is simply the shorter version of the word cyberlibrarian. I use both words to describe my profession. If the section in Chapter 4 didn't answer all your questions, here are the answers to the questions I get asked most often.

How do I become a cyberlibrarian?

It depends on what you mean by cyberlibrarian. Do you want a job with that title? Chances are you won't find many. However, you will find jobs with titles like information broker, special services librarian, and database researcher. All of these jobs can very well be cyberlibrarian jobs. When looking, judge it by the job description, not the job title.

If you are still in school, take whatever computer searching classes are offered. Wherever you do a get job will most likely use different databases (or use the same one you learned a different way) but the research skills can be applied to any new databases you learn. Having an aptitude for computer research is desirable. If you don't enjoy spending hours on the computer, trying to think in terms the programmer and indexer used, then don't go into this field. Each database you learn will have a different setup and you must keep hundreds of commands straight. One database will use a dollar sign to truncate a word; the next will use an asterisk.

I'm often asked if a Master of Science in Library Science (MLS) is necessary. It can't hurt but the necessity of it is dictated by your background and the type of company you plan to work for. If you want to work for a public or academic library, get one. In the commercial sector, a MLS may or may not be required. Many companies don't care if you have a MLS if you can do accurate, efficient research. If you already have a background in computers, you might be able to find a job without the library background.

I know some librarians who read this are cringing at that assessment. Library school teaches a lot more than computer searching (and many library schools offer only a class or two in computer research anyway.) Library school students learn how to evaluate resource materials (regardless of the medium it's in), reference interviews, ethics, collection development, and intellectual freedom principles. How will you know if there is a print resource that answers your question better than a computer database? Library school will teach you the knowledge and skills to determine the best resource to answer a question.

I'm also asked if a particular undergraduate degree is important. Again, it depends on the type of job you're seeking. A medical researcher might find a biology degree useful. However, a liberal arts education is sufficient. A minor (or even major) in computers might be handy.

Once you feel your education and experience has prepared you, start applying for jobs. You can learn of them in a variety of ways: classifieds, library school job files, professional associations, Internet LISTSERVs, and word of mouth. Emphasize your ability to find accurate information under deadline pressure. In interviews, give examples of actual searches you've conducted. A letter from someone happy with your research skills can help.

In the coming years, we are going to see the profession of cyberlibrarian grow. It will be a job title you'll see more often. (If you're already doing the job of a cyberlibrarian, consider asking to have your job title changed.) Some library schools have already responded to this trend by offering a more regimented program with the goal of students becoming cyberlibrarians.

How did you become a cyberlibrarian?

I suspect what people really want to know is the answer to the previous question, how do *I* become a cyberlibrarian? However, for those truly interested in my background, here's how it happened. I've been around computers all my life. I programmed a little, played games, and did my homework on them. I had been getting on computer bulletin boards as a teenager and when I went to college I found the Internet.

However, I did not get a degree in computers. My Bachelor of Science is in journalism. I worked as a technical editor for the computer department my senior year in college but still didn't plan on doing anything with computers professionally.

I went on to get my MLS because I discovered that I enjoyed the research aspect of journalism more than interviewing people in stressful situations, writing news articles on a deadline, or figuring out how to squeeze a headline into an ever-shrinking space. I planned to stay in the journalism field by becoming a news librarian. While in grad school, I did my second internship in a newspaper library. This time something was different; this news library had computers in it. After graduating, I got a job as a news librarian and for the first time started using my computer research skills for a job. Until then, it had been more of a hobby, although I had looked up information for class assignments on the Internet before.

I began writing for *Internet World* while still a news librarian. Soon, my Internet activities starting taking more of my time. I enjoy the free-wheeling nature of the Internet, and the friendliness of the Web. It's exciting to discover what's online. I enjoy showing others how they can use Web resources. This is a time of transition, as information is being directly relayed to the people. People are communicating in an environment where only your ideas and how you express them matter. I never felt quite comfortable in the academic halls of librarianship but cyberlibrarianship was like playing for a living, so I became a cybrarian full-time.

What's an editorial researcher?

It's another way to say news librarian. I worked in the editorial research department of *The Orlando Sentinel.*

Why didn't you tell me that my Web site was going to be in your column?

I get this quite often and there are two reasons. One of the reasons is that I don't have time to notify everyone before the column (or this book for that matter) goes to press. The main reason I don't tell Webmasters before publication is that their Web site might get pulled before *Internet World* gets published. This could happen for a variety of reasons. The most common one is that my column had to be cut to make space. I'd rather have Web site creators be surprised than disappointed.

Why didn't you include my site in your column?

There are many reasons I might not include a site that seems to the Webmaster to fit in with the subject I wrote about. One reason is that I might not have known about it. After all, there are millions of

Web sites and I cannot look at all of them. I try to be thorough but I could easily fritter away my time surfing from site to site without having the time to write about them.

Another reason is that I did look at it but didn't think it fit in with the subject matter. I try to write about places that offer information for free. On some level, most of what I write about is educational. A purely commercial site is not going to be profiled in my column.

One common reason that most people are not aware of is that the columns are written so far in advance that a site might not have been up and running. For example, a column on holiday sites would be written in August. A Webmaster didn't put up his Christmas Carol page until the middle of November. He reads my column in December and then writes to me and asks why I didn't include his site.

Will you visit my Web page and tell me what you think?

I am willing to visit Web pages to evaluate them for inclusion into my column. Some of my favorite Web sites were "discovered" when the Webmaster sent the URL to me. However, Web site design is subjective; my opinion isn't any more authoritative than your neighbors. Even if it doesn't fit into a cyberlibrarian column it might still be a good place to visit. Therefore, I don't rate sites for people.

Can you put me in touch with other librarians on the Internet?

If you're a librarian who wants to chat with colleagues, I suggest joining a LISTSERV related to your specialty. (I listed several in Chapter 6.) If you are trying to find a librarian to help you then you need to visit an online library.

Can you recommend a good Internet seminar/class?

Not really. I don't take classes or teach them, so I'm not familiar with what's available. If your ISP offers free classes and you are new to the Internet, it might be worthwhile. Online tutorials can also help you polish your skills. Classes and seminars that teach Internet skills can be expensive; make sure they give you your money's worth if you take them. Many computer stores and related businesses offer Internet training that turns out to be AOL training. Before signing up for a class, consider what you need to learn. You can learn a lot yourself just by reading FAQs and trying to do it yourself. Don't worry about making mistakes—everyone does at some time. There's no way you can permanently damage the Internet.

Please don't forget others who work in a library (paraprofessionals).

Outside the library profession, most people don't think about how a library runs. I have had people ask me, "You had to get a master's degree to check out books?" The person who checks your books out is most likely not the librarian, unless you patronize a tiny library. There are many other occupations in a library that have to be done—everything from shelving books to indexing. Usually, libraries hire non-librarians to do these tasks, with a librarian over-seeing the activity. The people who work in a library but aren't librarians are often called *paraprofessionals.*

I hear from paraprofessionals from time to time to remind me that they make a valuable contribution to libraries, both real and virtual. They're right. Without them, libraries wouldn't function. Some para-professionals have created Web pages that are just as valuable to researchers as the Web pages created by professional librarians. It is common for an experienced paraprofessional and professional librar-ian to do the same tasks and have the same skills. To those observing, there would seem to be no difference between the two.

Do you have a mailing list or home page that I can read?

At this writing, no. By the end of 1996 I will have a Web page. I've resisted doing one, but there seems to be a need for one now. Look for this FAQ, links to sites I have written about, and the obligatory pictures of my adorable daughter.

Experts on the Web

Although there's a wealth of information on the Web, you may not be able to find exactly what you're looking for. A Web site might come close, but still not answer your question. You may find the information you're seeking, but want to confirm it's still valid with someone working in the field. You can also have a specific question to your situation that needs personalized attention, not general information, or you might be looking for a person to interview.

The Web is full of experts on a variety of subjects. Many professionals have offered the benefit of their knowledge to Web researchers. Some have set up home pages, others have an e-mail link on a another's home page. Sometimes these experts are the ones with the idea to offer help online. Other times, their advice is solicited by an organization that provides a service. Usually, the experts are volunteering their time. Occasionally, ask-an-expert services are a "front" for a consulting service that will answer only basic questions and charges for more help. However, most of the ask-an-expert services are free.

It is common to have the frequently asked questions listed with the answers on a site; check the FAQs before sending off your query to an expert. The answer to your question might be sent to you via e-mail or posted to a Web page. You may have the option of asking for a direct reply even if the practice is to post to a Web page.

If you're a researcher who frequently looks for the answers to other people's questions, you might want to bookmark these sites and make your own index of experts. If you will be sending clients to an expert on a regular basis, you might want to cultivate a professional relationship with the expert. Some of these ask-an-expert services are not set up for heavy traffic, while others are designed for a large influx.

Expert sites tend to have a high turnover, probably because the expert cannot keep up with the flow of questions. You may have to update your links often. Also bear in mind that everyone who claims to be an expert isn't. If the expert in question is unable to list credentials or references, you may want to do a background check before sending patrons to him or her. A college degree does not make someone an expert; experience in a field is more important. In fact, many areas of expertise don't require degrees or certification: child rearing, sewing, carpentry, landscaping, etc.

There are experts in medical and financial fields who will answer questions. Remember that the advice you receive is not meant to replace the counseling you receive from someone who is actually dealing with your case. An answer to your medical question cannot replace a diagnosis by a doctor who examines you. An answer to your financial question cannot replace the guidance given to you by a financial consultant who has evaluated your investments.

The following is a subject list of experts on the Web who can answer your questions. Their advice is an invaluable Web resource. Before the Internet connected the world, it was much harder to get input from a worldwide forum of experts.

College and Career

Students have a lot of help from Web experts in finding the right career and preparing for it. Some sites guide students in choosing a college, while others chart the route to employment.

College Grad Job Hunter Ask the Expert

http://www.collegegrad.com/prep/expert

Brian Krueger answers questions from college students and recent graduates on how to find a job. Questions and answers cover interviews, dress codes, continuing education, and many other topics that graduates wonder about. The questions and answers are posted to the site and are updated on a weekly basis.

The College Guide

http://www.jayi.com/ACG/ques.html

The "Admissions Guru" answers questions about how to get into the college of your choice. The questions and answers are posted to the site. It's written in a casual style and organized in order of the questions asked. The systematization does make tracking down a previously asked question difficult. However, reading through the questions and answers can be useful to high school juniors and seniors (and their parents and teachers) who are facing the admissions process.

Finance

Although there are many consulting businesses online, some business experts offer their knowledge to the public for free. From individual finances to company tax laws, Web financial experts answer a variety of questions.

Ask-the-Expert

http://www.captive.com/Ask_The_Expert.html

Captive.com links you to several different business categories, such as accounting, investment management, and risk management. Each category is sponsored by a company who provides the expert. You can send questions via e-mail and receive answers through e-mail or by telephone. There is not an archive of previously asked questions.

Banks

Ask a Banker

http://www.oba.com/public/public.html

The Oklahoma Bankers Association has practical information for bank customers and allows researchers to ask a question if a topic isn't covered.

Ask the Banker

http://www.ljbank.com/ask031.htm

La Jolla Bank answers questions via e-mail. This site also has links to related banking topics.

Small Business

Entrepreneur Forum Ask the Expert

http://www.upside.com/forum/expert

Provided by Upside Online, business experts answer questions concerning finance, marketing, and laws that apply to people running small businesses (or just starting ones) in a technological field. Questions and answers are posted to the site and are divided into subject categories.

Wayne Brown Institute Ask an Expert

http://www.wayne-brown.org/doc/expert.htm

Professionals from the Wayne Brown Institute answer questions from small business owners. The questions are divided into categories, such as insurance and marketing.

Health and Medicine

Medical experts from a wide range of specialties will answer questions from Web users. In many cases, the most valuable service the doctors and nurses provide is emotional support to those going through a health crisis. They reassure patients that their feelings and responses to treatment are normal.

Ask-A-Doc!

http://www.rain.org/~medmall/ask/asklandon.html

Dr. Chris Landon answers medical questions and posts them to this site. Other doctors might answer the question or add to Landon's

answer when appropriate. Questions and answers are divided into subject categories. This service is part of Medical Mall.

Ask the Doctor

http://www.druginfonet.com/askmd.htm

Doctors that are "practicing, board certified, and not affiliated with pharmaceutical manufacturers" answer medical questions from Web researchers. A detailed form helps the information seeker make the request clear. Frequently asked questions are posted in subject categories (such as thyroid or allergies). Your identity is kept anonymous. Replies might take longer than a few days because more than one doctor might review your question.

Arthritis

Arthritis Foundation Ask a Question

http://www.arthritis.org/forms/ask.help.html

This site is part of the Arthritis Foundation's Web page. A detailed form helps researchers pose their question. Experts can answer via e-mail or call you. The AF Home Page has FAQs.

Cancer

About Breast Cancer

http://sadr.biostat.wisc.edu/bca/ask.html

The National Cancer Institute funds Breast Cancer Answers, which in turn allows researchers to ask questions. Cancer information specialists answer the questions via e-mail within a few days. This site also gives you a phone number you can call. Link to the BCA Home Page for more information, including FAQs.

Dentistry

Ask the Dentist

http://www.parentsplace.com/readroom/dentist/index.html

Dr. Kimberly A. Loos answers dental questions, primarily from parents concerned with good dental hygiene for their children. Questions and answers are posted to this site in easy to follow subject categories. You can search through the archive to see if your question has already been answered.

Ask Dr. Tooth

http://www.dentistinfo.com/aska.htm

Dr. Tooth answers questions via e-mail. There's a bit of a wait because of the number of questions but researchers can participate in a chat session with dentists.

Diabetes

Children with DIABETES

http://www.castleweb.com/diabetes/d_0d_000.htm

Doctors and nurses answer questions concerning children who have been diagnosed with diabetes. (Some questions about adults get slipped in too.) Questions and answers are posted to the site. The archive is arranged chronologically. You can decide to include your e-mail address in the post so that others who read the message can answer you. Names are not included on posts, however.

Hemophilia

World Federation of Hemophilia

http://www.wfh.org/doc.html

Dr. Clothilde of the World Federation of Hemophilia answers Web researchers' questions concerning hemophilia. Questions and answers are posted to this site and organized into subject categories. There is also a link to the WFH Home Page.

Infertility

FERTILITEXT

http://www.fertilitext.org/Question.html

Doctors and nurses in the field of infertility treatment will answer questions via e-mail. Although not anonymous (the experts have to answer you) it is kept confidential. The FERTILITEXT Home Page offers a wide scope of information on the subject.

Lifetime Online: RESOLVE Ask the Expert

http://www.lifetimetv.com/parenting/RESOLVE/expertad.html

RESOLVE is a non-profit organization founded in 1974 to help individuals facing infertility. RESOLVE's Home Page is **http://www.resolve.org**. The Ask the Expert page is part of Lifetime Online's Parenting section. A medical professional answers questions, but most of the posted ones deal with how people feel about their infertility rather than the medical aspects of treating it. For example, one woman asked how to deal with baby showers when facing her own inability to have a baby.

Medication

Ask the Pharmacist

http://www.wilmington.net/dees

Frank P. Purdy answers Web researchers' questions concerning prescribed medications. There's a small FAQ section and a form to fill out for questions. Purdy will answer questions via e-mail if the address is included in the request. A database of medications is planned for the future.

Neurobiology

Ask an Expert in the Field

http://www.neoucom.edu/DEPTS/NEUR/WEB/neuromail.html

Northeastern Ohio Universities College of Medicine Neurobiology Department invites questions from the curious. You can ask anonymously or request a reply via e-mail (in which case you have to reveal your identity). You can link to the Neurobiology Department's Web page and take a quiz as well.

Nutrition

Ask the Dietitian

http://www.hoptechno.com/rdindex.htm

Joanne Larsen, a registered dietitian with over 20 years of experience, answers questions of general interest. The answers are posted to the site; she is unable to give personal replies because of the volume of mail. Previous questions and answers are divided into topics for easy access.

Pediatrics

Answers from the Web Doctor

http://www.parentsplace.com/readroom/dr_answers.html

Dr. Robert Steele, a pediatrician, answers questions from parents concerning their children's health. Questions and answers are posted to this site. There is a searchable archive of previous questions and answers. The archive is divided into subjects for easier browsing. Occasionally, a response will be posted from other sources.

Psychology

Mental Health Interactive Ask the Expert

http://www.mhsource.com/interactive/interactive.html

Dr. Ron Pies answers questions about mental health. Recent questions and answers are posted to the site. A searchable archive allows researchers to read earlier questions.

Vision Care

Ask the Optometrist

http://www.visioncare.com/ask.htm

Dr. Steinberg will answer questions via e-mail. There's a form to aid researchers. This site is part of Internet Vision Care. You can also read the FAQs for general guidelines on exams and simple explanations of common vision problems and treatments.

Plants and Food

Agriculture and gardening may seem far away from the technology of the Web. However, many experts share advice and tips with researchers. Whether a commercial farmer or a backyard hobbyist, experts on the Web can help you with your green thumb.

Ask an Expert

http://www.ag.uiuc.edu/~stratsoy/expert/expert.html

Anything you ever wanted to know about soybean plants can be found at this site. Experts answer questions via e-mail. Questions and answers are also posted in an archive that is organized by subject.

Ask One of Our Experts!

http://www.perennials.com/qa.html

Heritage Perennials makes this site available to researchers to answer questions about perennial gardening. There is a small archive of previous questions in no particular order.

Ask Our Experts at the P&PDL!

http://info.aes.purdue.edu/ppdl/Ask_Expert.html

The Plant and Pest Diagnostic Laboratory at Purdue University has experts who answer questions about anything—disease or insect—that can blight plants. Questions and answers are posted to the site. You can also search the archive.

Ask the Experts

http://www.ars.org/experts.html

Rosarians answer questions about one of the world's most popular flowers. Each subject area is handled by a different expert. The expert writes about a particular rose care topic. If you haven't had your questions answered after reading the various areas, you can send a question to one of the experts.

Religion

You may have been advised never to talk about religion in public, but some Web experts want you to ask about religious practices. These sites are from amiable people and organizations who are eager to share what they know.

Ask the Amish!

http://padutch.welcome.com/askamish.html

This site could just as easily be called "ask about the Amish." The questions are answered by experts from the Mennonite Information

Center. You can read the archive to see if it answers your question before submitting one yourself. Someone could have asked the same thing you're wondering about already.

Ask a Bible Specialist

http://www.bibleinfo.com/question.html

Bible Information Online answers questions concerning the Bible via e-mail. A form is provided for researchers.

Ask Your Question on Judaism— Any Question

http://www.chabad.org/question.htm

Chabad-Lubavitch in Cyberspace answers questions concerning Judaism via e-mail. A form is provided for researchers.

Science

Science experts on the Web range from lab researchers to astronauts in space. Many of them have taken time from their projects to answer questions in their field. Often, the questions they answer are related to projects they're working on.

MAD Scientist Network

http://medinfo.wustl.edu/~ysp/MSN

Two hundred scientists from around the world have joined the MAD Scientist Network to answer questions from Web researchers. They refer to themselves as a "collective crania." You can search through a well-organized archive of previous questions or browse through the library before submitting a question of your own. A comprehensive form makes asking questions easy.

Astronomy

Ask an Astronomer

http://twsuvm.uc.twsu.edu:80/~obswww/o20.html

The Lake Afton Public Observatory offers this service. Besides e-mail, people can also send in questions through regular mail. There is not an archive of previously asked questions.

Ask the Astronomer

http://www2.ari.net/home/odenwald/qadir/qanda.html

Dr. Sten Odenwald answers astronomy questions sent via e-mail. The answers are posted to this site and organized into several different categories to make research easier. So far, Odenwald has answered over a thousand questions. This site is part of The Astronomy Cafe at (**http://www2.ari.net/home/odenwald/cafe.html**).

Chemistry

Ask the Chemistry Department

http://www.chem.lsu.edu/form.html

Louisiana State University's Chemistry Department sponsors this site. The faculty answers questions from Web researchers.

Geology

Ask-An-Earth-Scientist

http://www.soest.hawaii.edu/GG/ASK

Experts from the University of Hawaii Department of Geology and Geophysics answer questions concerning nature in Hawaii and the field of earth science, in general. Questions and answers are arranged by subject and can be read by the public. However, the scientists do answer questions through e-mail as well.

Ask-A-Geologist

http://walrus.wr.usgs.gov/docs/ask-a-ge.html

Experts from the U.S. Geological Survey answer questions on the earth sciences. This site does not list previously asked questions but directs researchers to read the newsgroup **sci.geo.geology**. Scientists answer questions via e-mail.

Ask a Volcanologist

http://volcano.und.nodak.edu/vwdocs/ask_a.html

Part of VolcanoWorld, this site lists previously asked questions organized into several different categories. You can also search for a question and answer. Three volcanologists answer most of the questions but if they get stumped they turn to scientists around the world.

Physics

Ask a Physicist

http://twsuvm.uc.twsu.edu/~obswww/o51.html

The Lake Afton Public Observatory offers this service. Besides e-mail, people can also send in questions through regular mail. There is not an archive of previously asked questions.

Ask Dr. Neutrino

http://nike.phy.bris.ac.uk:8080/dr_neutrino/ask.html

This site allows you to ask physics questions. You can browse and search the archive of questions or simply read the most recent ones. Several different people might respond to your question and you can respond to someone else's. Answers range from the articulate, well-informed ones to silly, off-the-cuff remarks.

Space

Ask an Astronaut

http://www.nss.org/askastro/home.html

The National Space Society has created a multimedia environment for learning about astronauts. A different astronaut is featured each month. You can ask questions and read the answers at this site. Speeches, pictures, biographical information, and related Web links are included for each astronaut. The identity of people who ask questions is kept anonymous.

Ask the Crew a Question

http://shuttle.nasa.gov/sts-69/crew/question.html

If you're curious about space travel, this NASA site lets you ask the space shuttle crew questions. The questions are relayed via air-to-ground voice communication while the astronauts are on a space shuttle mission. Because of time constraints, few questions are answered privately. You can read the FAQ and the more recent questions that have been answered. You can download audio clips of the astronauts' answers to questions.

School Subjects

Certain topics seem to be used more by students (and their teachers) in K-12 than the general public. Here are a couple of experts on the Web who can help students. Remember, they don't do homework!

Math

Ask Dr. Math

http://forum.swarthmore.edu/dr.math/dr-math.html

A team from Swarthmore College answers math questions from students and teachers. There's an easy to use search form for looking

through the archive. There's also a form for submitting questions. Students receive answers via e-mail.

Mythology

Ask the Folklore Expert

http://www.humnet.ucla.edu/humnet/folklore/archives/
expert.html

Experts at the University of California, Los Angeles answer questions on mythology and folklore. You can browse the archive index before submitting a question.

Zoology

Animals continue to fascinate both children and adults. You can visit the animal kingdom online and ask the experts your questions.

Earthwatch Online Resources

http://gaia.earthwatch.org/ed/olr/resources.html

Earthwatch has many different categories; most deal with animals but other subjects such as archaeology and folklore are also included. Each category leads to pictures, basic information, and a chance to ask the expert your questions about the subject. Answers come via e-mail. There is no archive of previously asked questions and answers.

Birds

Ask the Experts

http://www.upatsix.com/ask_experts/ask_experts.shtml

You can post your questions about aviculture here. The order is chronological but there is a search option.

Insects

Doctor Bug

http://www.orkin.com/bugdoctor.html

Doctor Bug's other name is F. Tom Turpin. An entomologist, each month he writes a short explanation of a featured bug. If that's not the insect you're looking for, you can send questions to Turpin. The questions and answers are posted to the site.

Marine Animals

Ask Shamu

http://crusher.bev.net/education/SeaWorld/ask_shamu/asintro.html

Sea World offers this site to educate researchers about ocean and marine animals. The archive is divided into subjects. The questions and answers are posted in the archive on a monthly basis. You can also join the Ask Shamu LISTSERV.

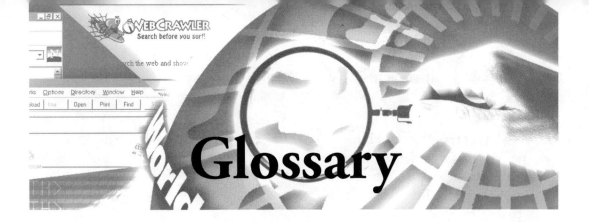

Glossary

The computer world has a love affair with jargon. It creeps into every technical conversation. Each profession develops its own language as well. Graph, chip, male/female, enhance: all of these are words that mean different things to different professions. Then there's the slang that develops among teenagers and college students. With so many companies coming on the Internet, joining students who have been there for years, it's no wonder that jargon has not only proliferated but thrived online. This glossary covers Internet terms used in this book that you may not be familiar with.

address—The URL that identifies a Web site and tells one computer on the Web how and where to call up the information on another computer.

bookmark—A Web browser feature that records addresses so a user can return to it easily. Saved addresses are called bookmarks and the act of saving an address is called bookmarking. Also known as a *hotlist*.

cyberlibrarian—Word coined for librarians who do research on the Internet and other online networks and databases. *Cybrarian* is a shorter version of the word.

e-zine—Electronic magazine. These publications are published on the Internet, not in print form.

FAQ—Frequently Asked Questions. Read these before posting a question of your own.

flame—A snide, scornful response to a message posted on a newsgroup. Usually done because the flamer was offended by the flamee's ignorance or rudeness.

Gopherspace—Refers to Gopher sites and information found on them.

home page—The main Web page of an individual or organization.

hotlist—Tells a Web browser to record the address so the user can return to it. Also known as a *bookmark*.

HTTP—HyperText Transfer Protocol. The Web uses it to transfer hypertext documents. In an URL, http indicates that the file is stored on a Web server.

hypertext—Text in a document that has a link to a word in another document. Hypertext links are the primary way that people move from one site to another.

index—A thematic list of Web resources organized in some manner (usually alphabetical) with links to the listed sites.

Internet Service Provider—A company that makes Internet accounts available to the public for a fee.

link—The hypertext word in a document that leads to another document.

LISTSERV—Technically an Internet application, in common usage it refers to a e-mail list that centers on a subject. Participating members subsribe to the LISTSERV.

junk e-mail—Unsolicited e-mail, usually tries to sell something. Chain letters are a subset of junk e-mail.

meta-index—An index of indexes. It leads to other indexes more often than actual resources.

mirror site—An exact copy of the original site's files are copied to another computer. When the original site is busy, the mirror site is often available.

mundane world—The "real" world. The physical world humans live in, not the virtual world.

netizen—Internet citizen. Someone who regularly participates in the Internet community. More flattering than newbie.

newbie—Someone new to the Internet and still learning how to use it. Sometimes used derisively.

newsgroup—A discussion centered (loosely) around a subject. Anyone on the Internet with access to a news server can read and post on a newsgroup. They are sometimes compared to electronic bulletin boards.

online library—Collection of full-text resources that use a classification system, have a collection development policy, and are maintained by at least one information professional.

protocol—The way one computer talks to another. It's a uniform format that stays the same regardless of computer.

robot—A software program used by search engines to seek out Web sites.

search engine—A database that uses robots to compile and organize as many sites as possible. Web users can look through the database for a particular site.

site—A page or group of pages by the same creator that are grouped together.

spam—The same message posted to many newsgroups, regardless of the content of each newsgroup.

top-level domain—The two or three letter part of an URL that indicates the type of site.

URL—Uniform Resource Locator. Used interchangably with "address."

virtual world—The computer world.

Webmaster—Someone who creates and maintains a Web site.

Index

from Prima Publishing, Products Division

ISBN	Title	Price	Release Date
0-7615-0801-5	ActiveX	$35.00	Available Now
0-7615-0680-2	America Online Complete Handbook and Membership Kit	$24.99	Available Now
0-7615-0915-1	Building Intranets with Internet Information Server and FrontPage	$40.00	Available Now
0-7615-0417-6	CompuServe Complete Handbook and Membership Kit	$24.95	Available Now
0-7615-0849-X	Corporate Intranet Development	$40.00	Fall '96
0-7615-0692-6	Create Your First Web Page in a Weekend	$24.99	Available Now
0-7615-0503-2	Discover What's Online!	$24.95	Available Now
0-7615-0693-4	Internet Information Server	$40.00	Available Now
0-7615-0815-5	Introduction to ABAP/4 Programming for SAP	$45.00	Available Now
0-7615-0678-0	Java Applet Powerpack	$30.00	Available Now
0-7615-0685-3	JavaScript	$35.00	Available Now
0-7615-0901-1	Leveraging Visual Basic with ActiveX Controls	$45.00	Available Now
0-7615-0682-9	LiveWire Pro Master's Handbook	$40.00	Fall '96
0-7615-0755-8	Moving Worlds	$35.00	Available Now
0-7615-0690-X	Netscape Enterprise Server	$40.00	Available Now
0-7615-0691-8	Netscape FastTrack Server	$40.00	Available Now
0-7615-0852-X	Netscape Navigator 3 Complete Handbook	$24.99	Available Now
0-7615-0751-5	NT Server Administrator's Guide	$50.00	Available Now
0-7615-0759-0	Professional Web Design	$40.00	Available Now
0-7615-0773-6	Programming Internet Controls	$45.00	Available Now
0-7615-0780-9	Programming Web Server Applications	$40.00	Available Now
0-7615-0063-4	Researching on the Internet	$29.95	Available Now
0-7615-0686-1	Researching on the World Wide Web	$24.99	Available Now
0-7615-0695-0	The Essential Photoshop Book	$35.00	Available Now
0-7615-0752-3	The Essential Windows NT Book	$27.99	Available Now
0-7615-0689-6	The Microsoft Exchange Productivity Guide	$24.99	Available Now
0-7615-0769-8	VBscript Master's Handbook	$40.00	Available Now
0-7615-0684-5	VBscript Web Page Interactivity	$35.00	Available Now
0-7615-0903-8	Visual FoxPro 5 Enterprise Development	$45.00	Available Now
0-7615-0814-7	Visual J++	$35.00	Available Now
0-7615-0383-8	Web Advertising and Marketing	$34.95	Available Now
0-7615-0726-4	Webmaster's Handbook	$40.00	Available Now

TO ORDER BOOKS

Please send me the following items:

Quantity	Title	Unit Price	Total
_____	_____	$_____	$_____
_____	_____	$_____	$_____
_____	_____	$_____	$_____
_____	_____	$_____	$_____
_____	_____	$_____	$_____
	Subtotal		$_____
	7.25% Sales Tax (CA only)		$_____
	8.25% Sales Tax (TN only)		$_____
	5.0% Sales Tax (MD and IN only)		$_____
	Shipping and Handling*		$_____
	TOTAL ORDER (U.S. funds only)		$_____

Shipping and Handling depend on Subtotal.

Subtotal	Shipping/Handling
$0.00–$14.99	$3.00
$15.00–29.99	$4.00
$30.00–49.99	$6.00
$50.00–99.99	$10.00
$100.00–199.99	$13.00
$200.00+	call for quote

Foreign and all Priority Request orders:
Call Order Entry department for price quote at
1-916-632-4400

This chart represents the total retail price of books only
(before applicable discounts are taken).

By telephone: With Visa or MC, call 1-800-632-8676. Mon.–Fri. 8:30–4:00 PST.

By Internet E-mail: sales@primapub.com

By mail: Just fill out the information below and send with your remittance to:

PRIMA PUBLISHING
P.O. Box 1260BK
Rocklin, CA 95677-1260

http://www.primapublishing.com

Name_____ Daytime Telephone_____

Address _____

City _____ State _____ Zip _____

Visa /MC# _____Exp. _____

Check/Money Order enclosed for $_____ Payable to Prima Publishing

Signature _____

...ent/Notice of Limited Warranty

...g the sealed disk container in this book, you agree to the following terms and conditions. If, upon reading
... following license agreement and notice of limited warranty, you cannot agree to the terms and conditions set
forth, return the unused book with unopened disk to the place where you purchased it for a refund.

License:

The enclosed software is copyrighted by the copyright holder(s) indicated on the software disk. You are licensed to
copy the software onto a single computer for use by a single concurrent user and to a backup disk. You may not
reproduce, make copies, or distribute copies or rent or lease the software in whole or in part, except with written
permission of the copyright holder(s). You may transfer the enclosed disk only together with this license, and only if
you destroy all other copies of the software and the transferee agrees to the terms of the license. You may not
decompile, reverse assemble, or reverse engineer the software.

Notice of Limited Warranty:

The enclosed disk is warranted by Prima Publishing to be free of physical defects in materials and workmanship for a
period of sixty (60) days from end user's purchase of the book/disk combination. During the sixty-day term of the
limited warranty, Prima will provide a replacement disk upon the return of a defective disk.

Limited Liability:

THE SOLE REMEDY FOR BREACH OF THIS LIMITED WARRANTY SHALL CONSIST ENTIRELY OF
REPLACEMENT OF THE DEFECTIVE DISK. IN NO EVENT SHALL PRIMA OR THE AUTHORS BE
LIABLE FOR ANY OTHER DAMAGES, INCLUDING LOSS OR CORRUPTION OF DATA, CHANGES IN
THE FUNCTIONAL CHARACTERISTICS OF THE HARDWARE OR OPERATING SYSTEM,
DELETERIOUS INTERACTION WITH OTHER SOFTWARE, OR ANY OTHER SPECIAL, INCIDENTAL,
OR CONSEQUENTIAL DAMAGES THAT MAY ARISE, EVEN IF PRIMA AND/OR THE AUTHOR HAVE
PREVIOUSLY BEEN NOTIFIED THAT THE POSSIBILITY OF SUCH DAMAGES EXISTS.

Disclaimer of Warranties:

PRIMA AND THE AUTHOR SPECIFICALLY DISCLAIM ANY AND ALL OTHER WARRANTIES, EITHER
EXPRESS OR IMPLIED, INCLUDING WARRANTIES OF MERCHANTABILITY, SUITABILITY TO A
PARTICULAR TASK OR PURPOSE, OR FREEDOM FROM ERRORS. SOME STATES DO NOT ALLOW
FOR EXCLUSION OF IMPLIED WARRANTIES OR LIMITATION OF INCIDENTAL OR
CONSEQUENTIAL DAMAGES, SO THESE LIMITATIONS MAY NOT APPLY TO YOU.

Other:

This Agreement is governed by the laws of the State of California without regard to choice of law principles. The
United Convention of Contracts for the International Sale of Goods is specifically disclaimed. This Agreement
constitutes the entire agreement between you and Prima Publishing regarding use of the software.